IMAGES
*of America*

# AZLE

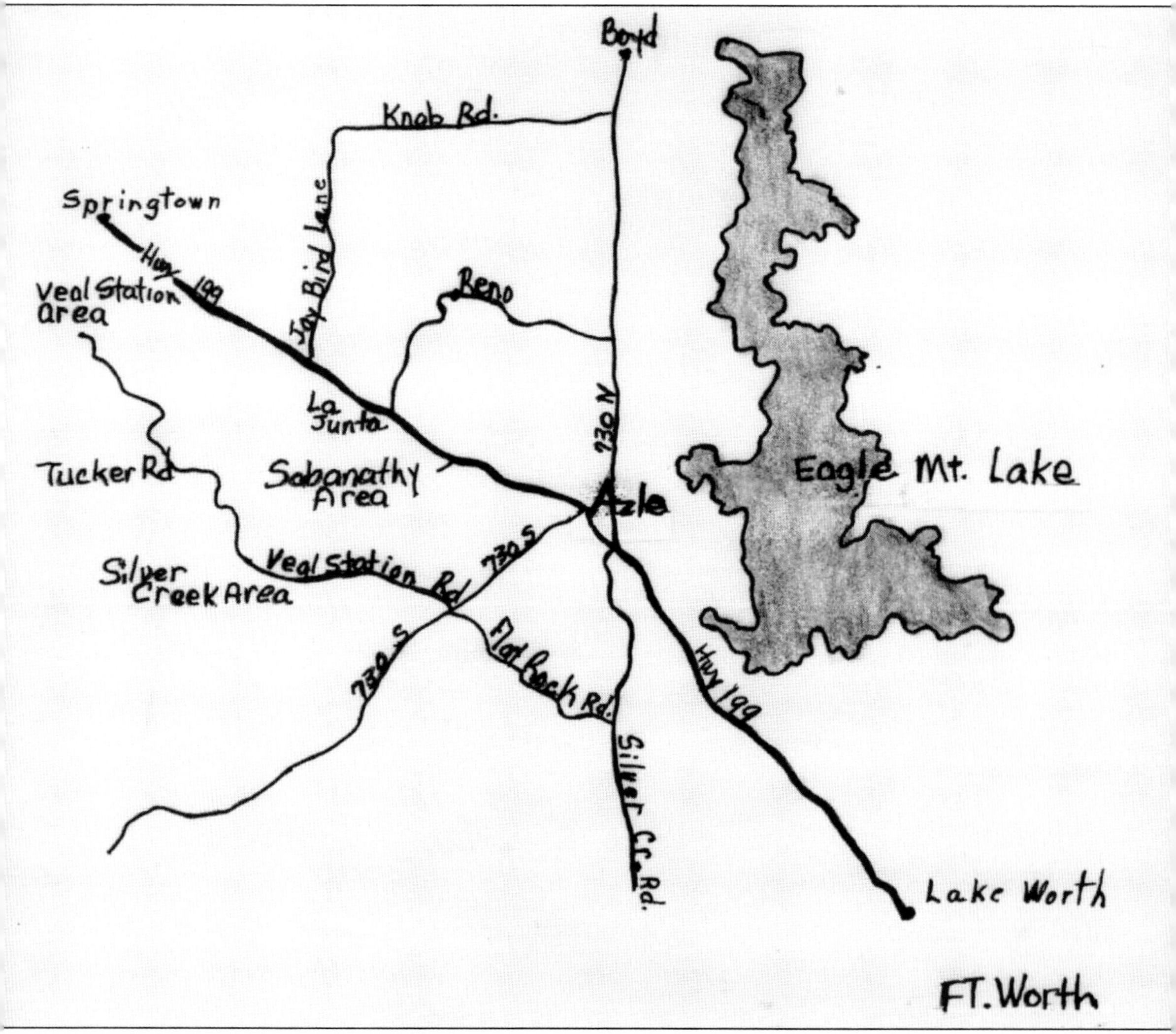


Azle lies in both Tarrant and Parker Counties. A third county, Wise, also shares Azle's school district. Eagle Mountain Lake provides the city's eastern boundary. This area map shows the small communities where early settlers built their homes and the roads leading to them. The Veal Station area is approximately nine miles from Azle, the Sabathany area is about four miles away, and Silver Creek area is three miles away. The city of Azle is 20 miles northwest of Fort Worth, Texas. (Azle Historical Museum.)

**On the Cover:** In 1956, these students exited Azle school buses and entered what was then Azle High School. The building, on School Street, now serves as a junior high. While clothing for boys has not changed much in more than half a century, girls' fashions—long, full skirts, penny loafers, and bobby sox—certainly have. (Azle Historical Museum.)

IMAGES
*of America*

# AZLE

Azle Historical Museum

ARCADIA
PUBLISHING

ISBN 978-0-7385-9592-4

Published by Arcadia Publishing
Charleston, South Carolina

Printed in the United States of America

Library of Congress Control Number: 2012940638

For all general information, please contact Arcadia Publishing:
Telephone 843-853-2070
Fax 843-853-0044
E-mail sales@arcadiapublishing.com
For customer service and orders:
Toll-Free 1-888-313-2665

Visit us on the Internet at www.arcadiapublishing.com

*The current board members of the Azle Historical Museum would like to dedicate this book to the past board members who began the museum and began the preservation of Azle's history, as well as to the early pioneers who laid the foundation.*

# Contents

# ACKNOWLEDGMENTS

The members of the Azle Historical Museum would like to thank the residents of Azle for their tremendous response to our historical calendars over the past 10 years, which preserved a bit of Azle's past. This book is an attempt to go further and provide a more permanent "keepsake" record of our town, from its mid-19th-century beginning to the present.

We also wish to thank two of the officers, president Rex Ballauer and secretary J'Nell Pate, for teaming up to do the majority of the work on this photographic story of Azle's history. Other officers provided help as well, including vice president Debbie Hall, who gave excellent computer and photography advice, and treasurer Patsy Glover, who provided her always-capable money management and support.

The remaining board members—Nancy Davis, Kim Dunaway, Hurene Morrow, Dicey Rowden, and Christine Sellers—suggested images, provided answers to questions, helped check facts, and double-checked proofs. Several of these ladies are descended from Azle's earliest settlers.

Thank you also to Jerry Bales Ludwick, who helped us struggle through image test-scans early on; Lynda Scott and Britt Eason, who helped proofread; and to everyone who provided images for this book.

Unless otherwise noted, all images are courtesy of the Azle Historical Museum.

# Introduction

Located approximately 20 miles northwest of downtown Fort Worth, Texas, the small city of Azle originated as a farming settlement of immigrants from the South, many from Tennessee, in the mid-1850s. One of the earliest to arrive, John Giles Reynolds, came from Tennessee a few years earlier to check out the land, returning in 1854 with a wife and three children to settle on a creek that subsequently became known as Reynolds Branch.

On one of his 160 acres, he constructed a log house with native rock chimneys on each end that remains standing at 612 South Stewart Street, although he later built a frame house around it. Descendants of Reynolds still own the house today.

Also from Tennessee, Dr. James Azle Steward, born in 1831, became the first doctor in the community when he arrived in 1858. Two years later, he married Mary Fowler, and people called the small community of settlers Marysville in honor of their beloved doctor's wife. For a time, a Mr. Moore had a general store, so people called the tiny community Mooresville.

A few years later, Joe Fowler, Mary's brother, ran the only general store in the area, carrying needed merchandise for the rural community. In the late 1870s, people began calling a group of buildings—a gristmill, church, and school—Fowler's Store. In 1871, Ash Creek Baptist Church was organized by 48 settlers, and has survived to the present day.

William O'Bar owned a ranch in the area and worked hard to acquire a post office, which was approved in 1881. Consequently, the US government designated the town O'Bar, and Fowler's Store housed the post office, with Joe Fowler serving as postmaster.

The name of the town changed again, for the last time, in 1883, to Azle. Dr. James Azle Steward promised to donate five acres of land for two blocks of Main Street, but he also donated land for a cemetery and for Azle Christian Church. Dr. Steward died in 1889 at age 58.

The first drugstore came to Azle in 1882 through the efforts of Lewis Thomas Wigfall "Wig" Reynolds, a son of John Giles Reynolds. James Walker bought it in 1888, tearing it down in 1900 to construct a two-story frame building in its place. That building still stands at 117 West Main Street, the oldest storefront in downtown Azle.

In the 1920s and 1930s, Azle schools incorporated with numerous rural common school districts in the surrounding area. These included Promised Land, Sabathany, Steele, and Slover. Because a larger schoolhouse was needed, local residents sought New Deal Works Progress Administration (WPA) funds to build a concrete and rock structure in 1939 called the Rock School. All grades were held there until 1953, when a new high school was built on School Street.

In 1930, the population of Azle was 146 and the town had 10 commercial businesses and three churches—Baptist, Christian, and Methodist.

Texas governor James Allred came to Azle on April 3, 1936, to celebrate the arrival of electric service to the town's 250 residents. The construction of Eagle Mountain Lake in the early 1930s brought more people to the area, as did World War II later. In 1946, after the war, the population hit 400.

In 1957, locals heard a rumor that Fort Worth might annex Azle, so they incorporated as a city. The first mayor was Dan Jarvis, a descendant of an early family who had owned a plantation. By 1960, the population had reached 3,000.

After it grew to 5,000 a decade later, the city applied to the state for Home Rule status in 1971. This meant that the community could pass its own ordinances and select the type of city government it wanted. Towns with populations under 5,000 were governed under rules set by the state. In the 2010 census, Azle's population was 10,947.

# *One*

# Pioneer Families

The first settlers started arriving in the 1850s and settled beside Ash Creek, which wound through the countryside, beginning in the hills southwest of Veal Station and emptying into the Trinity River. Today, it empties into Eagle Mountain Lake, which was built in the early 1930s. Indians said that the creek never went dry; it provided a reliable watering source for livestock and crops, attracting many families who built homes along its banks.

Azle was settled by a hardy bunch of pioneers mostly from Tennessee, Arkansas, Missouri, and Kentucky. An extended list of some of the citizens in early Azle includes Gregg, Rumsfeldt, Jarvis, Fowler, Moore, Steward, Rowland, Reynolds, O'Bar, McDonald, Walker, Grigsby, Scrimshire, Fletcher, Myers, Dunaway, Cantrell, Hoggard, Gilley, Goode, Young, Crow, Porter, Gipson, Rice, Rogers, Snodgrass, Daugherty, Kitchens, O'Donald, McBride, Nation, Pierce, Smith, Parker, Ross, Kimbrough, Crane, Clingman, Neuman, Dodson, Tucker, Aaron, Myers, Dent, Patterson, Hill, Cozby, Jackson, and Helm. These and other early families moved onto farms in the rural area that would later become Azle. Many descendants of these families still live in the area and have seen Azle develop from a "stop in the road" to a fast-growing city.

The lives of the early pioneers were hard and filled with unending work, but it was customary for families to help each other. The pioneers of Azle had a unity of purpose that helped the community to grow, building a town with a faith in God and a hope for prosperity. Some came and only stayed a short time, but for others, this new settlement was the place they wanted to be.

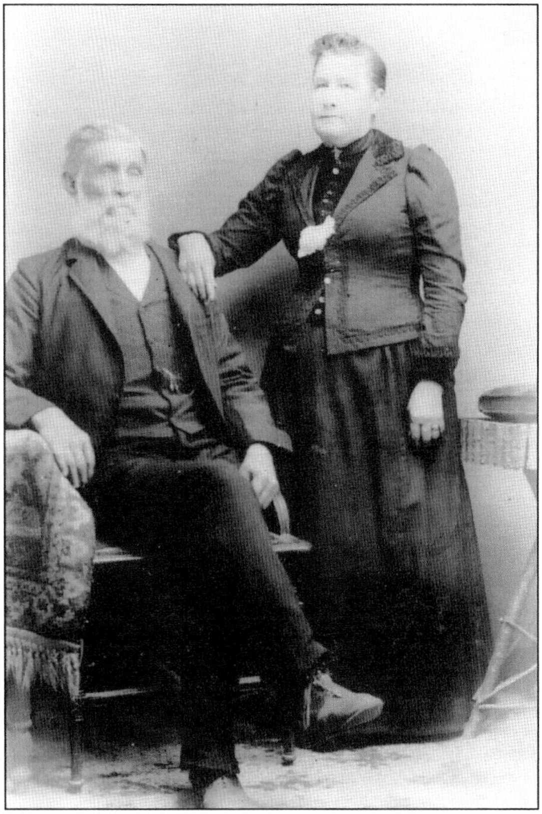

One of Azle's first settlers was John Giles Reynolds, who arrived in 1854. He built the first school, which was also used as a church, and donated land for Ash Creek Cemetery. He also built the first gristmill west of the Mississippi. He was married three times and widowed twice. His wives' names were Frances Ham, Martha Hart Tucker, and Mary Nichols (seen here).

Benjamin Franklin Reynolds was the fourth child of John Giles and Frances Ham Reynolds. He was born in 1854, shortly after his parents moved to Parker County, and was the first white child born in this newly named county. He is shown here with his wife, Matilda Isobell Hoggard, who was born in Parker County in 1856. Both families have many ancestors still living in the Azle area.

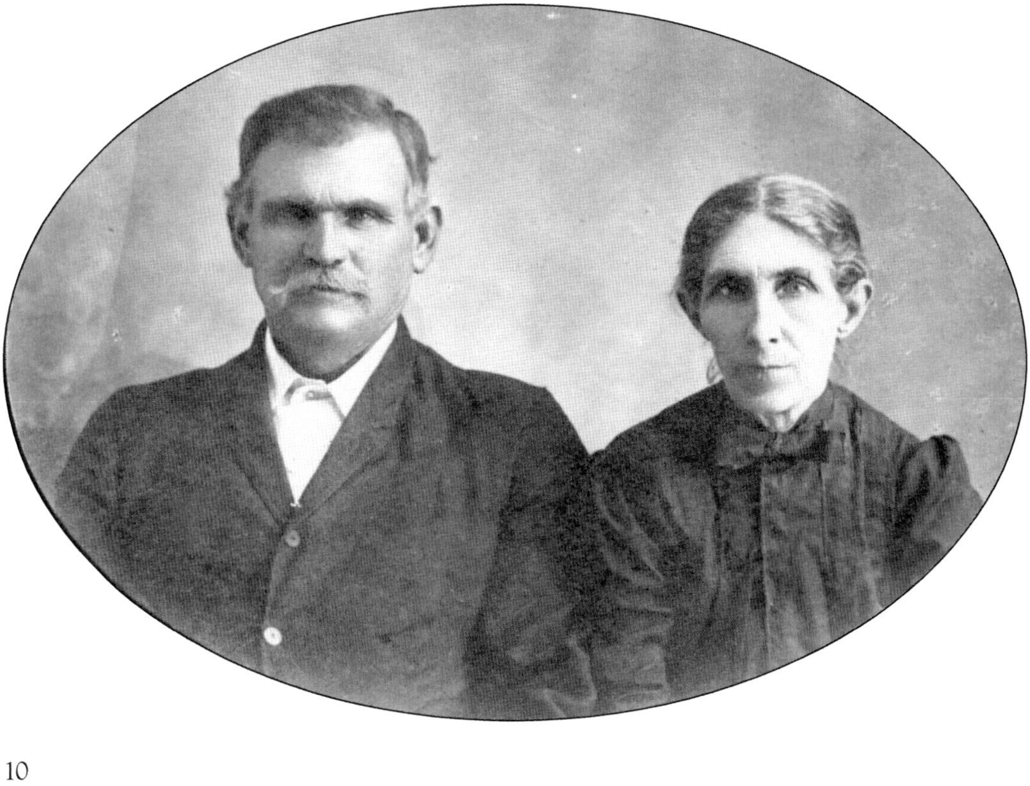

Dr. John Morgan Reynolds was the son of John Giles and Martha Hart Tucker Reynolds. He married Susan Alma McColluch in 1896 and began his medical practice in Keller, Texas. After a short time, he moved to Azle, where he practiced for a number of years, before eventually moving to Reno, Texas, in 1912.

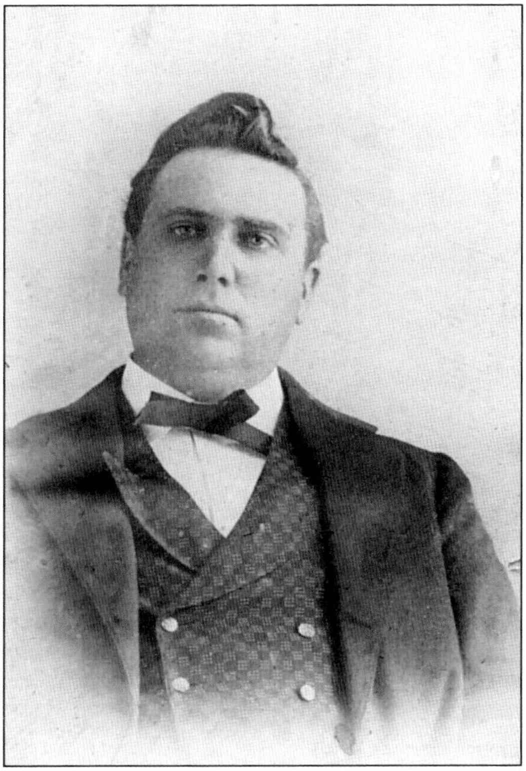

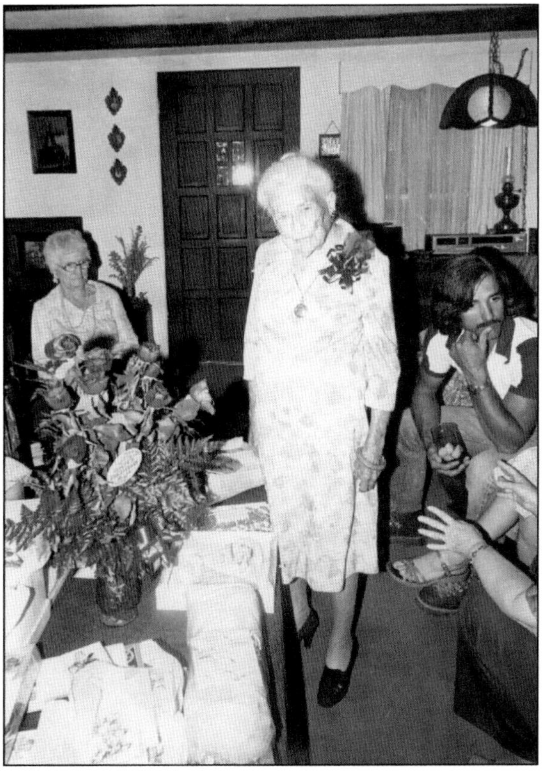

Blanche Dameron Scrimshire was born on June 23, 1890, in Azle and was the granddaughter of John Giles Reynolds. Her husband, Floyd Ira Scrimshire, moved to Azle in 1909, and they married in 1911. The Scrimshires were dairy farmers for 30 years. She was known as the local historian, writing histories of the town, the schools, and Ash Creek Baptist Church. She passed away in 1984.

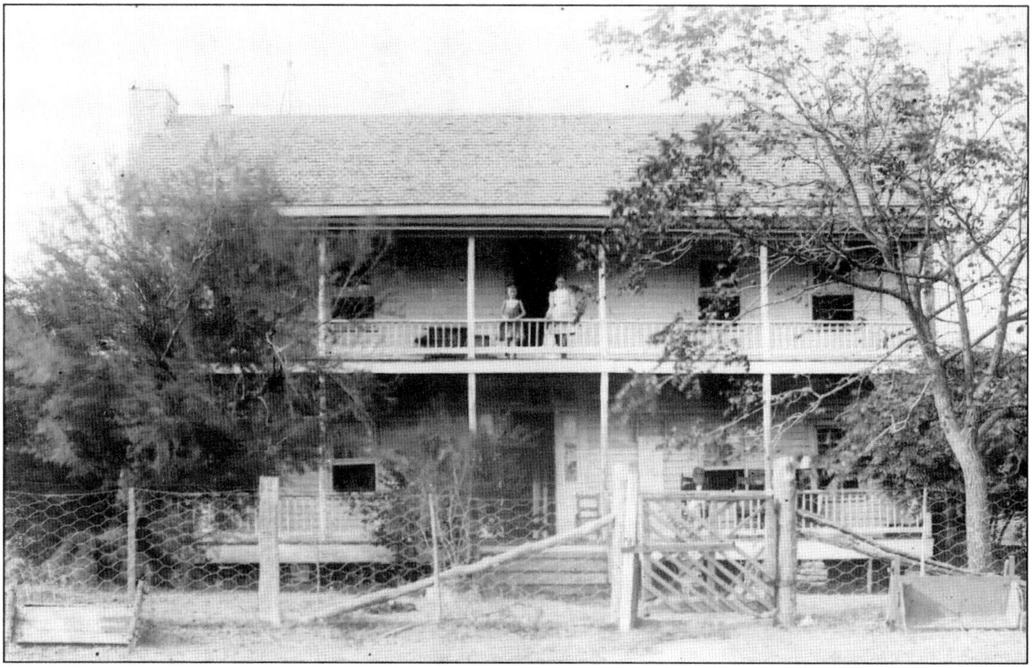

This two-story house at 612 South Stewart Street, the home of John Giles Reynolds and his family, was built in the early 1860s. The lumber was hauled from Houston by oxen and took three months to arrive. It was the first plank house in the area. The house was built with two and a half rooms on each floor and with fireplaces at both ends of the house, both upstairs and downstairs. There were double porches across the front and a large kitchen was at the back of the house. The top floor was removed in the 1930s, as seen in the bottom photograph. The oldest home in Azle, it is owned by Reynolds's great-great grandson Charles Conwell. The original smokehouse was donated to the Log Cabin Village in Fort Worth.

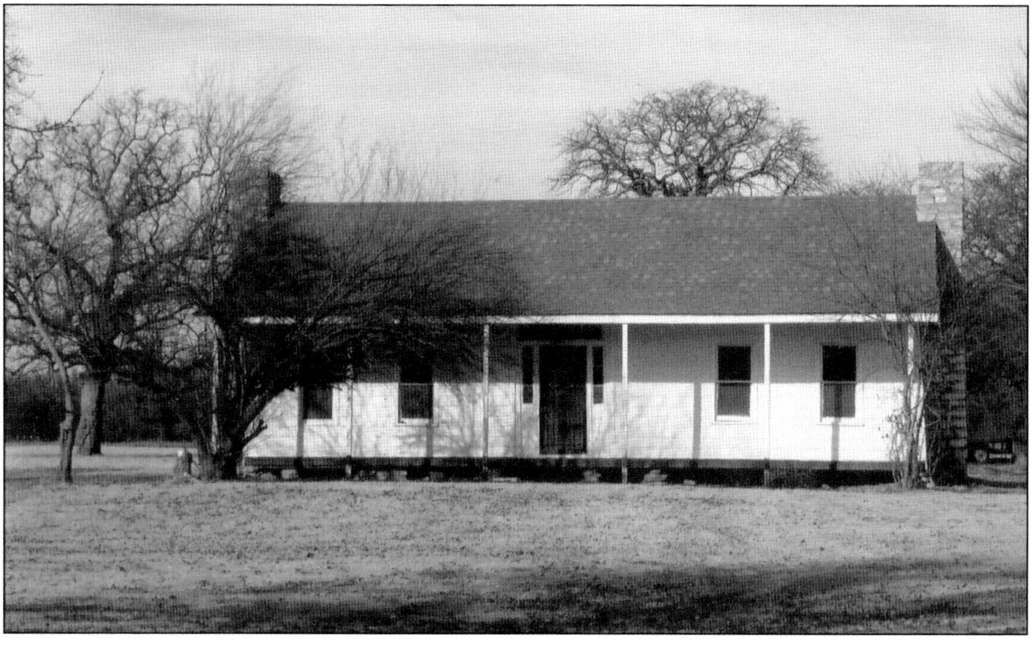

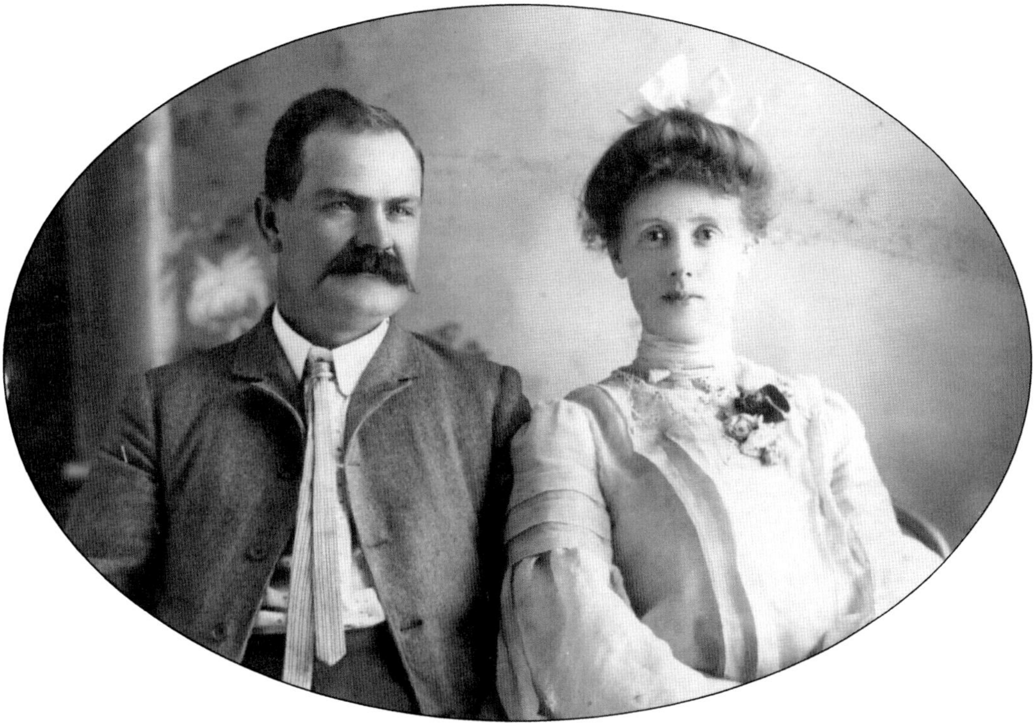

John Robert Parker and his wife, Anna Kimbrough, were both born in 1872 to prominent early families in Azle. John's father, Andy K. Parker, was Azle's first blacksmith and handed the shop down to John. Anna's grandparents William and Matilda Thompson Kimbrough had settled in the area in 1837. William traded his property in 1842 for the Kimbrough family farm one mile east of Azle.

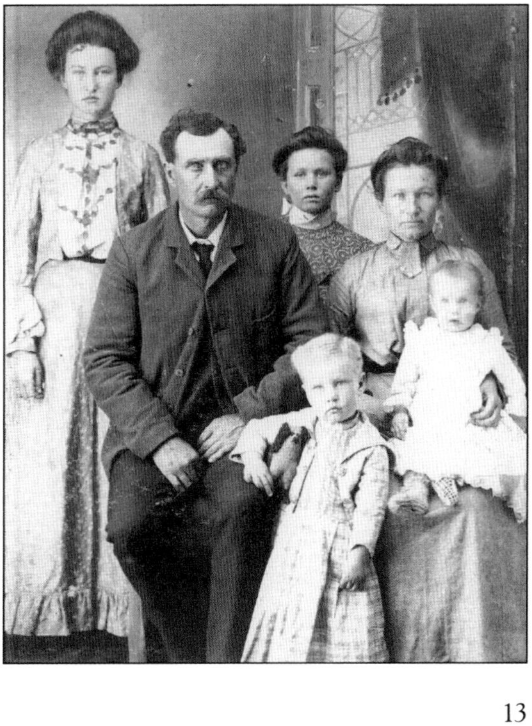

James Stuard Rowden's parents, Ezekiel and Francis Rowden, bought 299.2 acres in Azle in the 1860s. Ezekiel sold off some acreage, but upon his death, the rest was deeded to his children, with 119 acres going to James for caring for his mother. This photograph shows the Rowden family, from left to right, (seated) James Rowden, with son Noble, and Florence Tennessee Rowden, with baby Iva; (standing) Beulah Rowden Horton and Ola Rowden Dugan.

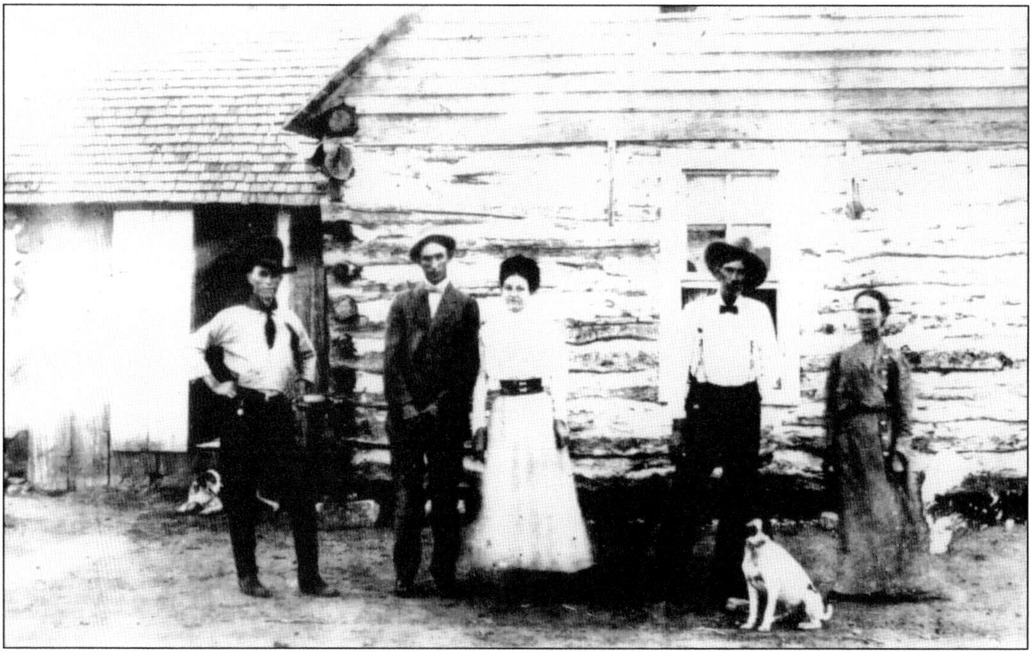

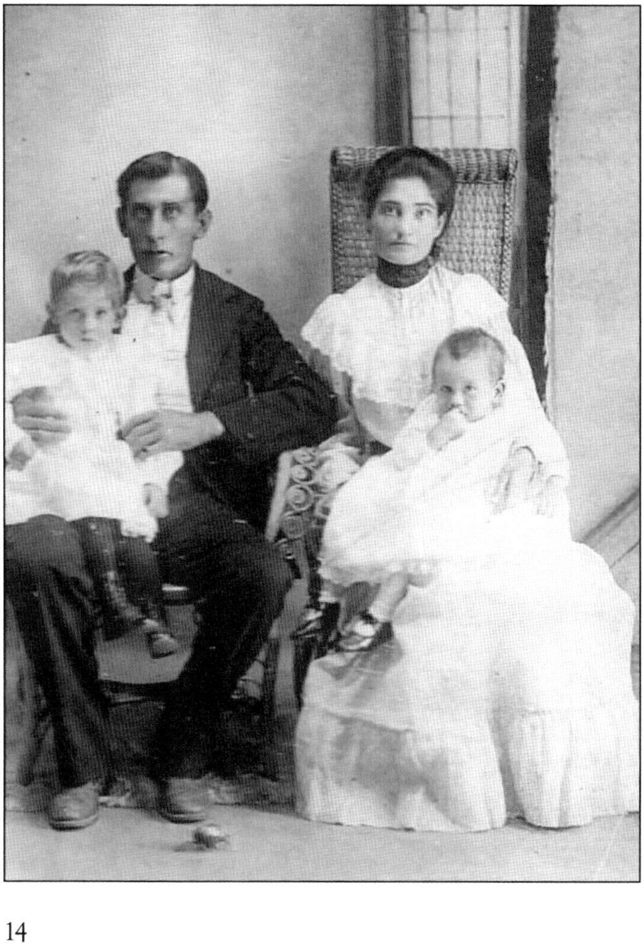

Jackson D. Crow and his wife, Elmettie Davis Crow, were early settlers on Ash Creek. They are shown here in front of their log house. From left to right are son Ben S. Crow, Joe W. Kitchens, Alice Crow Kitchens, Jackson, and Elmettie. Jackson was a peddler throughout the country and grew a productive peach orchard for many years in Parker County.

The Sabathany area was the home of Jessie Andrew and Amanda Rose Gilley's family around 1857. Jessie's father was a Texas Ranger and Amanda's father, Wilson Rose, fought in the Civil War. They helped organize the Presbyterian Church in the Sabathany community. They had five children, two of whom, Carl Adrian (left) and Henry, are seen here with their parents in 1906.

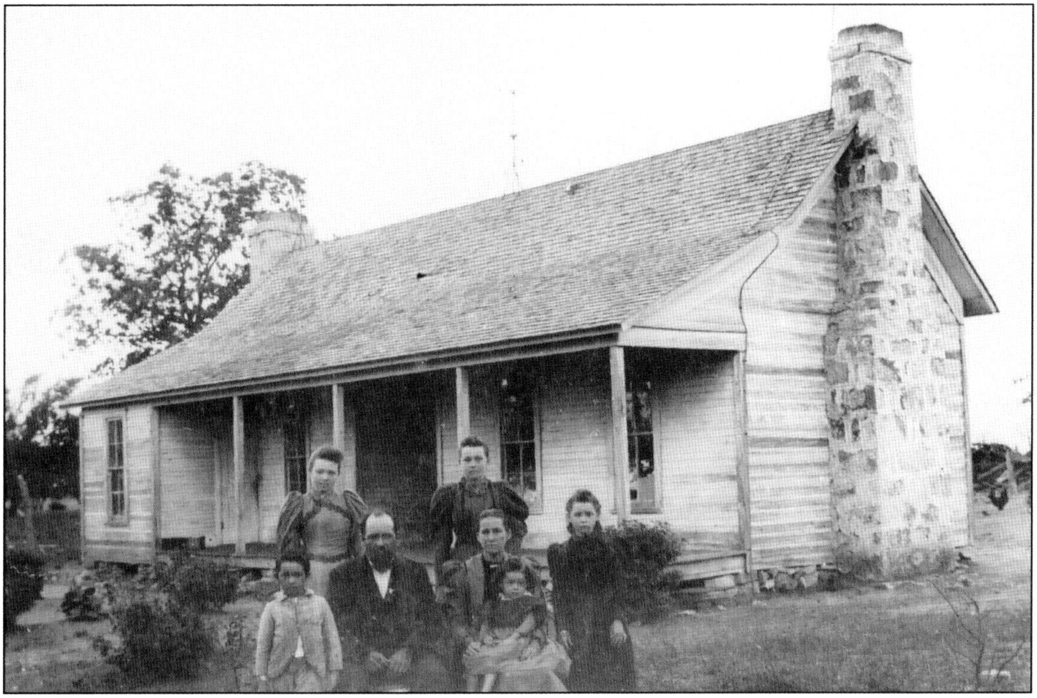

The Van E. Admire home, built in the mid-1880s, sat on a hill facing south on what is now Sandy Beach Road. The family lived in it until 1922, when Van died. The children attended the old Liberty School. Van is seated here with his wife, Nancy Elizabeth Barnes Admire, and some of their children.

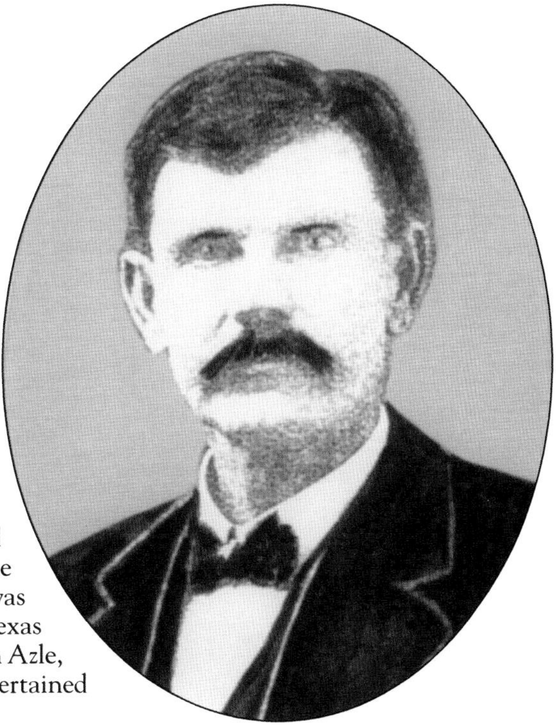

John Jeremiah "Coho" Smith and his wife, Nancy Jane Hoggard, settled in Azle in 1861. Smith's earlier need for adventure led him to Dallas to help lay off the town site. He participated in several Indian campaigns, was held captive by the Comanches, and was a Texas Ranger. In his later years, he taught school in Azle, had a gunsmith shop on Main Street, and entertained children with puppet shows.

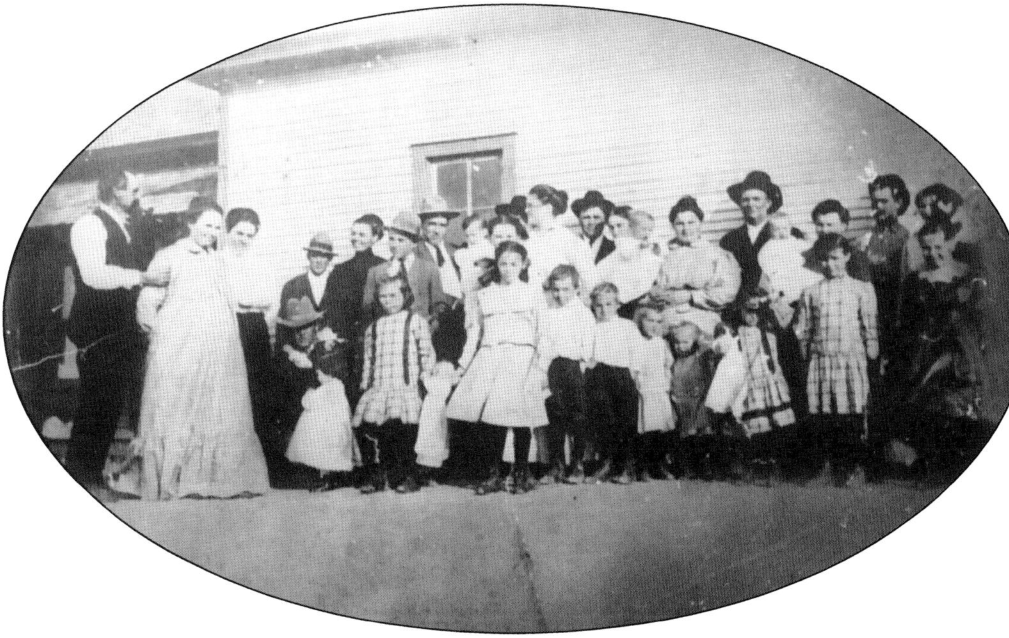

This 1910 photograph shows Soloman "Saul" Gilley and his wife, Belle (both far left), with some of their family. They were the parents of 15 children, 12 of whom survived to an old age and had large families of their own. Saul was a farmer and taught at Veal Station College, which was chartered in 1877.

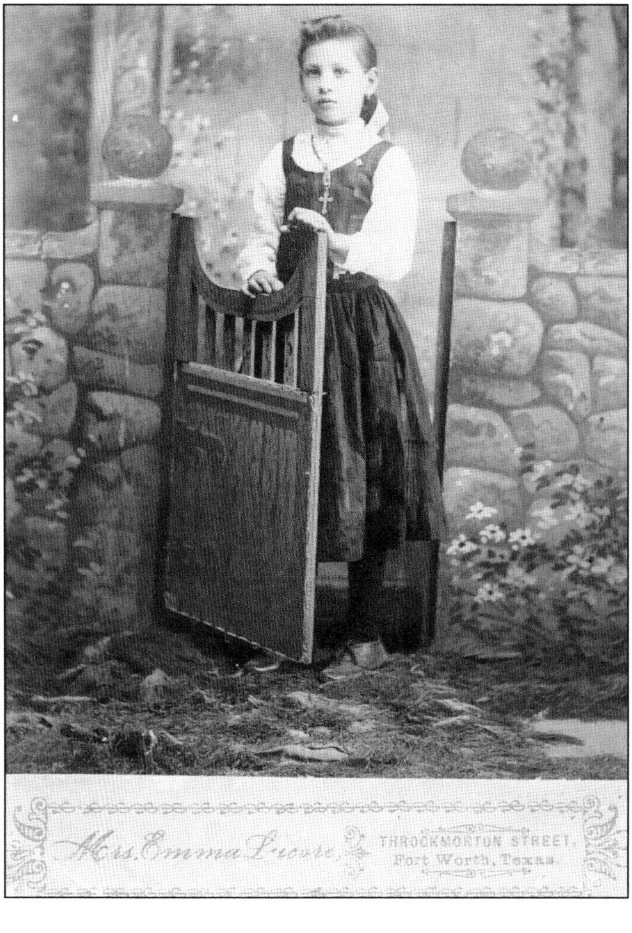


Hattie Lou McKinsey, the daughter of Jasper McKinsey, was born at Veal Station in 1880 and was nine years old in this photograph. She joined the Christian church when she was 12 years old and was baptized in the Chance Baptizing Hole in the Reynolds Branch of Ash Creek. She married Frank M. Fowler in 1895 and they had 11 children. Most of the Fowler descendants still live around Azle.

Edward L. Huster stands in front of his two-story white house on East Main Street. The house and land were purchased from the family of Azle's namesake, James Azle Steward, around 1899. The house was torn down in 1967. Edward married Valeria Helen Winstead in 1905. She died in 1922, leaving him to care for their two children alone. He remarried much later to Eda Houphogel, in 1944.

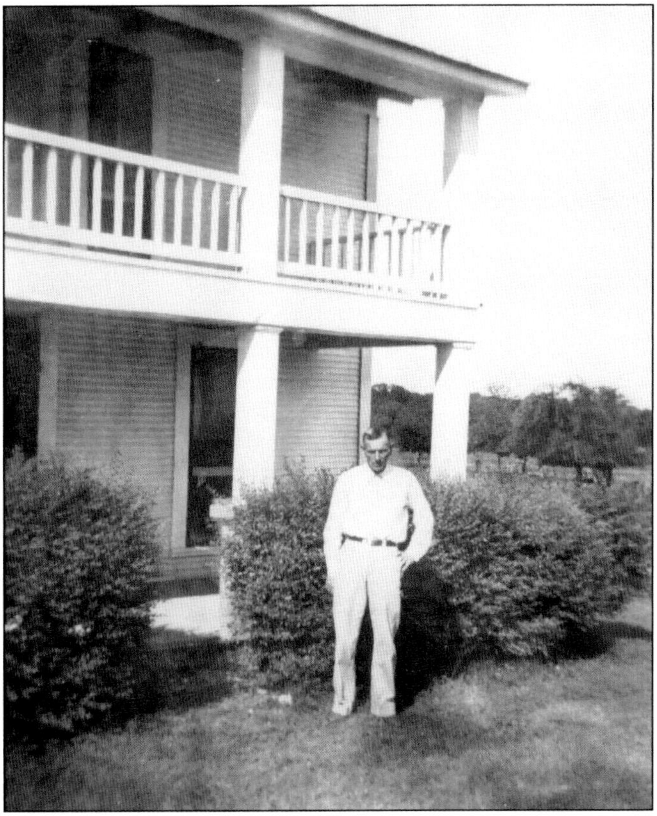

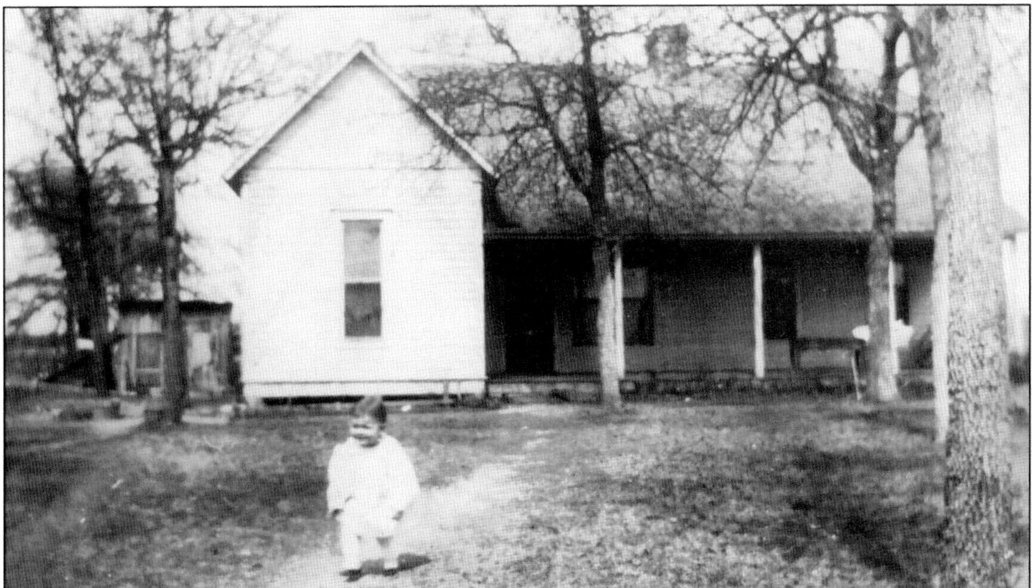

The original homestead of William and Frances Scrimshire was built in the late 1800s. William and his son Floyd owned a general store on Azle's Main Street in 1909. Their daughter Dellaware "Della" and her husband, Jody Tipton "Tip" Couch, purchased the home and lived in it until 1980. The home was located at 501 North Stewart Street. The old oak tree seen here still stands.

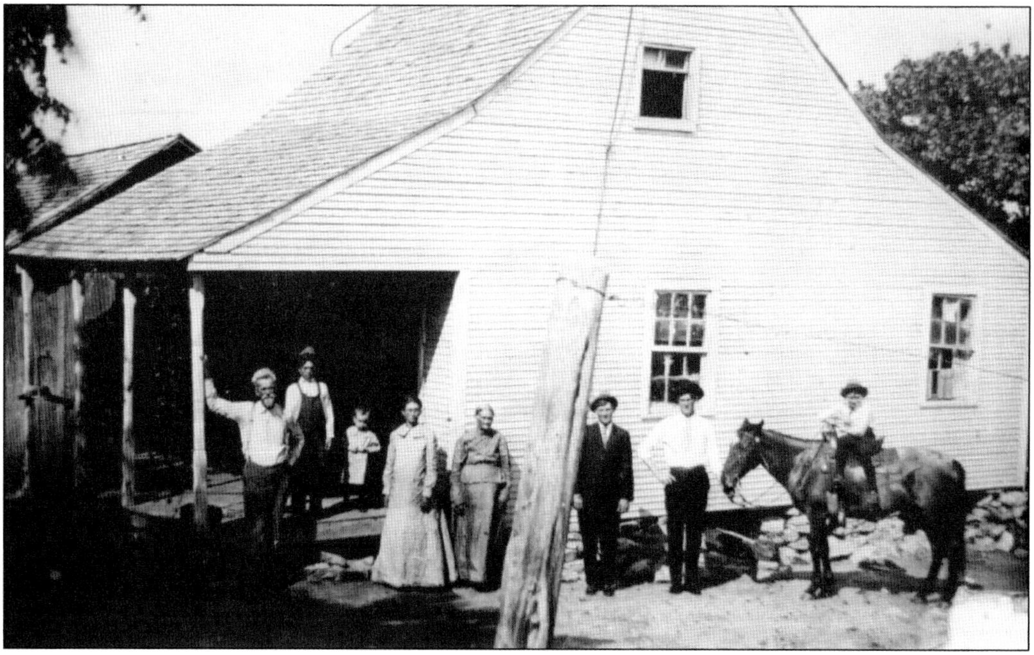

The Davis-Giles home was west of Azle on Veal Station Road. These family members are, from left to right, J.C. Davis, Jimmie Giles, Jesse Davis, Helen Giles Davis, Amanda Giles, Archie Giles, Pete Davis, and Lewis Giles. The house was torn down in the mid-1980s. Today, the property is owned by Azle Historical Museum board member Dicey Davis Rowden, a descendant of the family.

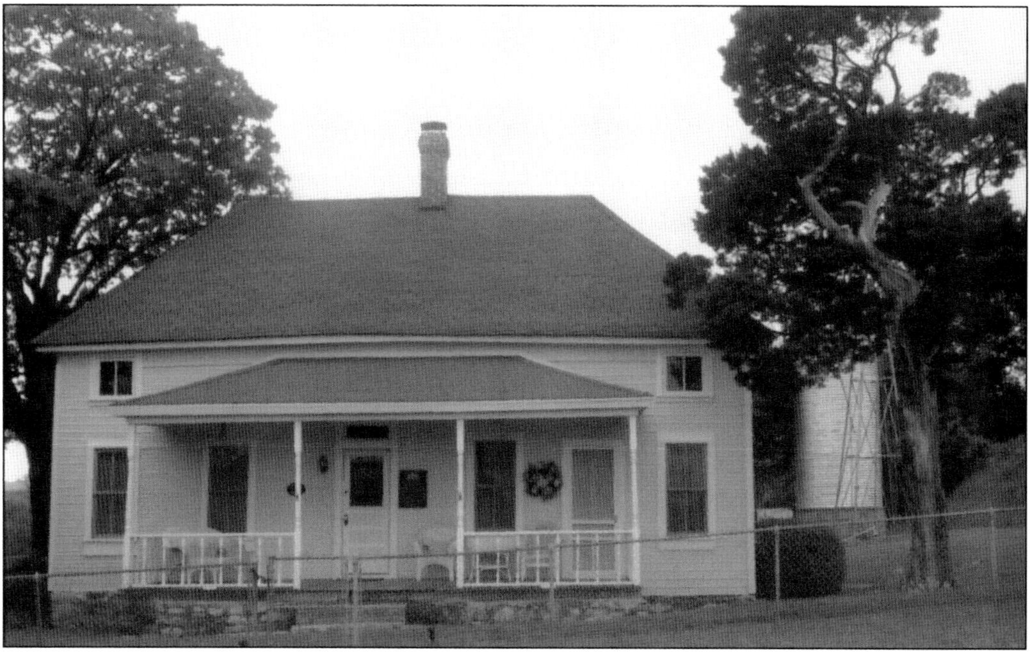

The Tucker house was originally built by brothers Jerry and Virgil Tucker around 1889. Jerry owned it first but sold it to his brother after a few years. Virgil and his family lived in the house until his death in 1946. The descendants owned the house until they donated it to the Silver Creek Heritage Society in 1999.

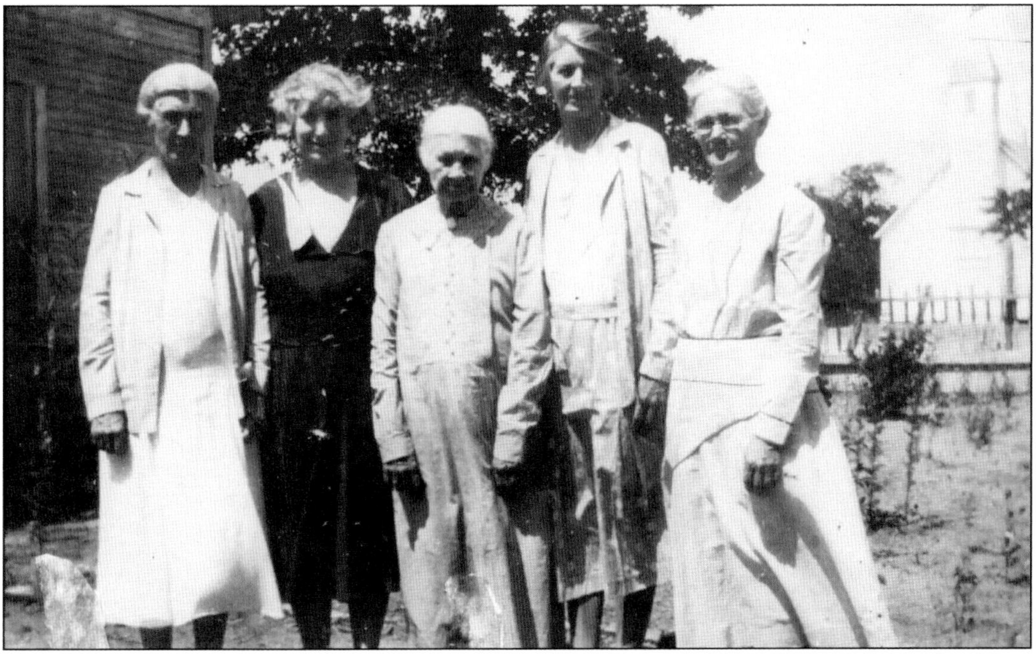

The first member of the Rice family to come to the area was J.M. Rice, who settled in the Silver Creek community in 1872. He opened a day school, charging $2 a month per child. He later married one of his pupils, Leatha Jane Moseley, and died in 1907. Leatha Jane is seen here with her daughters (in no particular order) Emma, Annie, Lizzie, and Ellen—all Azle schoolteachers.

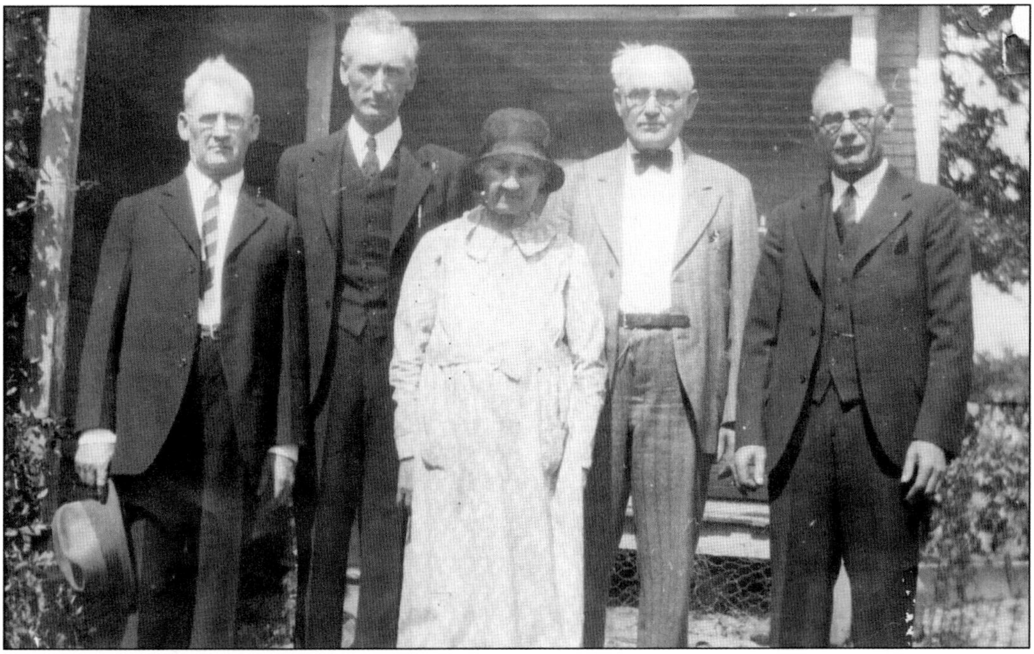

Leatha Jane Moseley Rice and her sons (in no particular order) stand in front of the house her husband, J.M. Rice, built south of Azle on Jacksboro Highway. It was known as the "house by the side of the road." Edmund was a Baptist preacher; Jessup worked in the Memphis, Texas, post office; Frank worked in the Azle post office; and Curt was a mail carrier in Granbury, Texas.

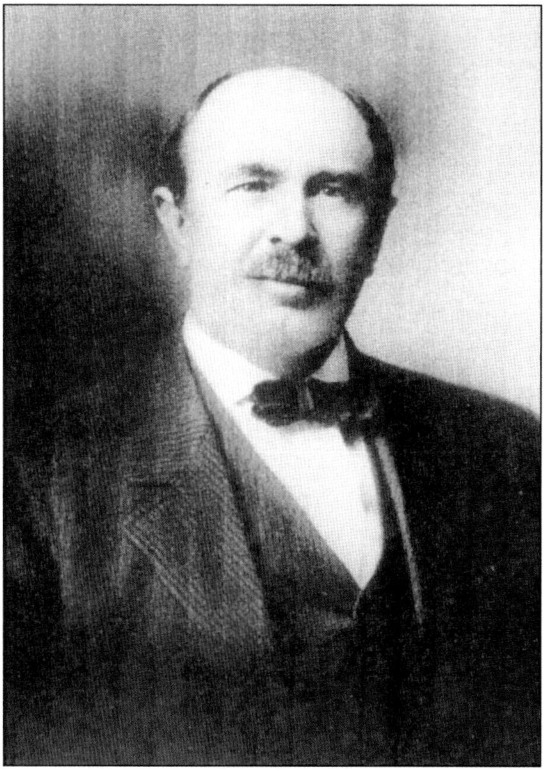

Dr. James Allison Cozby and his wife, Cynthia Mildred, came to Azle in 1891. He bought the house and furniture of the previous owner, Dr. James Dameron, who had left Azle for health reasons. Dr. Cozby made long drives in his horse and buggy to see patients. The Cozbys had nine children.

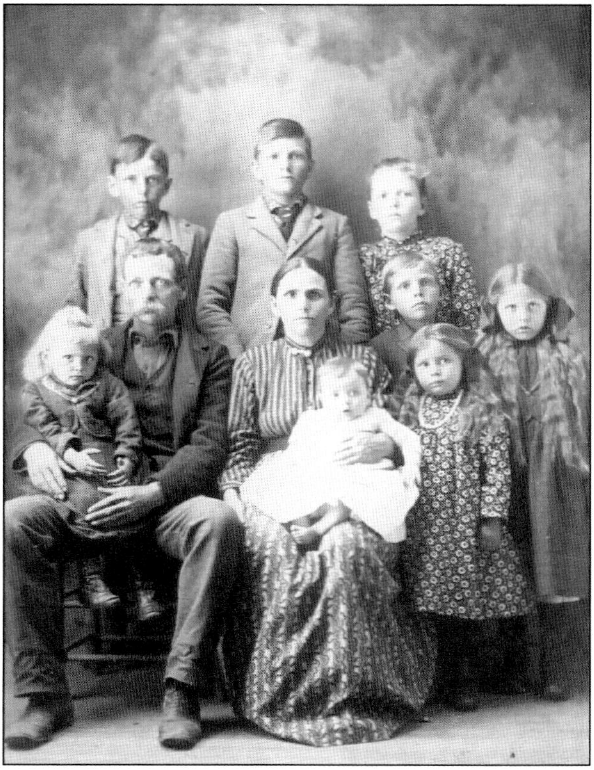

William Thomas and Sarah Rebecca Good Gipson moved to Azle in 1898. In 1903, Sarah died, leaving behind eight children. William was able to see two of his daughters become postmasters, three children become postal employees, two become schoolteachers, and one become a preacher before his death in 1948. These children, posing for a photograph in 1902 with their parents, are, clockwise from left to right, Charlie, Samuel, Laura, Martin, Mamie, Elsie, William, and Beatrice.

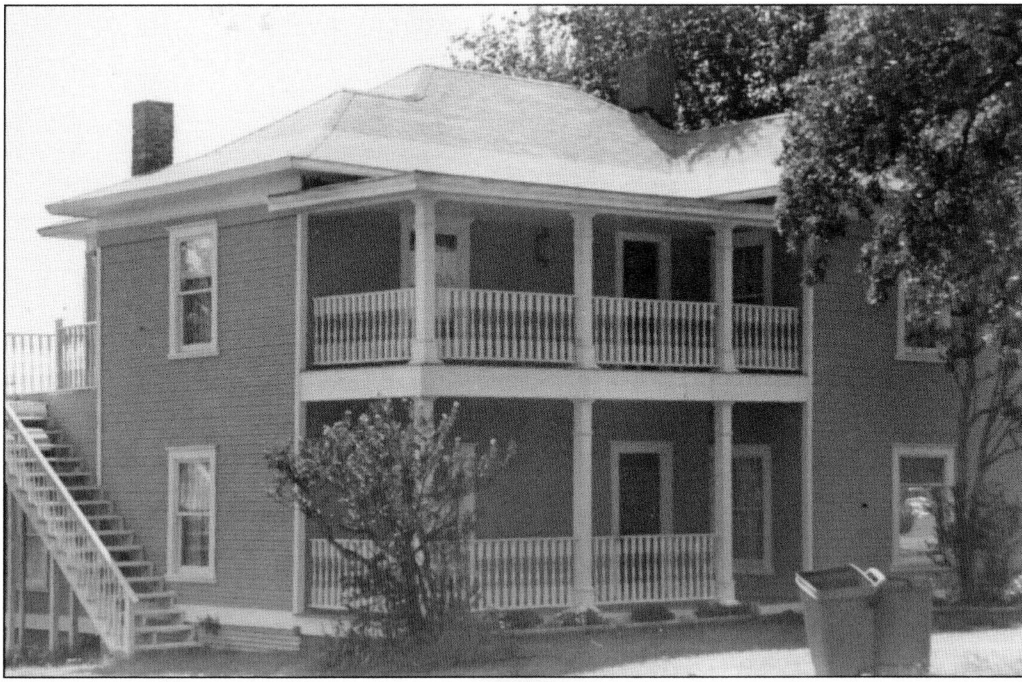

This two-story building at 173 West Main Street was built in 1907. It was the home of Dr. Robert Smith, one of the few physicians in the Azle area in the early 1900s. It was sold in 1919 to Jerry Sessions, a successful farmer and landowner. Today, it is the office of Ronnie Feemster, CPA.

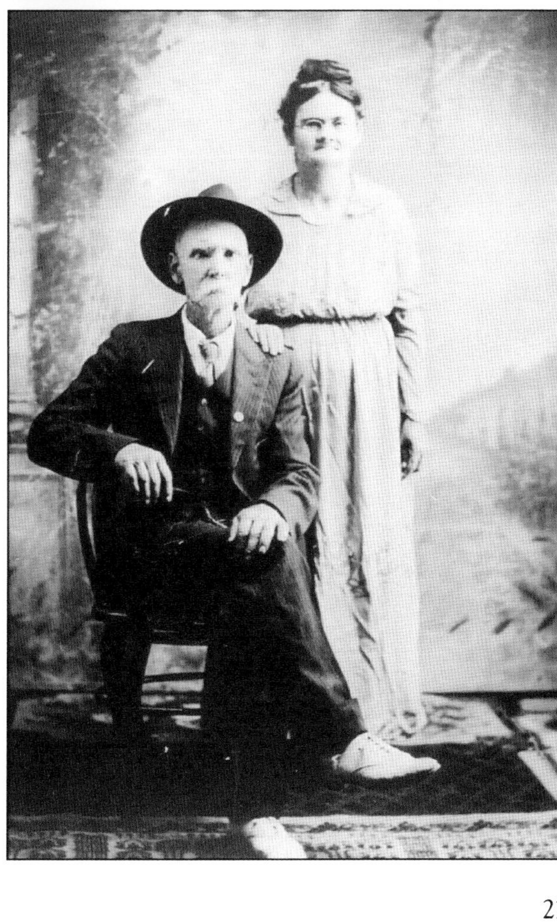

Adelbert A. and Katy Elizabeth Baker Porter settled on a farm south of Azle in 1905. They arrived with a suitcase, a lunch basket, a canary bird, and seven of their 12 children. Their children were named Willie J., Ethel Mae, Leorenzo Clay, Carrie Fay, Harry Ray, Winnie Gay, Nellie Gray, Emma Fray, Mellie Kay, Lora Laray, Glen A., and Florence Essay.

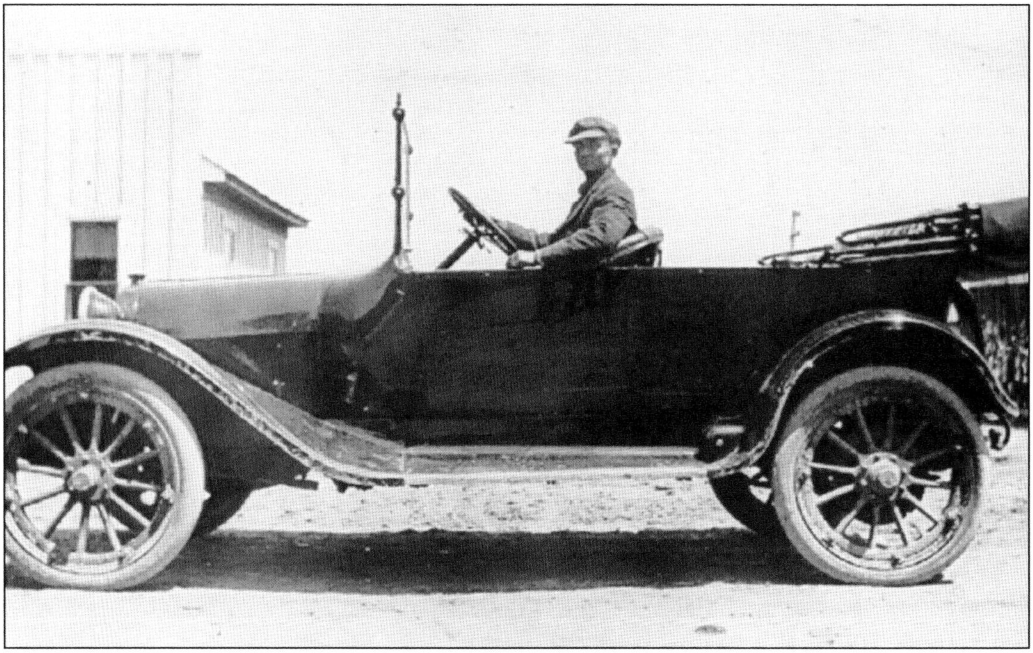

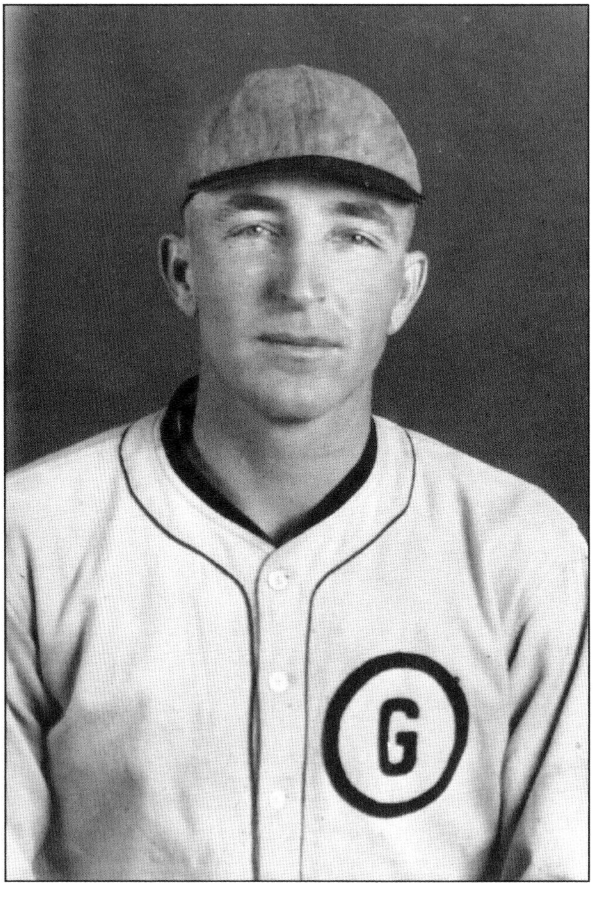

Rev. Pleasant Tackett, came to Parker County with his wife, Kezia, and a small band of settlers. Having seen the rolling hills around what is now Veal Station, they settled there, calling the community Carter. Pleasant was a Methodist preacher and started many churches. His grandson Houston Tackett is seen here in this touring car.

Atlas Carter was born in Reno, Texas, in 1897 and had a successful baseball career in Texas and Oklahoma. He pitched for the Azle team during its Saturday afternoon games. After pitching against the Fort Worth National Bank team and striking out 21 men, he signed with the Rangers in the West Texas League. After his ball-playing days, his family built the first house on the newly surveyed Jacksboro Highway.

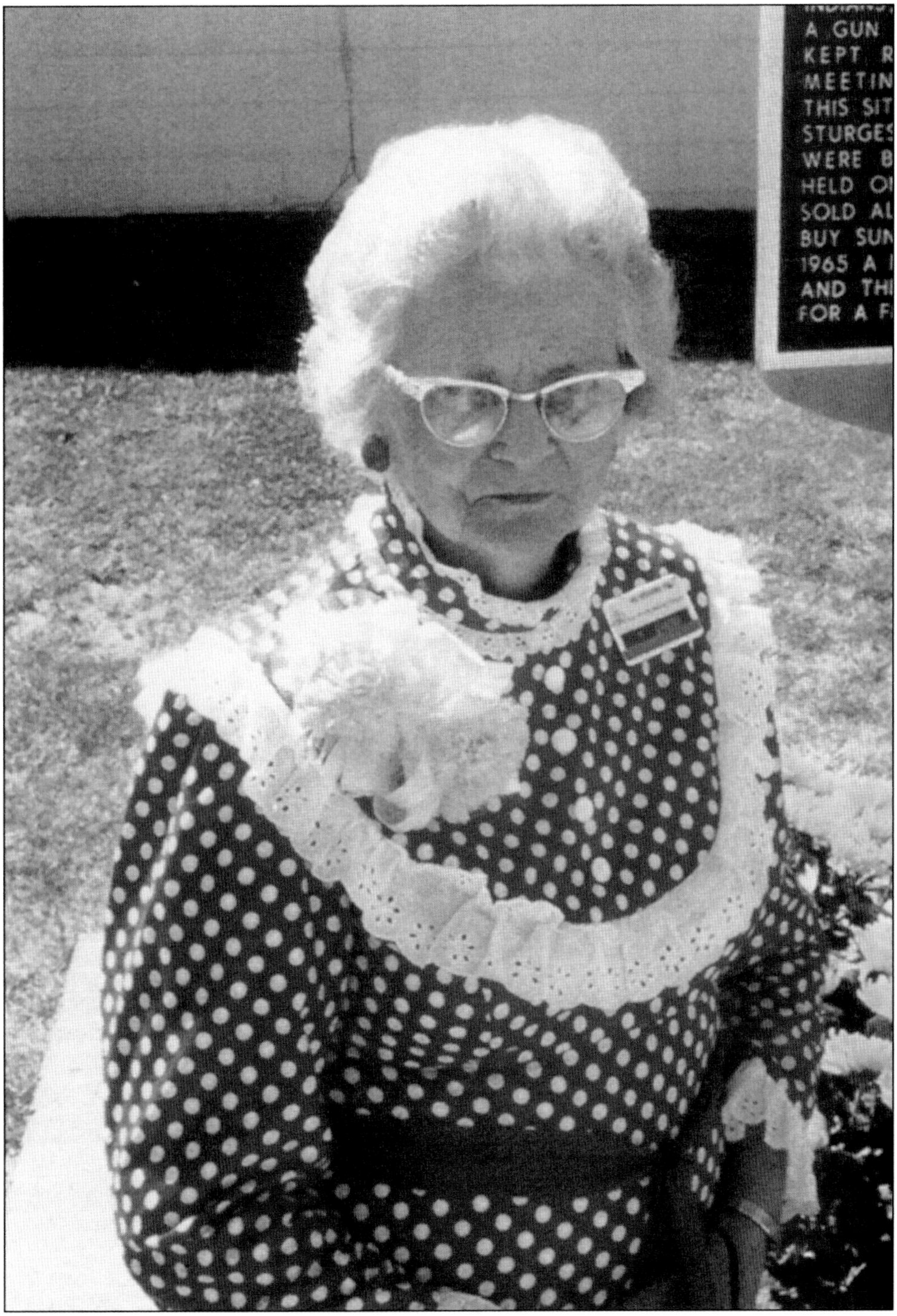

Beatrice Gipson Carter, the daughter of Thomas and Sarah Gipson, was born in Azle in 1899. She married Atlas Carter in 1918, and they had three sons. Beatrice wrote the book *My Home Town* in 1968, and it soon became a must-have book on Azle's history. It included memories of her carefree days as a child in Azle, brief biographies of 120 families, and short histories of neighboring towns.

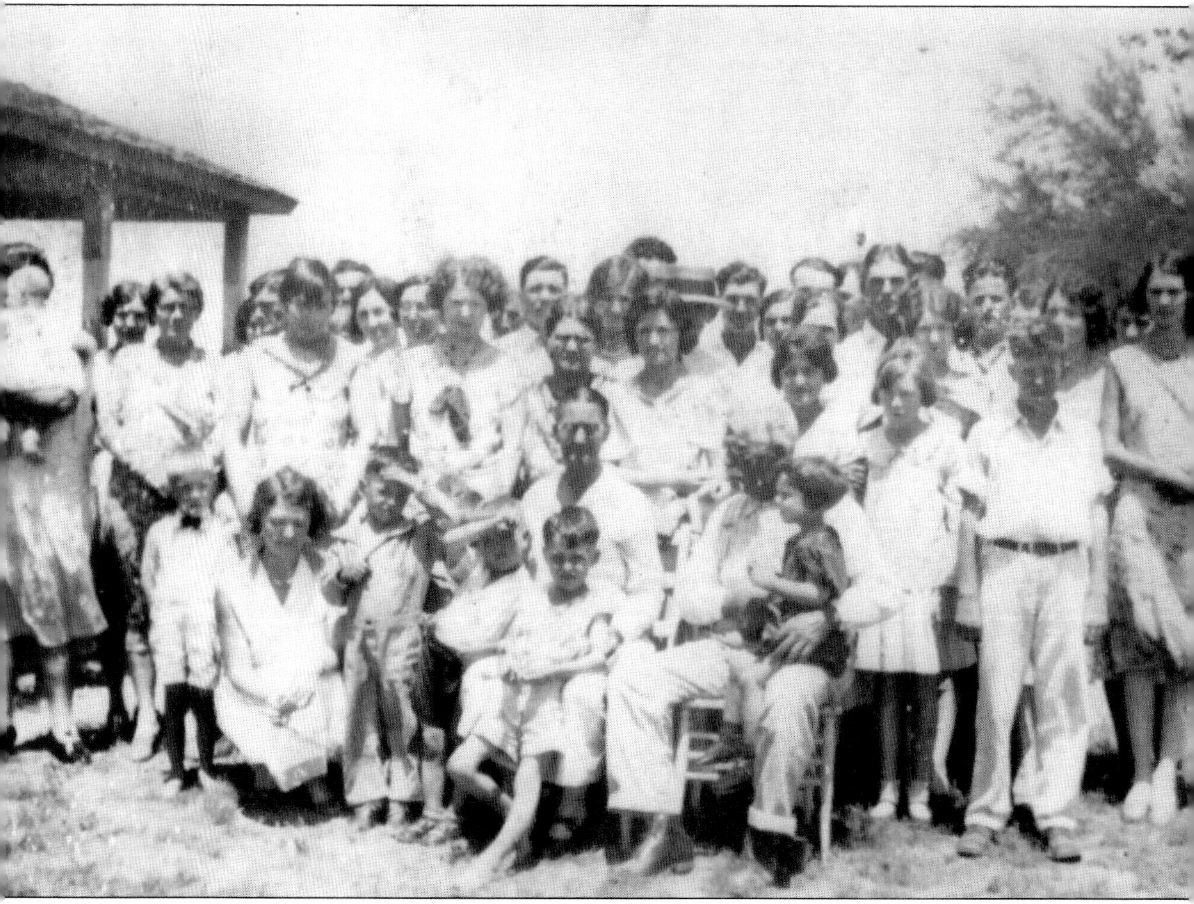

James M. and Josephine Daugherty settled on 228 acres on Mill Creek, seven miles south of Azle, around 1870. After Josephine's death, James married Margaret McBride. At age 16, James had been herding Longhorns across Missouri when Jayhawkers stampeded the cattle and captured him. They let him go because of his young age, and he returned to camp and continued on his way. This photograph shows James (seated) with his large family.

# *Two*

# Schools

Schools were built for the children of early settlers shortly after those first families arrived in the area. John Giles Reynolds, who arrived in 1854, built a log house on what became Reynolds Branch. He also constructed a one-room cabin on his land after a few more families came to serve the dual purpose of being a school on weekdays and holding church services on Sunday. Many early communities followed that same pattern.

The second building to be used as a school, and the first one built solely for that purpose, was called the Picket School. Small trees could be used for construction if the logs from them were set vertically in the ground in a trench dug for that purpose. In this school, children sat on benches made out of logs, with no back support. The Picket School was located on land that later became the Coho Smith farm. Smith enlarged the original schoolhouse and made it into a home for his family. The farm currently is incorporated within the boundaries of the city-owned Cross Timbers Golf Course. A historical marker notes the previous location of the Picket School–farmhouse, a cellar, and a rock fort. The unique rock-lined well is still there.

A third early school was built in 1871 at Ash Creek Baptist Church, at 300 South Stewart Street. Only the last names of two of the teachers survive, a Mr. McIntire, and his successor, a Mr. Rowland.

By the 1880s, two schools existed in Azle: Ash Creek, with 15 students, and Walnut Creek, with 35. The schools extended only through eighth grade. William Lipscomb built a college in 1882, which eventually admitted younger boys and girls. Later, the college consolidated with the Azle School, and in 1884, a new building was erected at what is now 209 West Main Street in Azle. The frame structure had a Gothic arch over the entrance and a belfry. It was expanded to three rooms, which incorporated a high school, a grammar school, and a primary school. A separate school for African Americans was in operation by 1891.

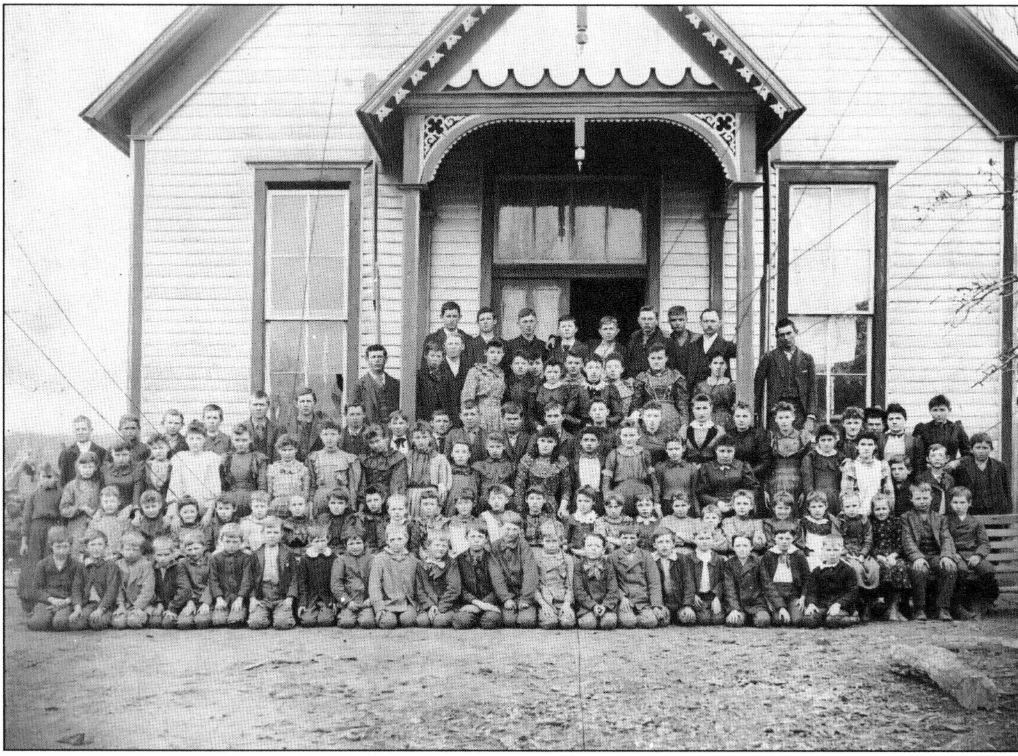

The entire school population lined up for this 1906 photograph when the school building was this white frame structure at 209 West Main Street. The principal that year was a Mr. Stubblefield. Today, a private residence is there.

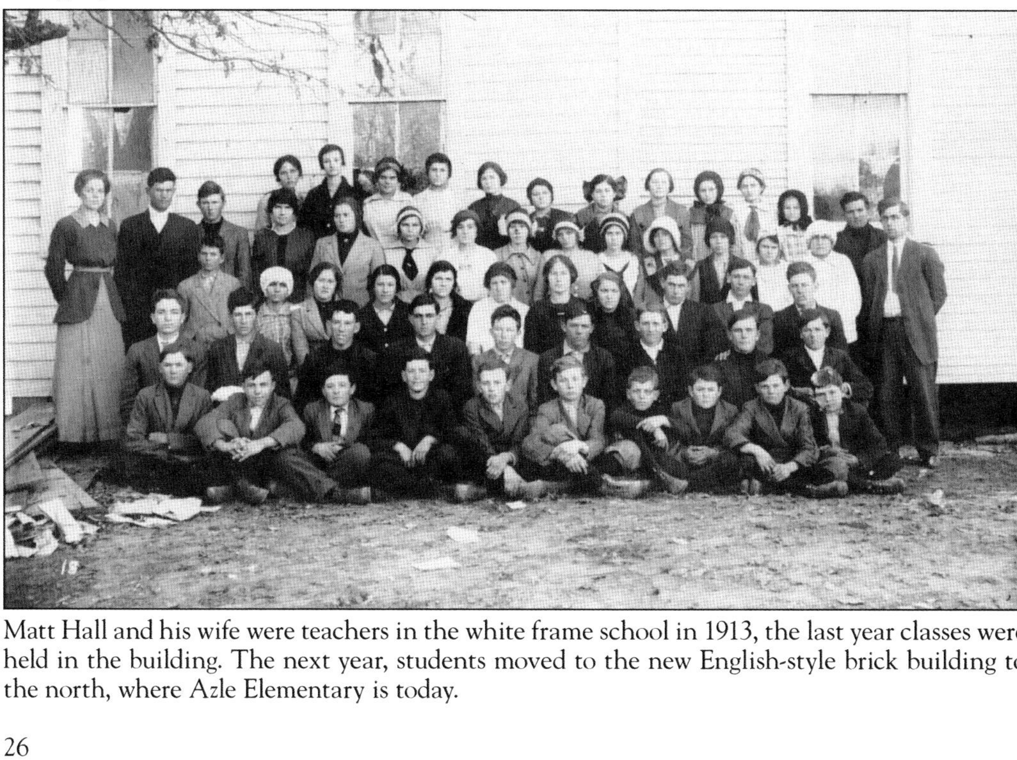

Matt Hall and his wife were teachers in the white frame school in 1913, the last year classes were held in the building. The next year, students moved to the new English-style brick building to the north, where Azle Elementary is today.

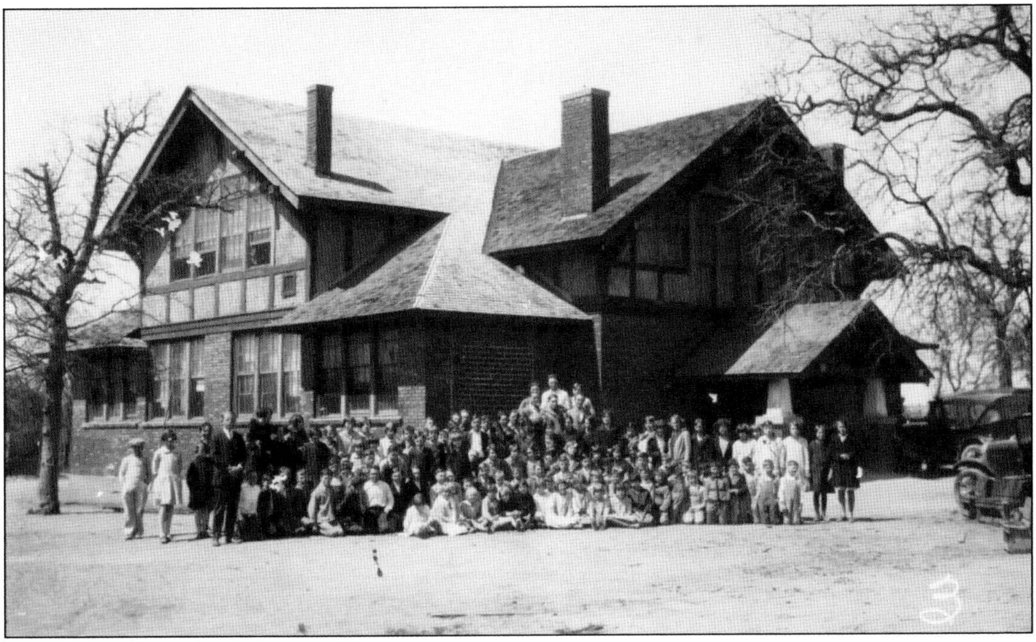

The two-story "Red Brick School," as folks called it, was Azle's first school built to house all grades. The English-style building was completed before the 1914 school year and opened with four classrooms downstairs and an auditorium upstairs. The first superintendent was W.A. Meacham, who had just graduated from North Texas State Teachers' College in Denton. Meacham later taught in Fort Worth, where a middle school now bears his name.

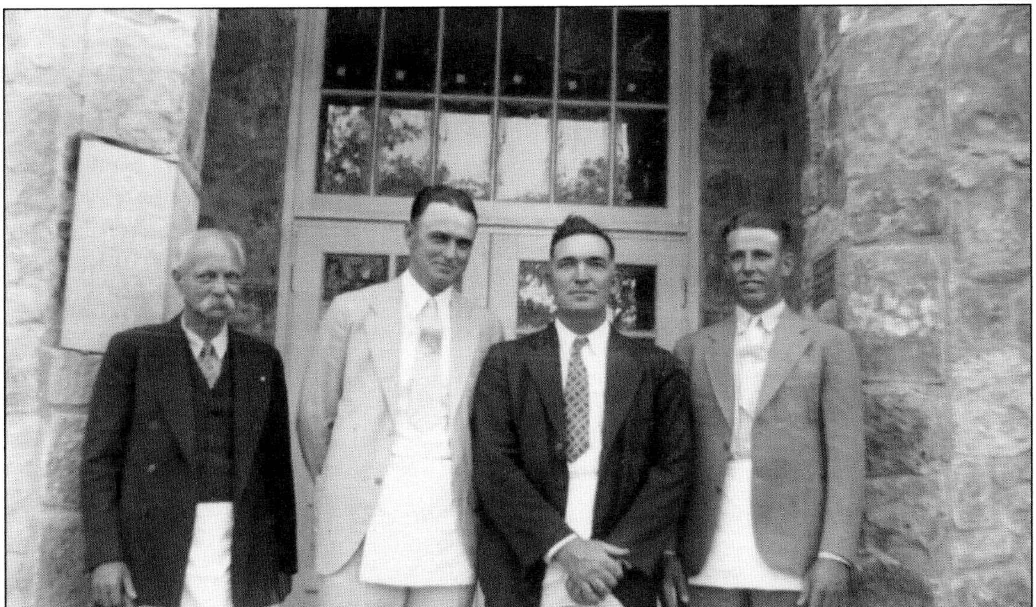

Masonic Lodge members in Azle often officiated at dedications and cornerstone layings within the community. Seen at the laying of the cornerstone for the Rock School in the late 1930s are, from left to right, W.T. Gipson, Johnny Lee King, Willie Speers, and Faris Ross, all members of the local lodge.

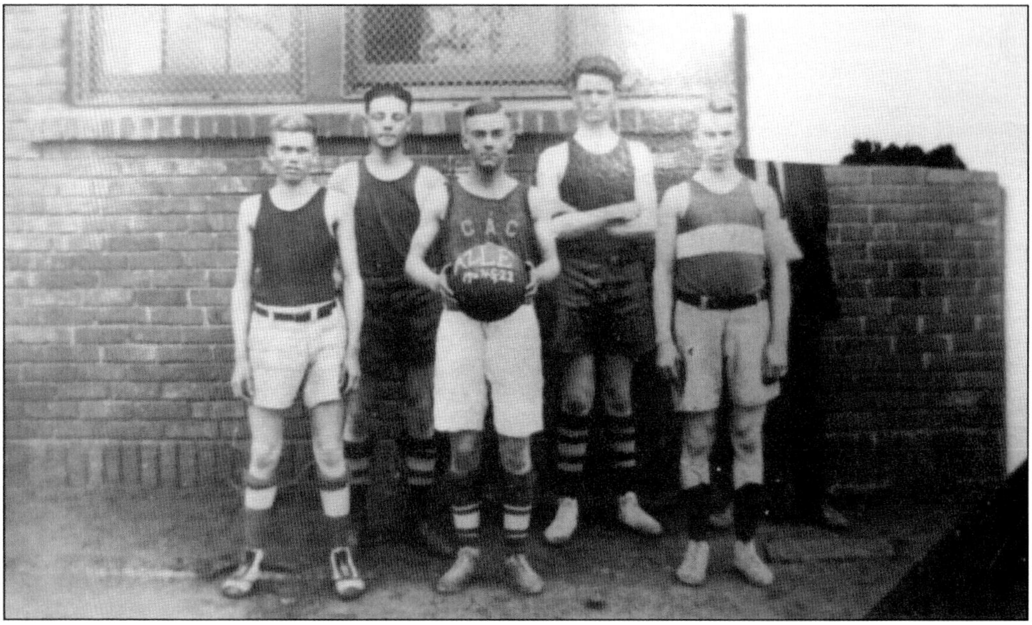

In 1922, Azle's basketball team included, from left to right, Martin "Scoopy" Dolman, Harry Pierce, Nolan Seyster, Robert Floyd, and Martin Parish. The entire team could travel in one car to out-of-town games. With hamburgers costing only 5¢, they could all eat for a quarter.

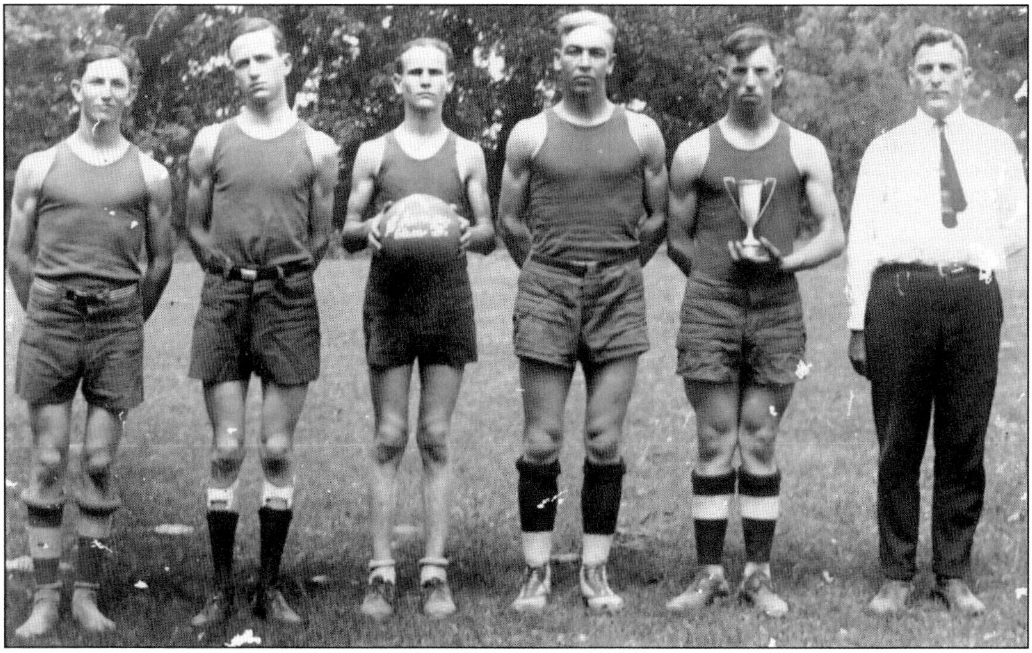

Coach Grover McAlister led these Azle High School players to a championship season in the mid-1920s. They are, from left to right, George Dunaway, Ray Dunaway, Joe Sessions, Carroll Rowden, Malcolm Walker, and Coach McAlister. Today, a street in Azle is named after the Dunaway family.

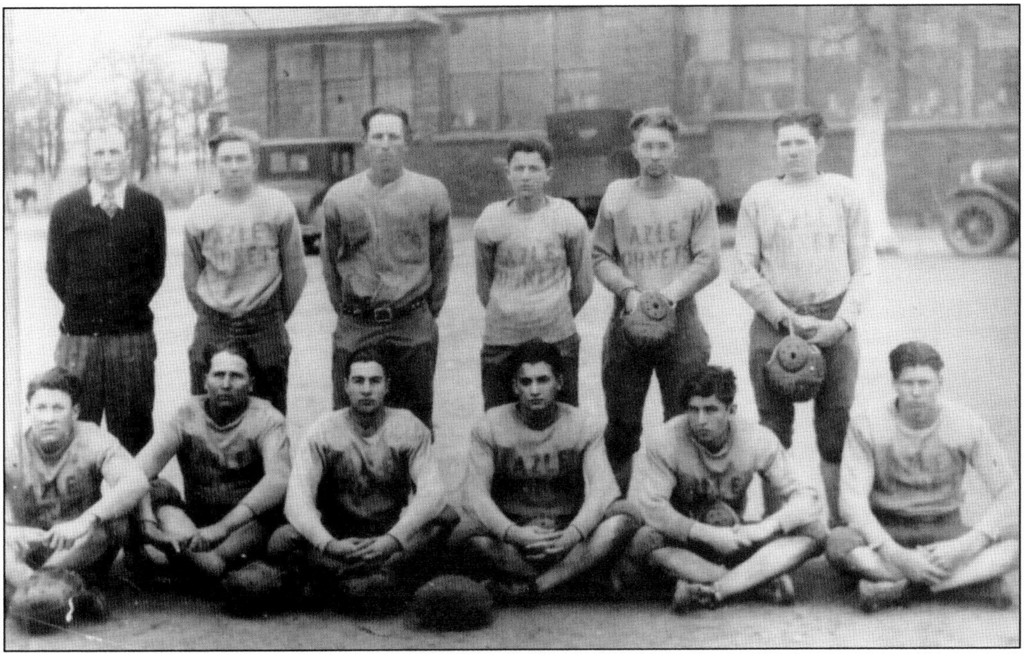

The Azle Hornet football team in 1929 barely had 11 players, including, from left to right, (first row) F.G. Brittian, Elbert Chandler, Orman Kimbrough, Claudie Newsom, Clingman Thompson, and Floyd Cummings; (second row) Coach Frank Young, Gail Scrimshire, Wilburn Ansley, Douglas Phillips, O.D. Wilms, and Hershel Scroggins.

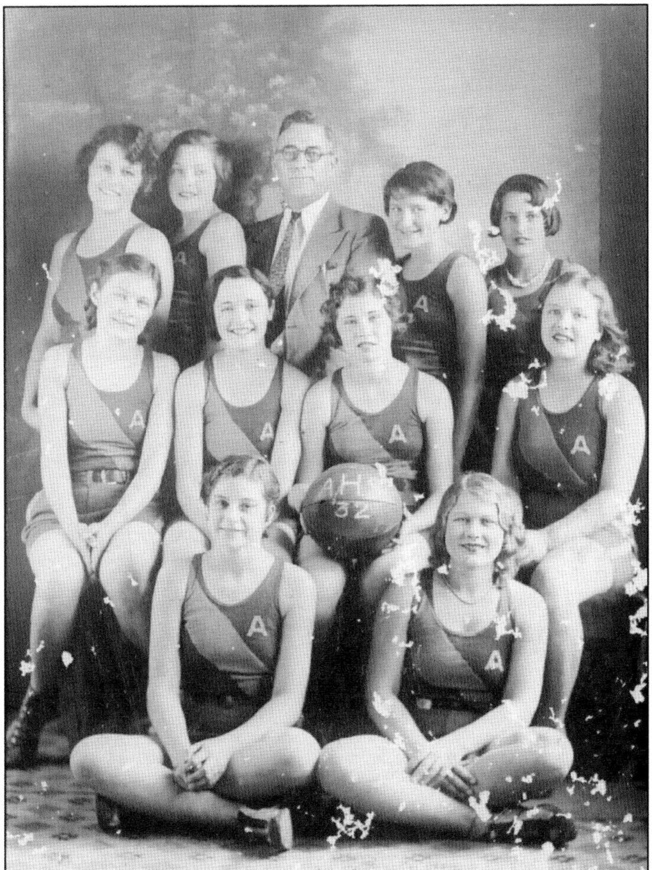

In 1932, Grover McAllister coached the Azle High School Girls' basketball team. The team included, from left to right, (first row) Nadie Murphy and Mary Page; (second row) Iva Mae Parker, Maggie Parker, Rebecca Thompson, and Pauline Admire; (third row) Helen Warn, Marjorie Scoggins, McAllister, Lorena McDonald, and Marie Tucker.

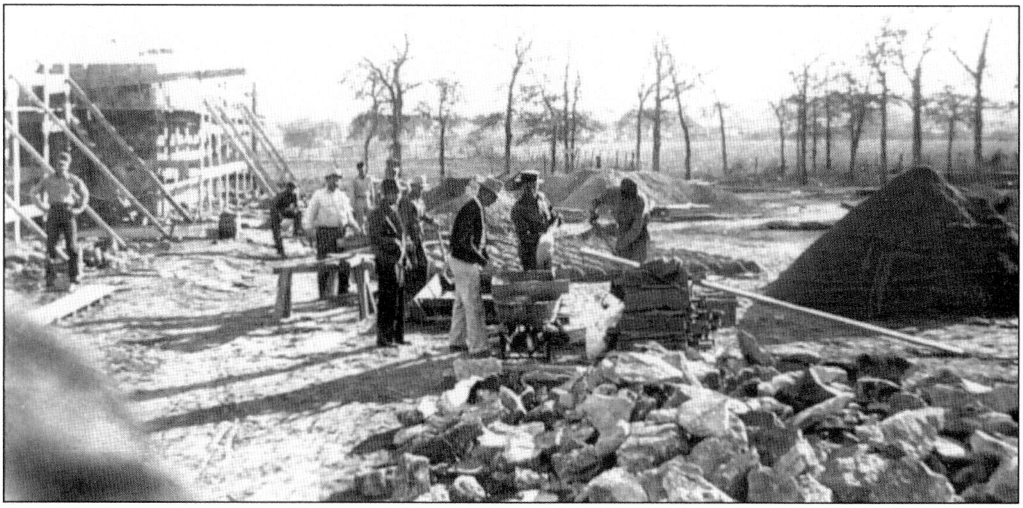

A work crew in the late 1930s built what is now Azle Elementary, which currently includes fifth and sixth grades. Long called the Rock School, it originally held all grades, from its opening in 1939 until 1953. Written on the back of this original photograph are the words, "Granpa Reed building the Azle rock school." (Courtesy Roy Woodruff.)

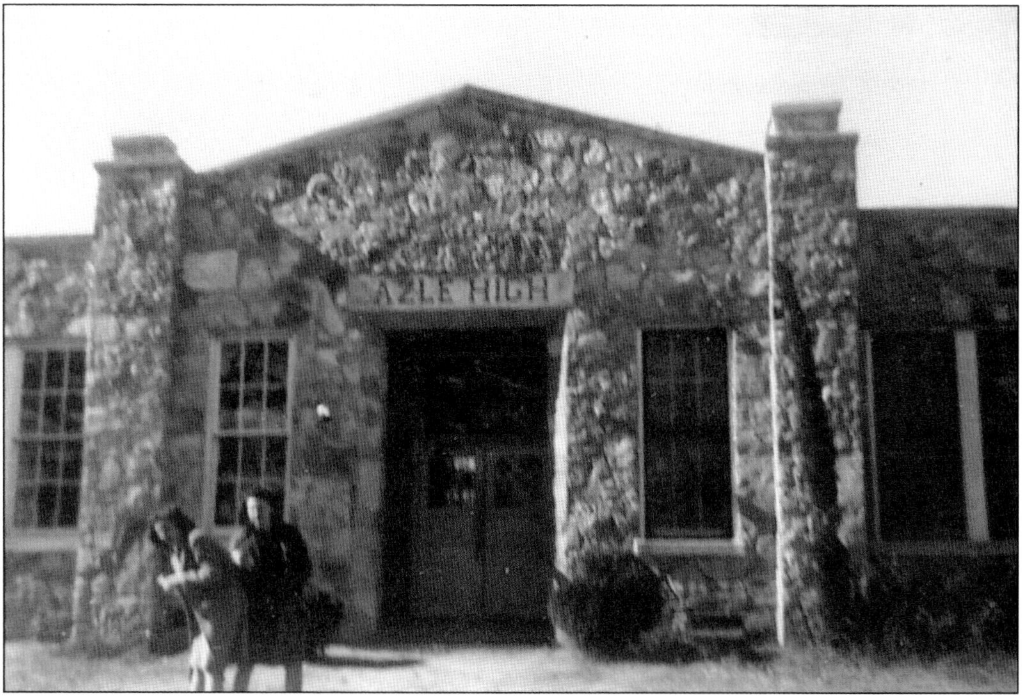


This close-up photograph of the Rock School features the words "Azle High" embedded in concrete above the door. The class of 1939 became the first to graduate from the Rock School. In 1953, a new high school opened on School Street.

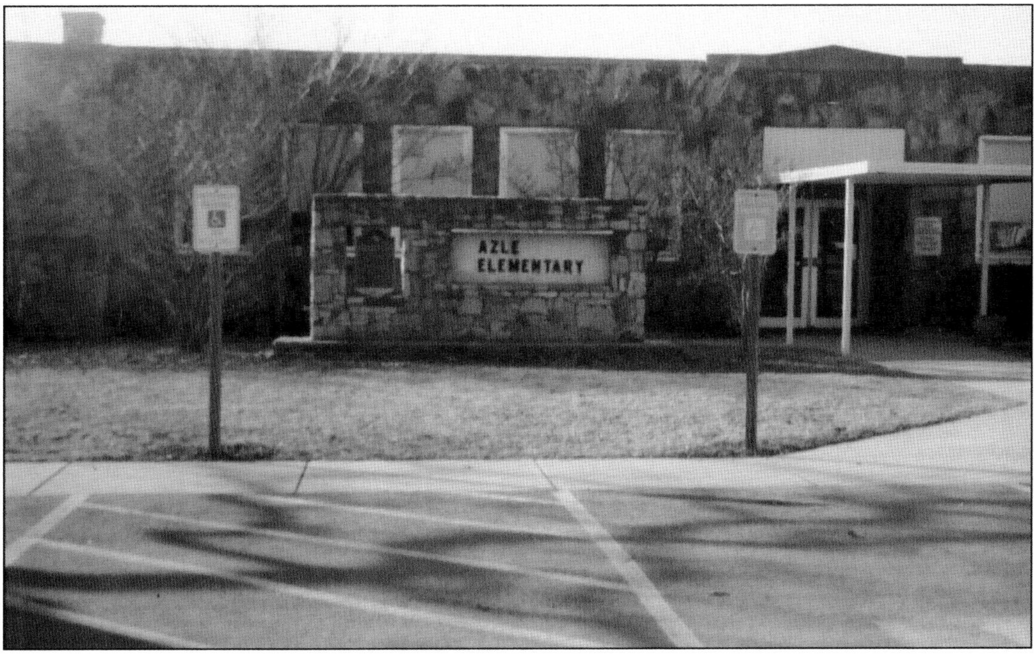


After the Azle Historical Museum Society pursued placing a historical marker for the old Rock School, the Azle Independent School District constructed a rock structure in front of the school as a marker, with a sign indicating that the building now houses Azle Elementary.

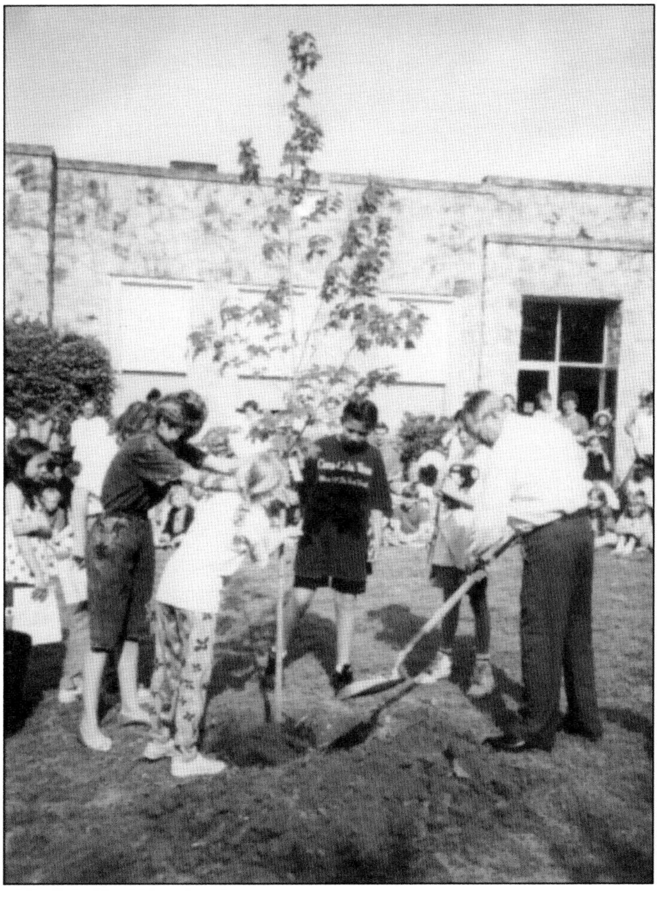

The students of Azle Elementary went outside on this beautiful spring day in May 1993 to plant a tree on the lawn in honor of principal Charles Richardson's five years of service. The red maple was donated by the Cobb and Rogers families and Janice Williams.

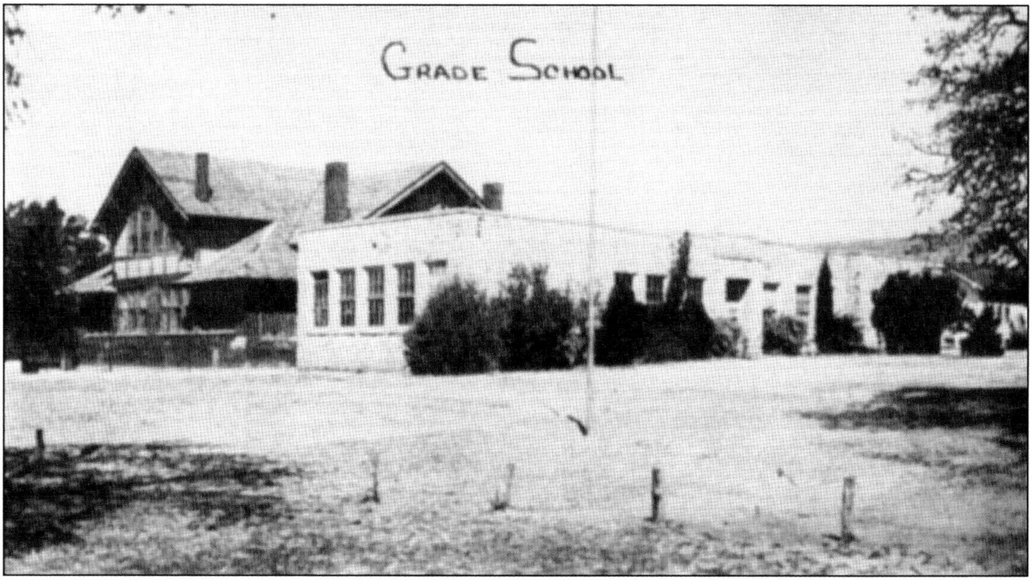


In 1946, the old Red Brick School served as the grade school and was still located behind the Rock School, which housed the high school. Later, the second story of the redbrick building was removed and the lower floor was connected to the Rock School. The white frame building pictured below served as the gymnasium for all of Azle's schoolchildren in 1946. The trees to the right provided welcome shade while the children played outside at recess.

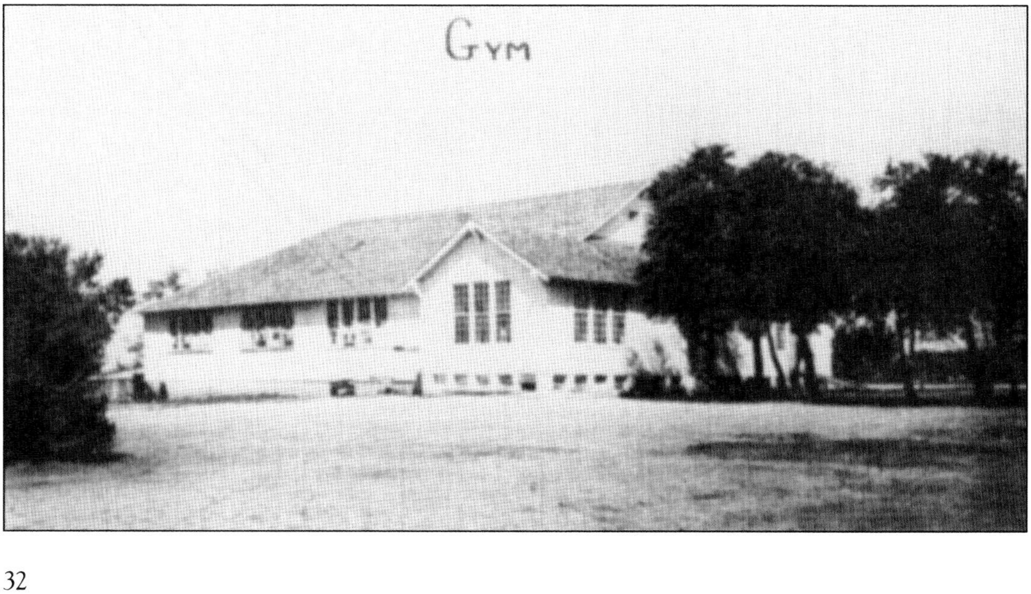

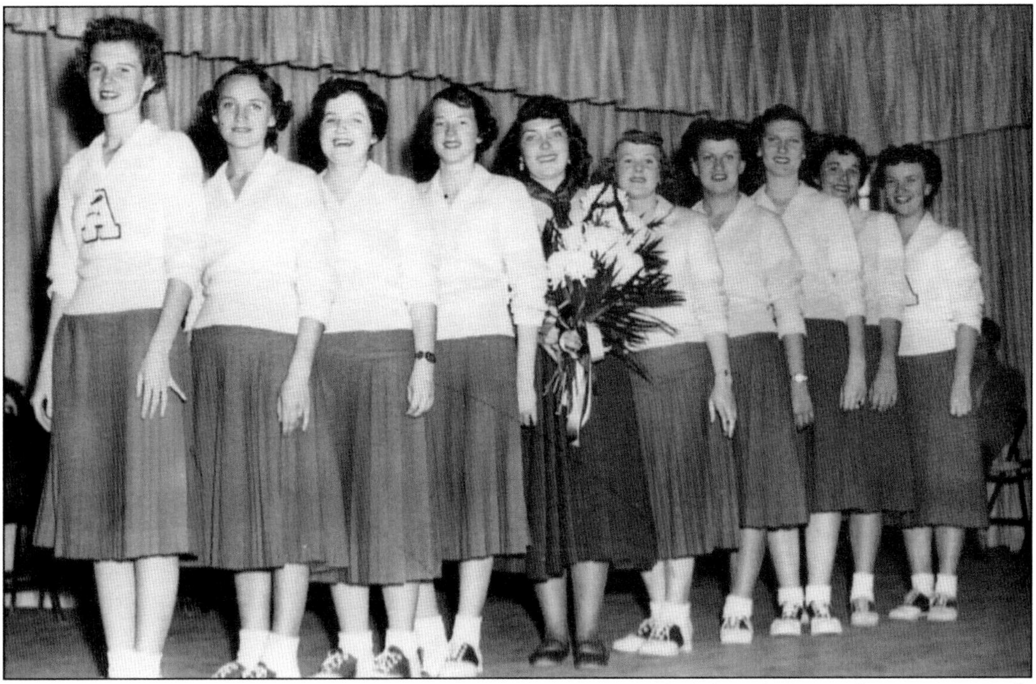

In the 1951–1952 school year, the Azle cheerleading team included, from left to right, Juanita "Red" Phillips (senior), Marjorie Dusek (junior), Annette Deats (sophomore), Betty Yates (sophomore), Jeanne Pearson Wright (sponsor), Ethel McMullin (senior), Laverne Reynolds (sophomore), Carolyn Bell (junior), Ann Looney (senior), and Dorothy Berry (senior). Junior Eva Gottlob, not pictured, was also a cheerleader.

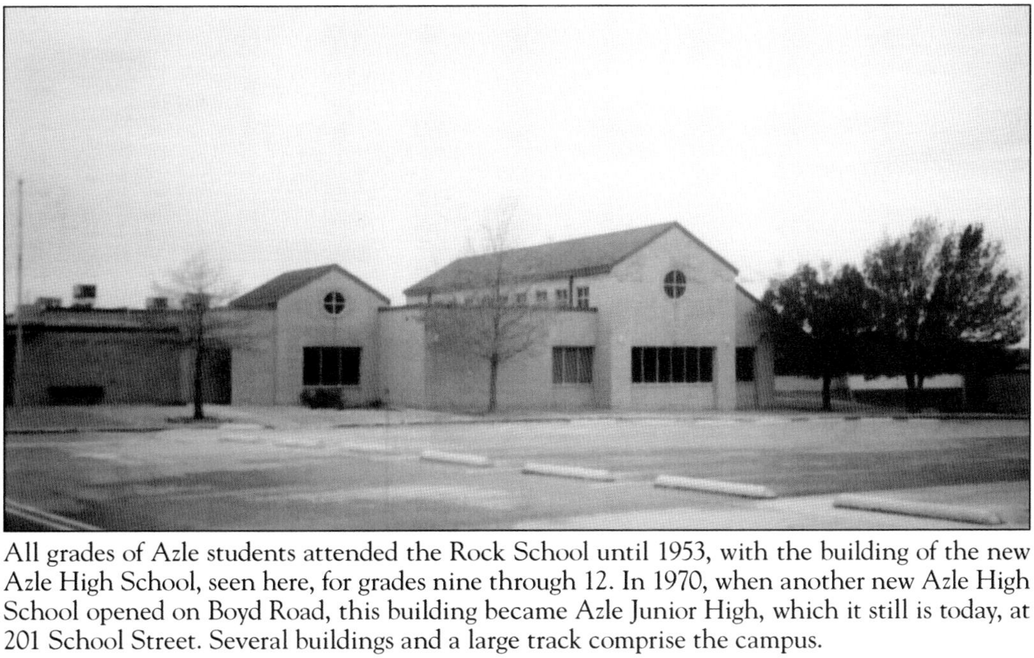

All grades of Azle students attended the Rock School until 1953, with the building of the new Azle High School, seen here, for grades nine through 12. In 1970, when another new Azle High School opened on Boyd Road, this building became Azle Junior High, which it still is today, at 201 School Street. Several buildings and a large track comprise the campus.

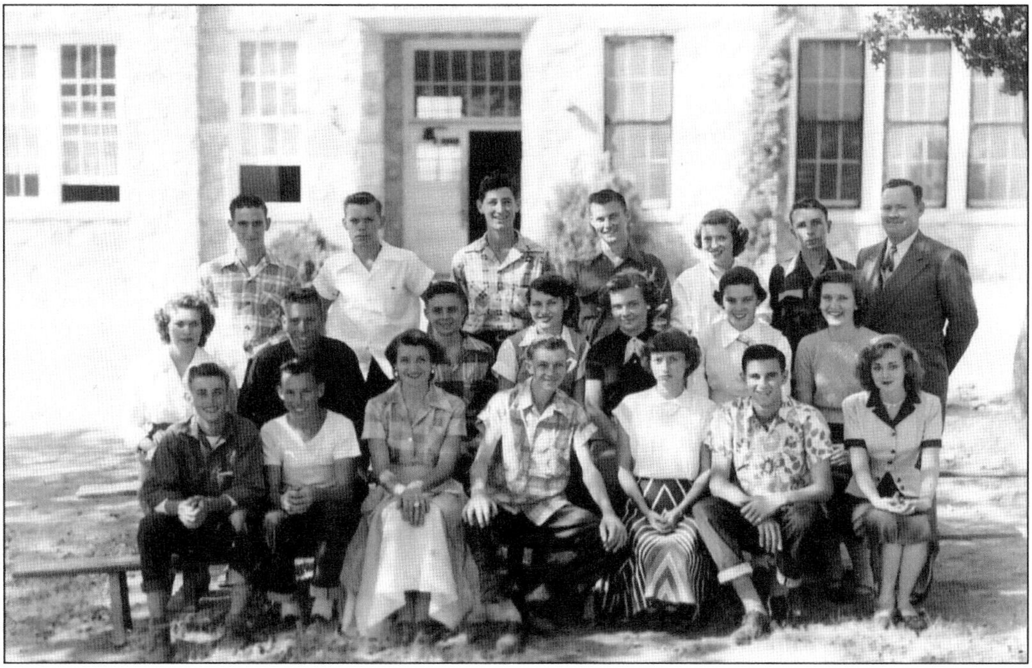

In 1951–1952, the Azle High School junior class included, from left to right, (first row) Tommy Henderson, Cleyon Davis, Marjorie Dusek, Bobby Thomas, Mona Gilley, Ed McDuff, and Joan Ingram; (second row) Barbara Banks, Aerl Jernigan, Dale Guthrie, Eva Gottlob, Jacqueline Emanuel, Carolyn Collins, and Carolyn Bell; (third row) James Gilley, Loyd Dennis, Fred Weaver, Melvin Chandler, Ruth Brister, Frank Horton, and R.W. Simmans, sponsor.

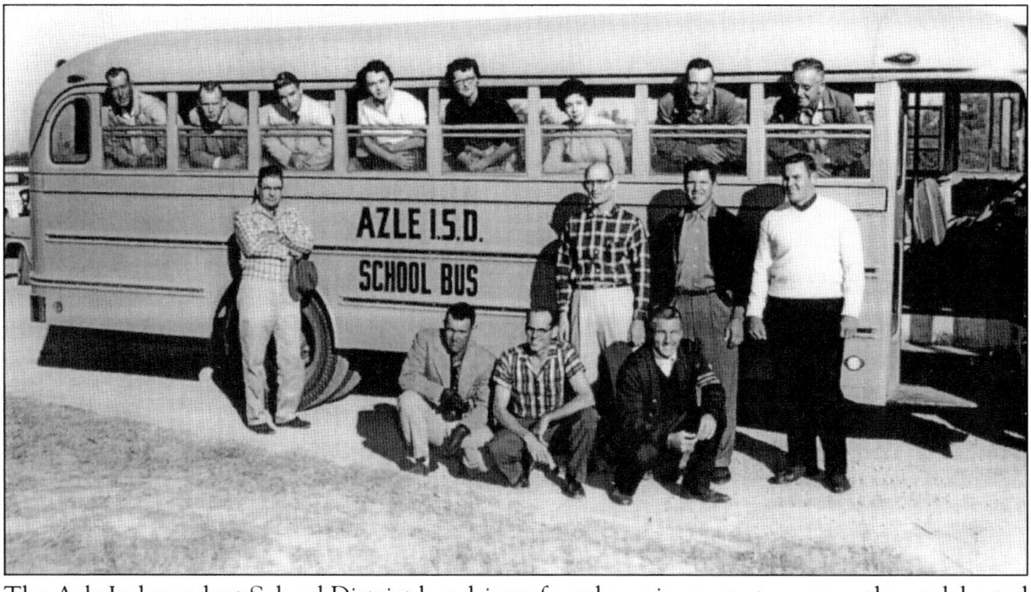


The Azle Independent School District bus drivers found a unique way to pose as they celebrated the purchase of a new bus. They are, from left to right, (kneeling) Gene Thomason, John Miller, and Don Hood; (standing) Fred Admire, John Webb, Al Merritt, and Larry Ward. Peeking out of the windows are, from left to right, Fred Howard, Harden Ray, Bill Barber, Alleene Admire, Mamie Dusek, Jeanine Irby, Jessie Howard, and Fred Kahler.

William B. Smith served as Azle High School principal from 1957 to 1961. This photograph came from the 1959–1960 Parent Teachers Association scrapbook, which is housed in the Azle Historical Museum.

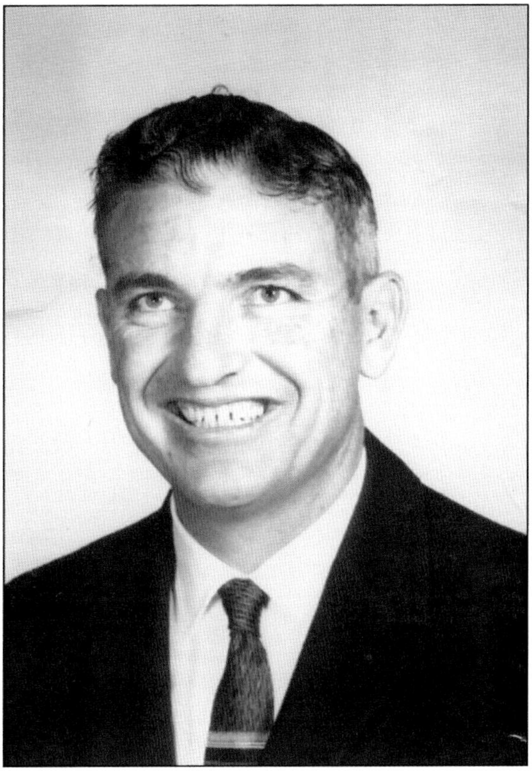

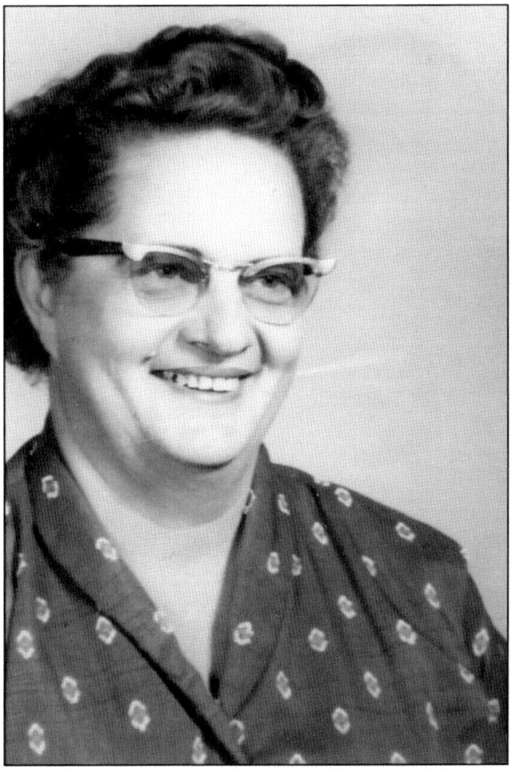

Hallie Harmon, seen here, served as Eagle Heights Elementary principal from 1960 to 1964. Berniece Finney followed her as principal in 1964, and Bobby Boyd took over in 1972.

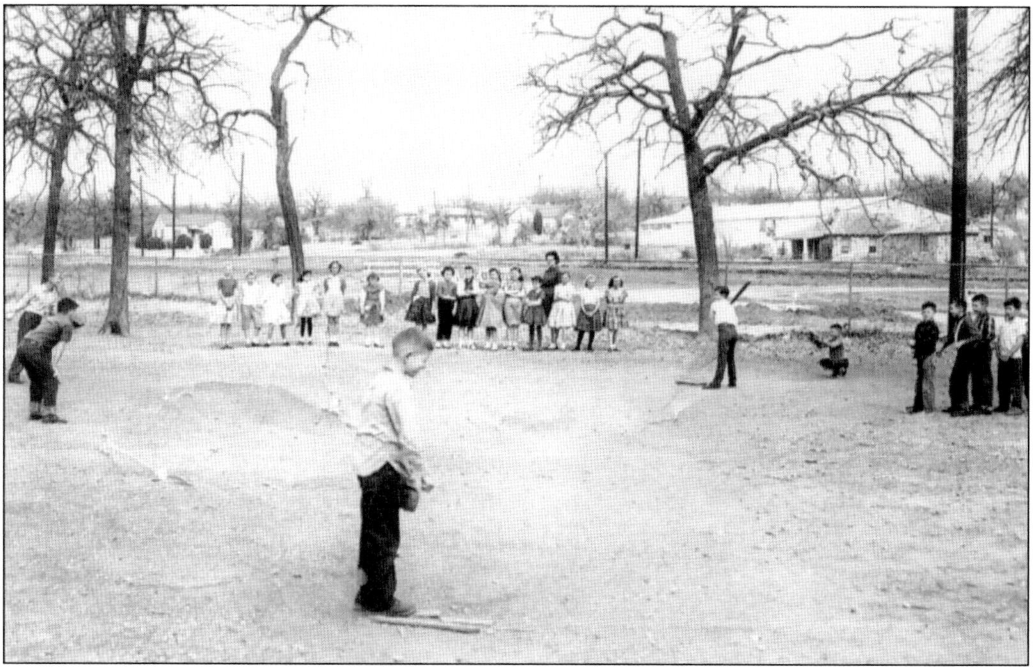

This baseball team plays on the Azle Elementary School playground during the 1959–1960 school year while the girls and their teacher stand and watch. Perhaps these girls, who all wore dresses to school in those days, formed a cheering squad.

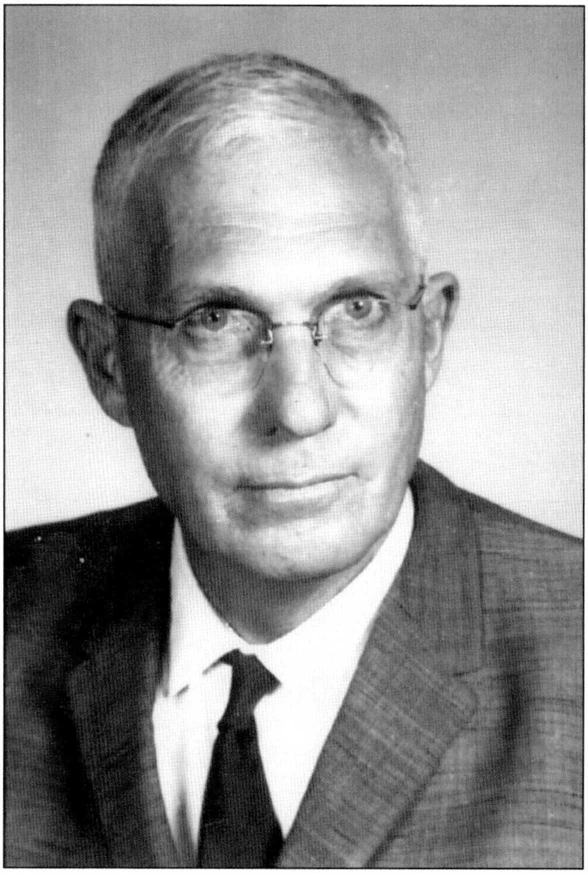

Louis McGregor served as superintendent of the Azle Independent School District from 1949 to 1961. This photograph appeared in the 1959–1960 Parent Teachers Association scrapbook, which is in the Azle Historical Museum. The museum also has numerous Azle High School annuals.

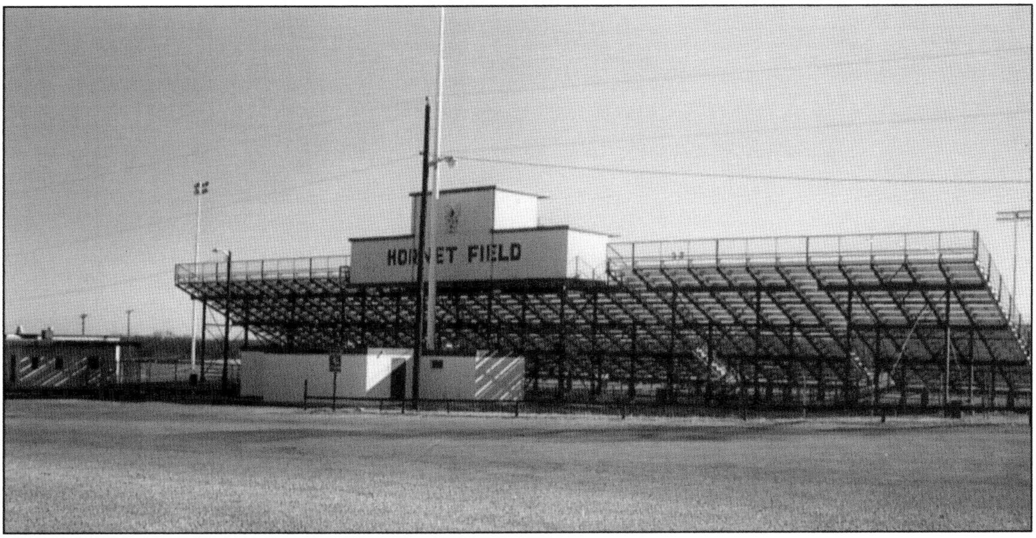


An early photograph of Hornet Field supplements the current Azle High School complex on Boyd Road. The field was constructed in 1965 before the high school opened in the fall of 1970. Prior to 1970, the high school was located at 201 School Street, where the Azle Junior High is today. By the early 2000s, the Azle Independent School District had seven elementary schools, two junior high schools, and Azle High School. (Courtesy Azle Chamber of Commerce.)

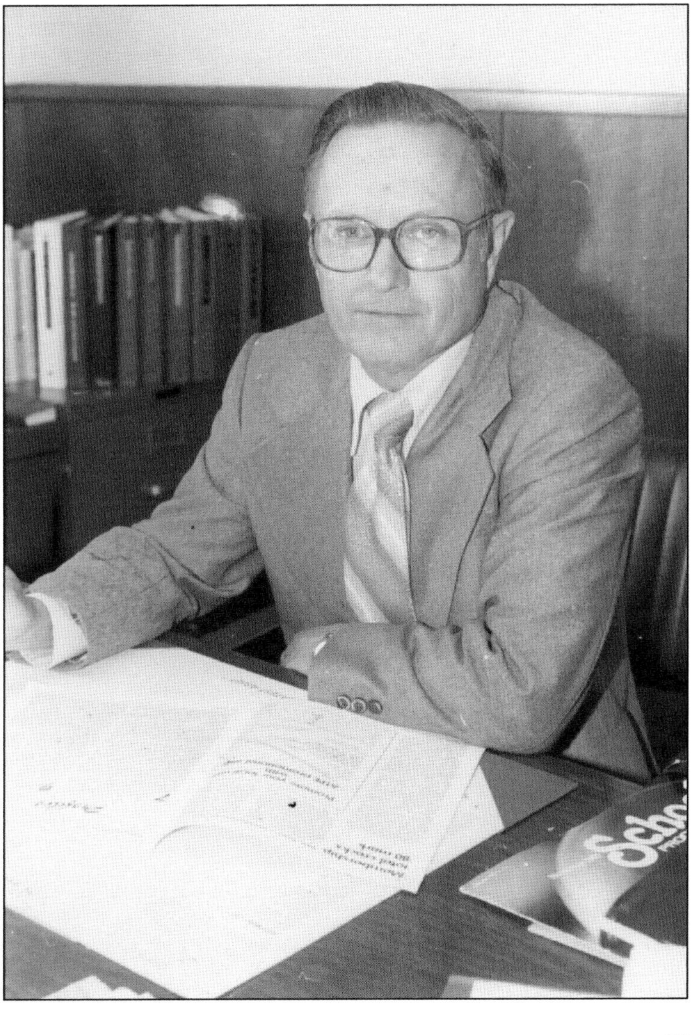

Wendall Hoover served as principal of Azle Elementary—the Rock School—from 1953 to 1961. Previously, he taught for a year and a half in Springtown. From 1961 to 1985, he was superintendent of all the schools in the growing Azle Independent School District. An elementary school in Azle now bears his name.

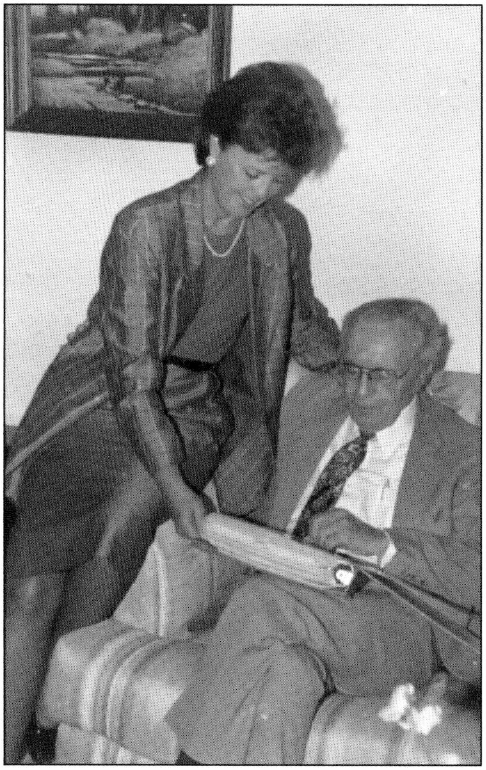

Chelsa Holder and her dad, G.C. Holder, reminisce about his days at the Rock School. She followed in his footsteps, many years later, becoming principal at the same school, then called Azle Elementary. Mr. Holder spent six years as principal at the Rock School when it housed all the grades. In 1957, he left the Azle schools to work for the Texas Education Agency and the Texas Rehabilitation Commission, retiring in 1974.

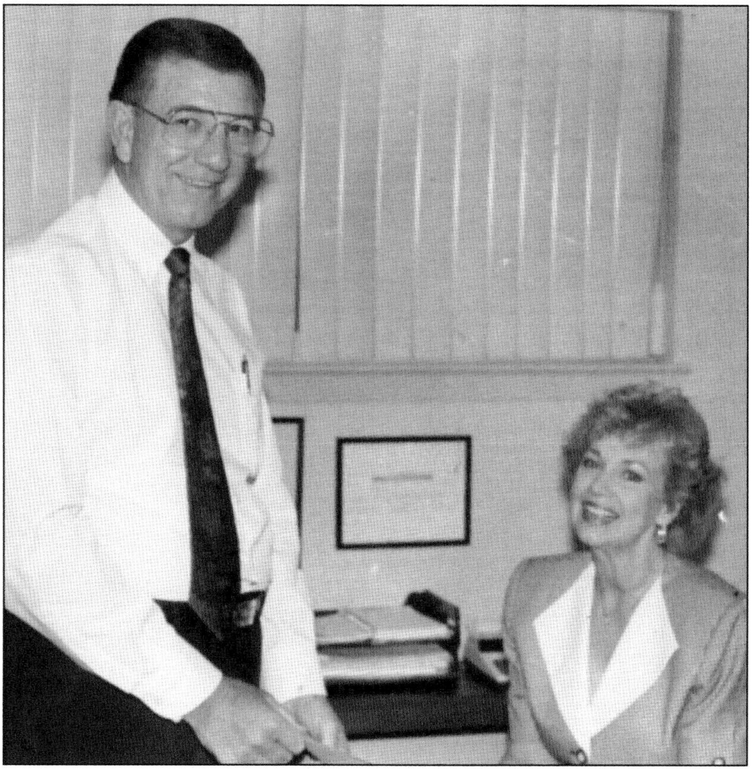

In this photograph, William Ortego, superintendent of Azle ISD from April 1985 to June 1994 confers with his secretary, Camilla Spruill, before a 1992–1993 board meeting when the trustees approved the school budget.

# *Three*

# Churches and Historical Markers

In the years leading up to 1900, Azle had Baptist, Methodist, and Christian churches. Since that time, religious institutions have multiplied in Azle, and today, several churches in those denominations exist, as well as many others.

The Texas Historical Commission was created in 1953 as the Texas State Historical Survey Committee before changing its name in 1972. Its mission is to identify important historic sites across the state with the purpose of preserving them if possible. An educational responsibility has also been added. The state commission relies on local citizens to help with this identification and preservation process.

Since its establishment in 1976, the Azle Historical Museum Society, along with its museum responsibilities, has applied to the Texas Historical Commission for historical markers. Along with those requested by others, the city now has 15 such markers. Most of these are site markers rather than building or landmark designations.

For example, in clearly marked spots around Azle, historical markers commemorate a Kiowa raid that occurred in the 19th century, honor an early African American cemetery, point out the burial site of a hero of the Texas Revolution who later lived in Azle, and mark the location of an early post office.

Additional historical markers honor the city's namesake, Dr. James Azle Steward, and indicate where Azle's first school and an early farmhouse existed. An actual rock-lined well forms a part of that site. Several Azle churches whose original buildings are still standing have also obtained historical markers through the help of the Azle Historical Museum and the Texas Historical Commission.

Intermediary agencies of the commission are the county historical commissions throughout the state. Because much of Azle falls in both Tarrant and Parker Counties, the historical commissions of both counties have been involved depending on the location of the marker.

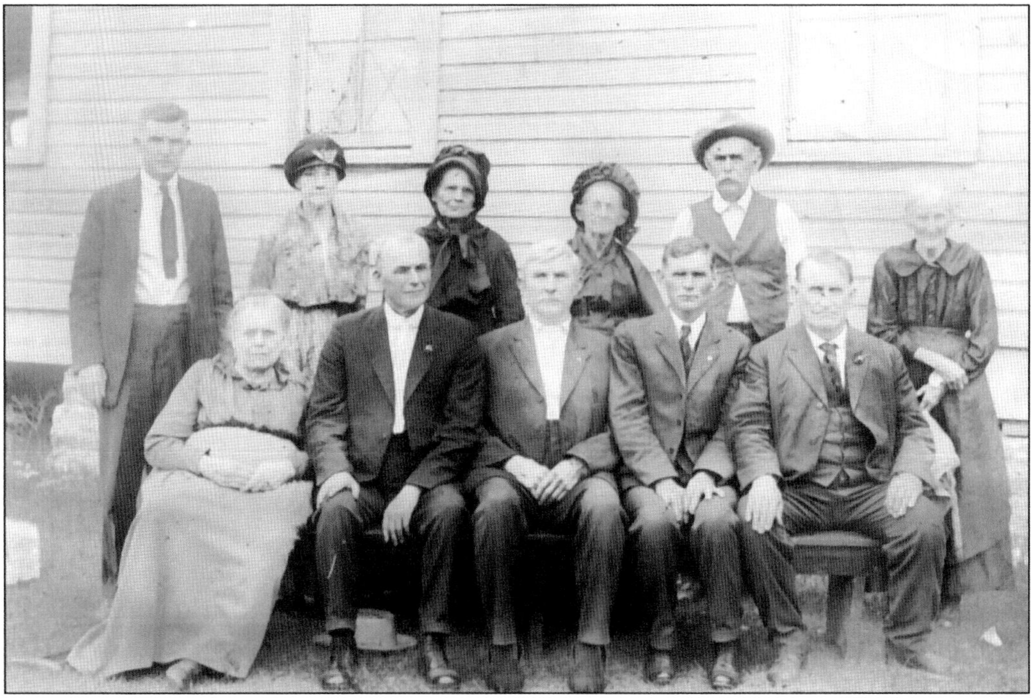

This 1906 photograph shows some of the charter members, deacons, and former pastors of Ash Creek Baptist Church. From left to right, they are (seated) Lottie Smith, Brother J.L. Ward, Deacons T.A. Woodruff and Pat Rogers, and Brother J.R. Goode; (standing) Deacon Charlie Ledbetter, Mattie Rowland, Leora Parker, Pliny Reynolds, Dave Reynolds, and Haskey Dent.

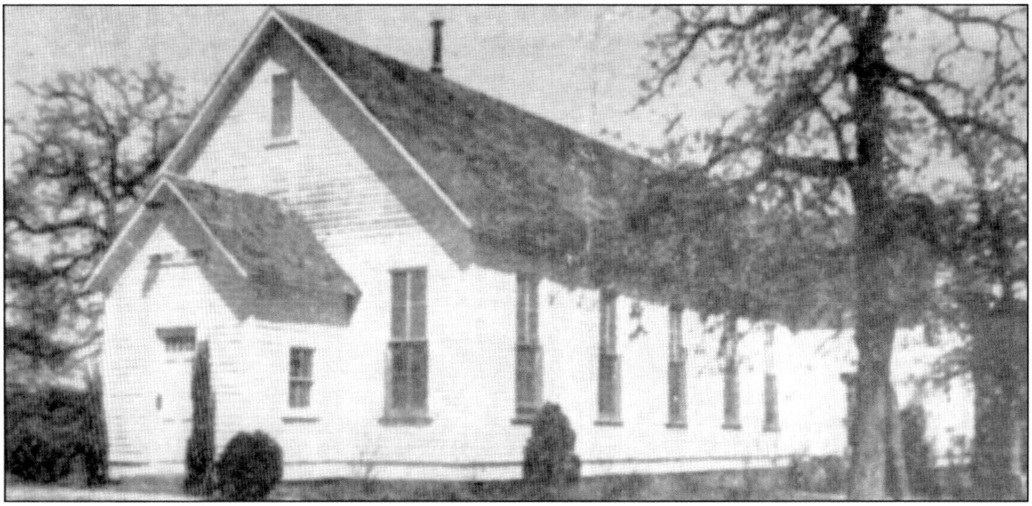

First United Methodist Church of Azle is one of the oldest Methodist congregations in Tarrant County. In 1895, the Promised Land Church held a revival in the abandoned United Brethren Church building in Azle. Rev. J.F. Sherwood organized the first Methodist congregation in October 1895. Rev. W.A. Stephens was called as the first pastor.

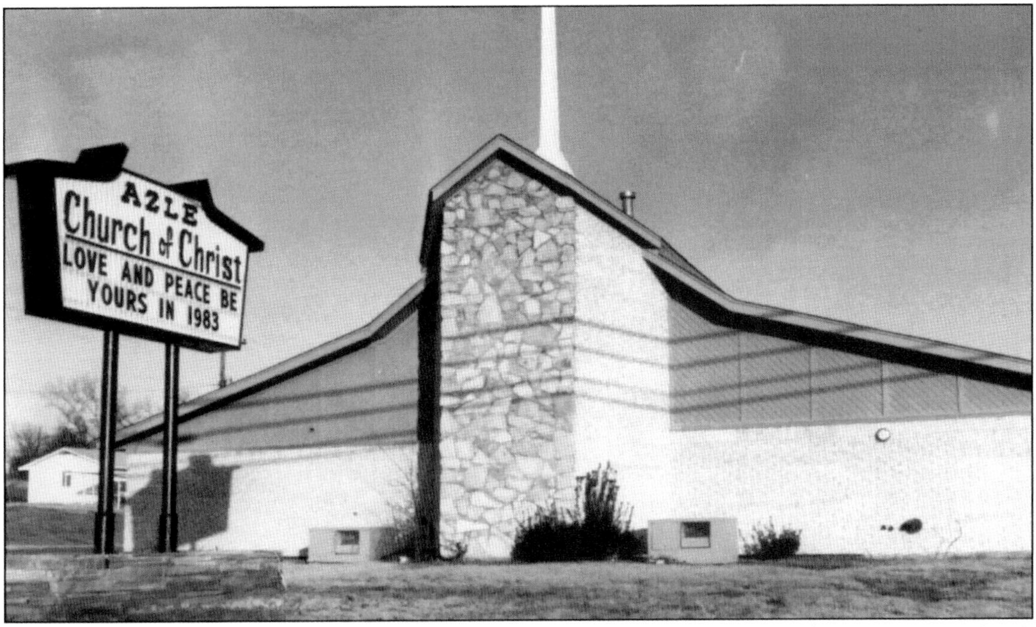


In April 1949, a small group of Christians began meeting together to worship in M.G. Huling's service station. The group made up the beginnings of the Azle Church of Christ. A frame church was completed in September 1949 at 336 Northwest Parkway. As membership increased, a larger meetinghouse, seen here, was completed in 1959. The first full-time preacher was Lee A. Kreidel, who served from 1953 to 1957.

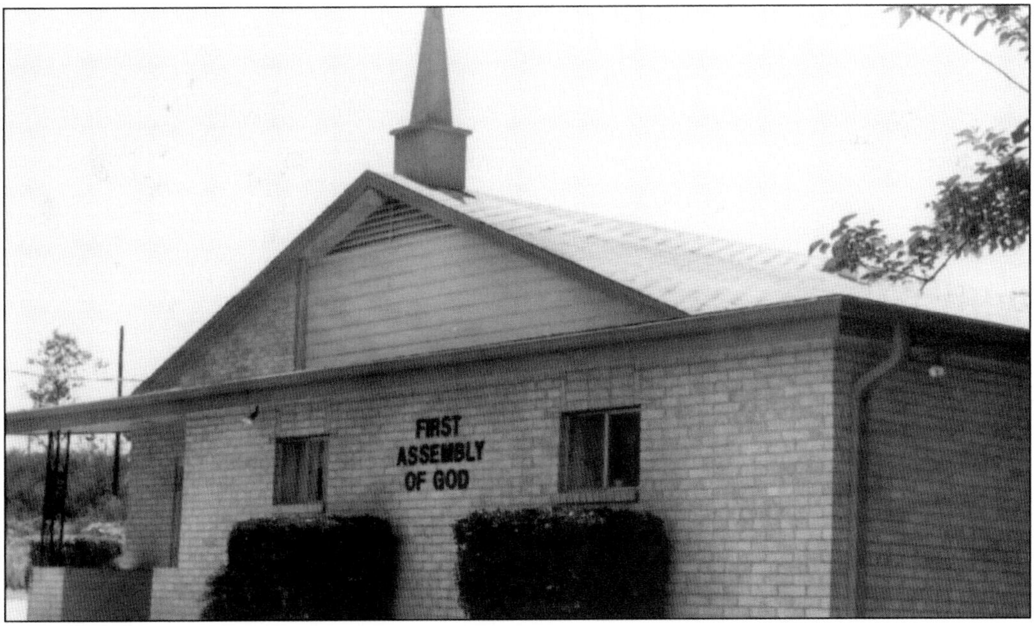


A small group of people met in 1953 at 114 Porter Drive to establish Azle First Assembly of God with Rev. A.E. Stevens as its first pastor. It dedicated a new church building in June 2001 and celebrated 50 years in Azle in 2003. Tim D. Stevens, the current pastor, spent most of his childhood in Africa as the son of missionaries in Botswana.

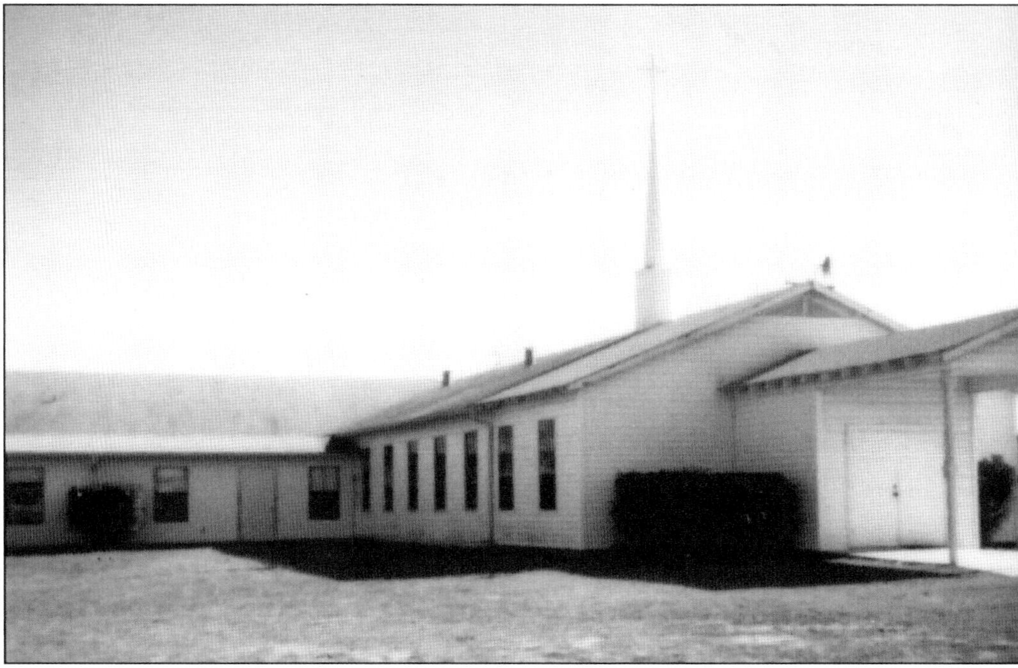

First Baptist Church of Azle began in 1904 as West Fork Baptist Church. The name changed in 1957 under pastor V. Odell Lene. The first pastor was S.M. Edwards, who served for two years. The church is seen here in 1995 at 1016 Boyd Road. A beautiful new sanctuary and classrooms were built across the road at 1017 Boyd Road in 2008.

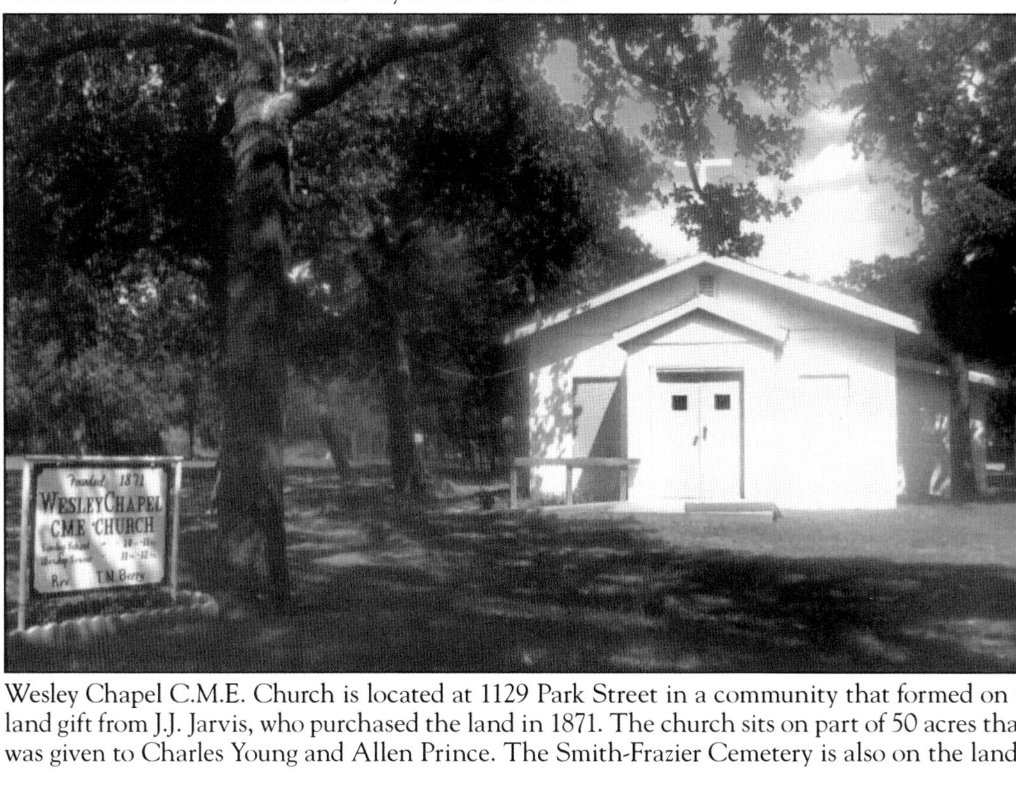


Wesley Chapel C.M.E. Church is located at 1129 Park Street in a community that formed on a land gift from J.J. Jarvis, who purchased the land in 1871. The church sits on part of 50 acres that was given to Charles Young and Allen Prince. The Smith-Frazier Cemetery is also on the land.

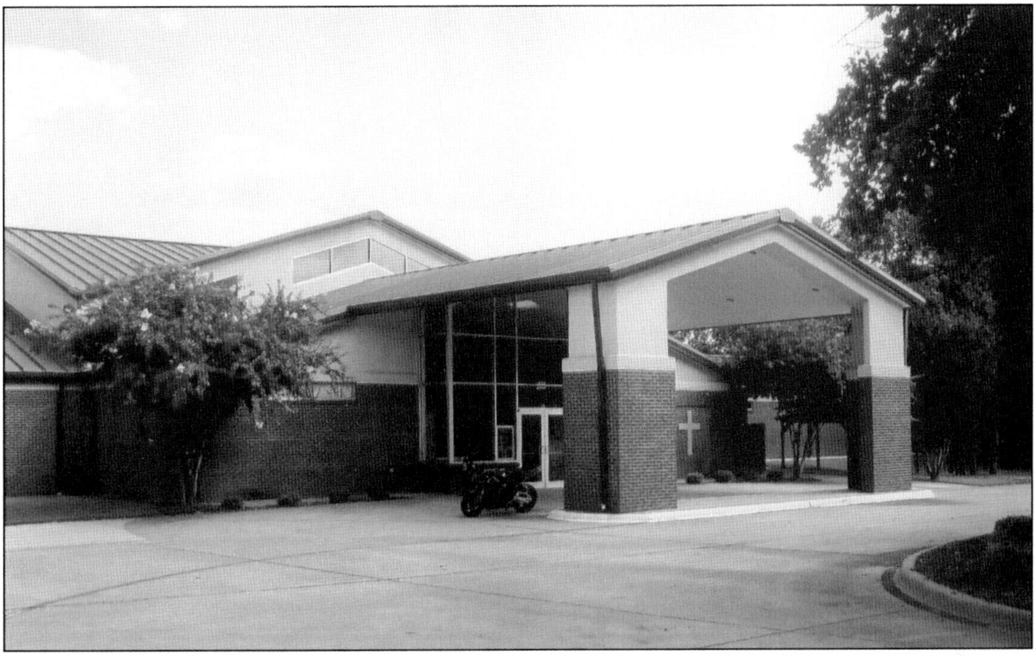

Holy Trinity Catholic Church was organized on November 20, 1982. Followers met in two area churches until they purchased 12 acres of land in August 1990 at 800 Highcrest Drive in the Azlewood development. The building was officially dedicated on June 22, 1996, and the church's membership includes about 250 area families.

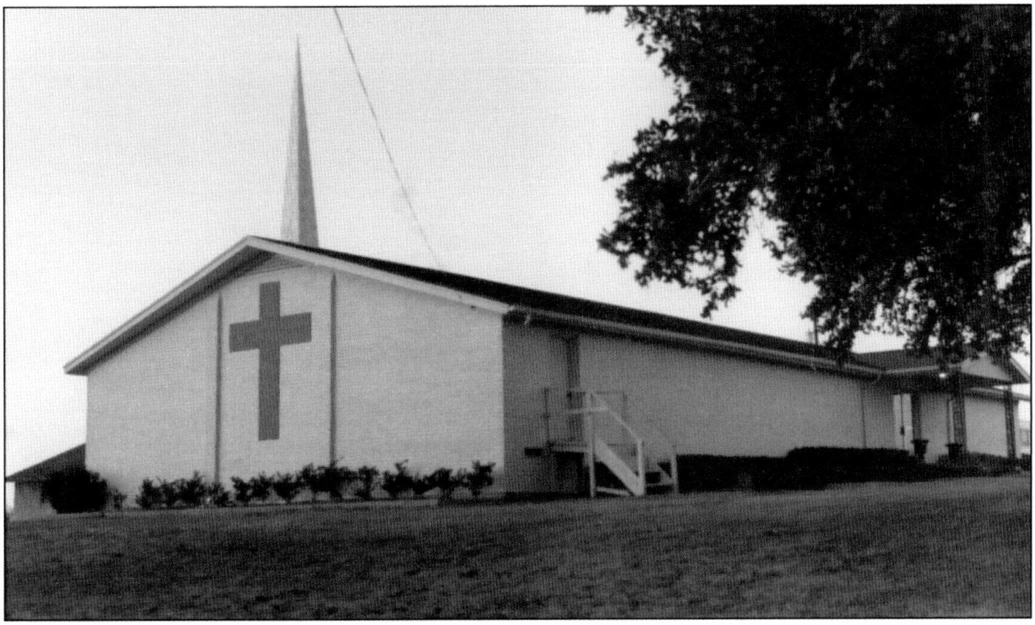

West Parkway Baptist Church began with the prayer and faith of 12 Azle families. The church formally organized in November 1969, first adopting the name Victory Baptist Church. John Beard served as its first pastor. The church auditorium and education building, at 836 Northwest Parkway, was first used in September 1971. The church name was changed to West Parkway Baptist in September 1975.

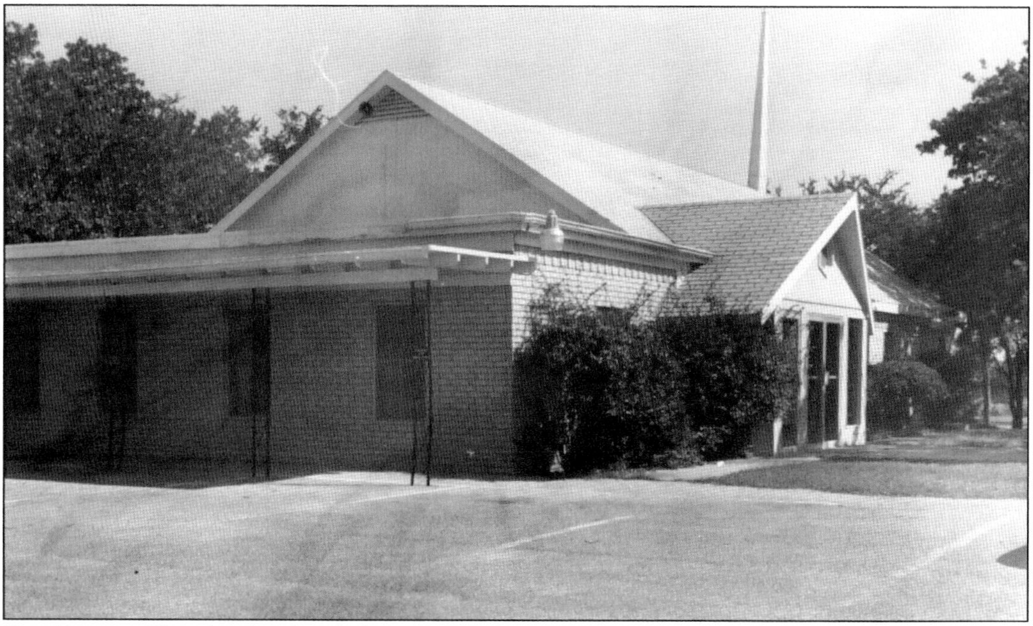

First Baptist Church of Lakeside began with former members of Young Station Baptist after it disbanded in 1965. Handley Baptist Church assisted them in forming the Handley Baptist Mission. The present name was adopted in 1966, when it moved into this building at 8801 Jacksboro Highway. Rev. Cecil Gammill was the first pastor, serving 10 years.

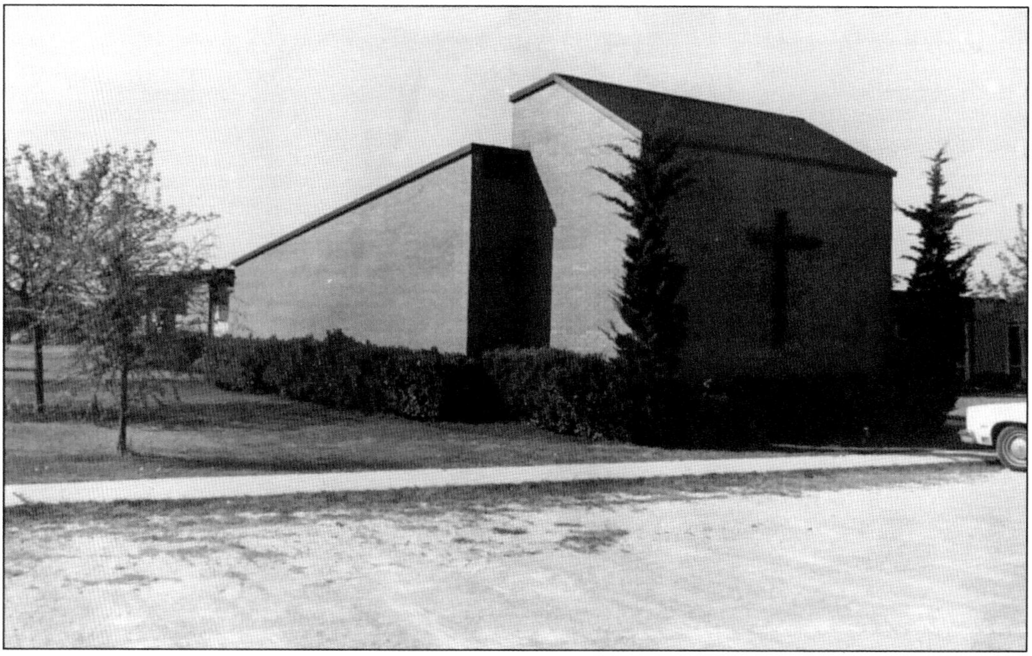

Good Shepherd Lutheran Church began when interested persons were invited to a meeting in November 1962 by Rev. Keith Fox, the pastor of Redeemer Lutheran Church in Fort Worth. Sixty-six people attended their first service on December 2, 1962, at Azle Family Center. Seven acres were purchased at 1313 Southeast Parkway and ground was broken for the church building in March 1966. A new sanctuary was completed in 2011.

This historical marker states, "Tennessee native James Azle Steward came to Texas prior to 1860. He and his wife, Mary E. Fowler Steward, were among the early settlers of this area. Steward was a well-known, respected pioneer physician. The settlement, which had been known by several different names at various times, was renamed Azle when Dr. Steward gave land for a town site in 1883. He was also instrumental in the establishment of Ash Creek Cemetery. Azle Christian Church was built on land donated by the doctor. A Mason, he was buried in Ash Creek Cemetery."

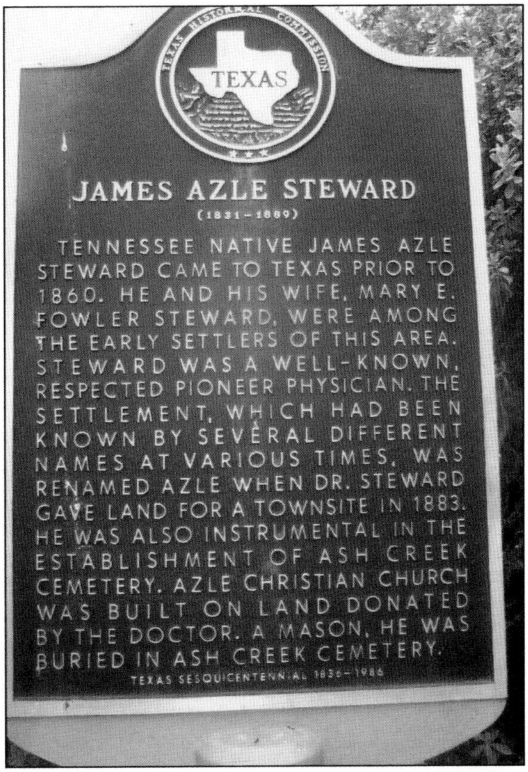


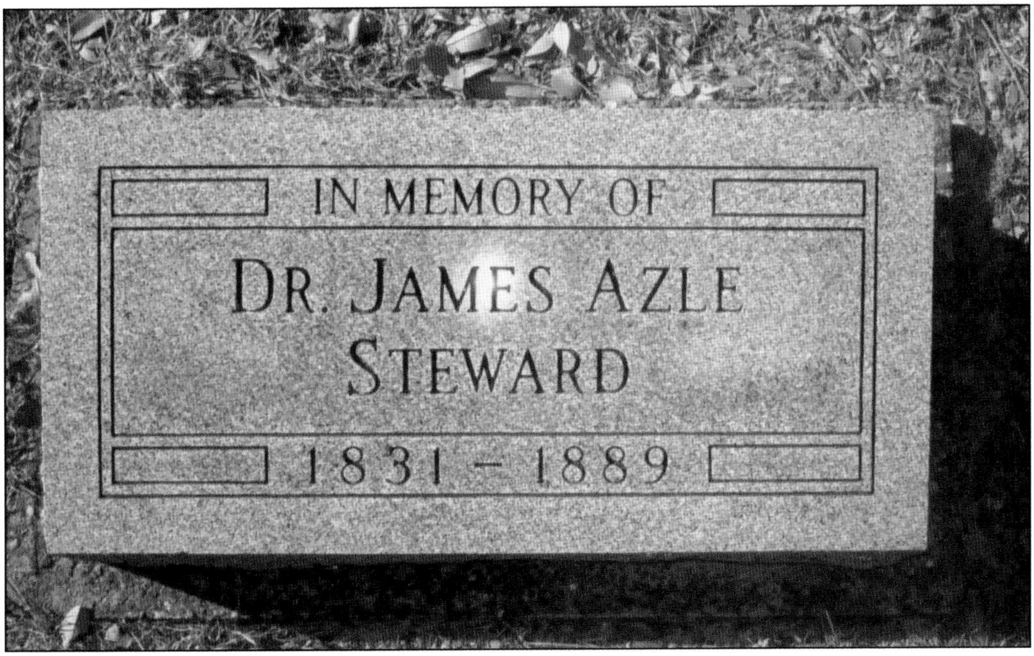


Dr. James Azle Steward's grave finally received a marker after 99 years of almost total obscurity and even confusion of the correct spelling of his last name. Local workers had some trouble locating the grave in order to install the marker. It is located in Ash Creek Cemetery on land that he originally donated.

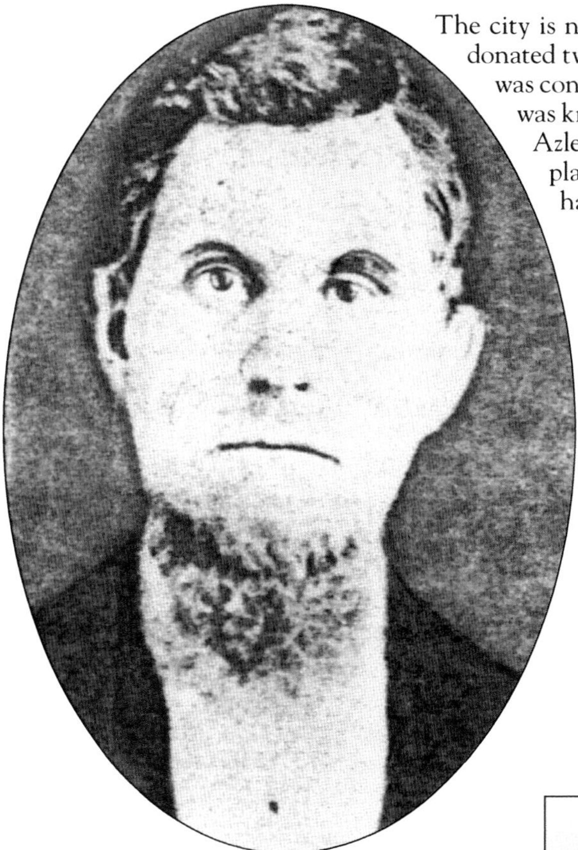

The city is named after Dr. James Azle Steward, who donated two acres of land for a townsite. Later, there was confusion over the spelling of his name, and it was known as "Stewart" in some books for years. Azle Historical Museum members discovered a plat map of the 1890s in which the name was handwritten as "Steward."

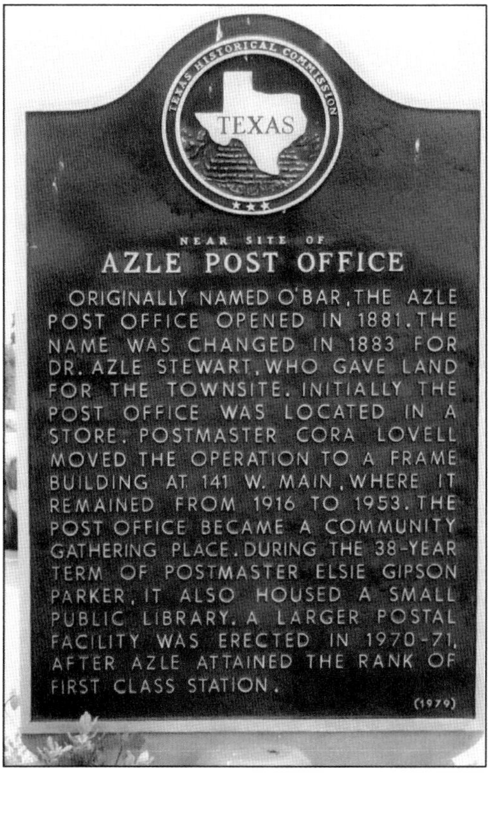


Azle's post office was once just a window in a general store. Later, it operated from a tiny, white frame building on West Main Street before moving twice more in the coming years. Unlike many towns, Azle's name is unique, as no other town in the nation bears the same name. This historical marker states, "Originally named O'Bar, the Azle Post Office opened in 1881. The name was changed in 1883 for Dr. Azle Stewart (sic), who gave land for the town site. Initially the post office was located in a store. Postmaster Cora Lovell moved the operation to a frame building at 141 W. Main, where it remained from 1916 to 1953. The post office became a community gathering place. During the 38-year term of Postmaster Elsie Gipson Parker, it also housed a small public library. A larger postal facility was erected in 1970–1971 after Azle attained the rank of first class station."

This marker states, "This congregation was organized in 1867, led by the Rev. J.C. Power. Worship services were first held in a log cabin. In the 1870s, a larger log cabin, which served as a church and school, was built on the banks of Walnut Creek in the community of Parker's Shop (now Reno). The congregation moved to a site south of the second log cabin in the late 1880s and built a frame sanctuary. Adjacent property was acquired in 1947, and has been the site of several buildings. Beginning as a rural church, Walnut Creek Baptist Church has continued to serve a growing congregation."

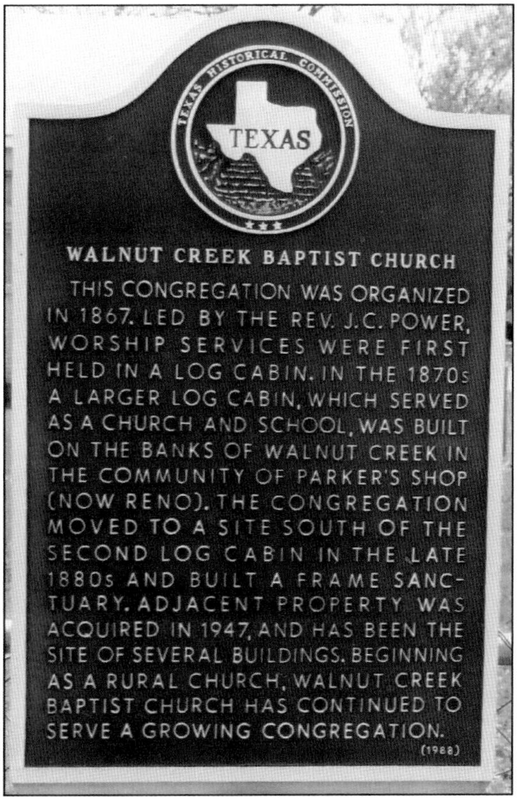


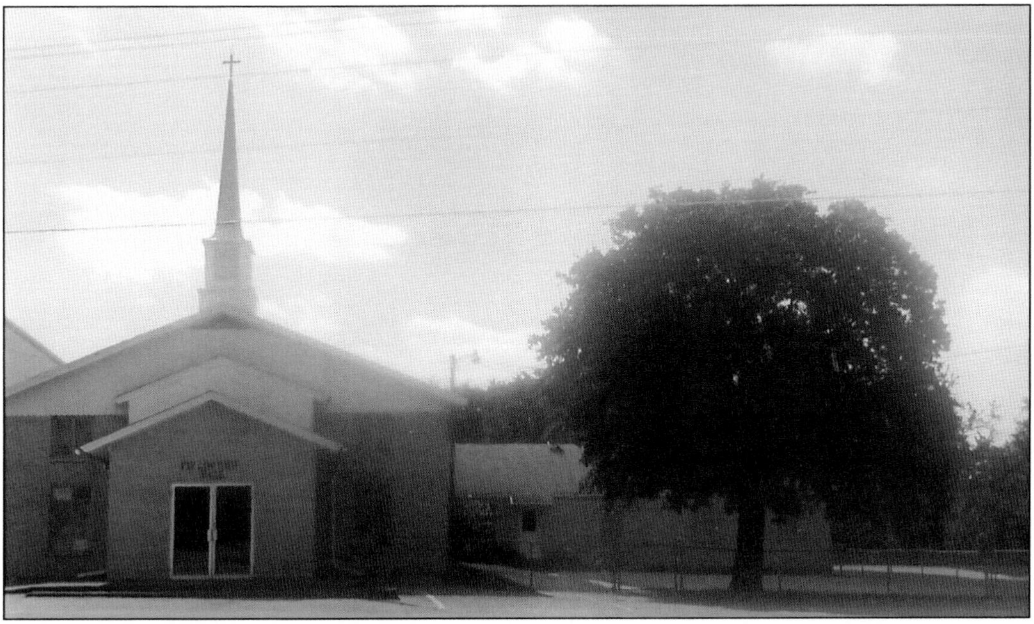

Walnut Creek Baptist Church, located at 220 West Reno Road, got its name from the creek on which it was built. The church family has held services in at least four different buildings since 1867. A small log cabin was the humble beginning of a congregation that recently totaled 300 resident members. The marker was erected in 1988 and stands west of the building complex.

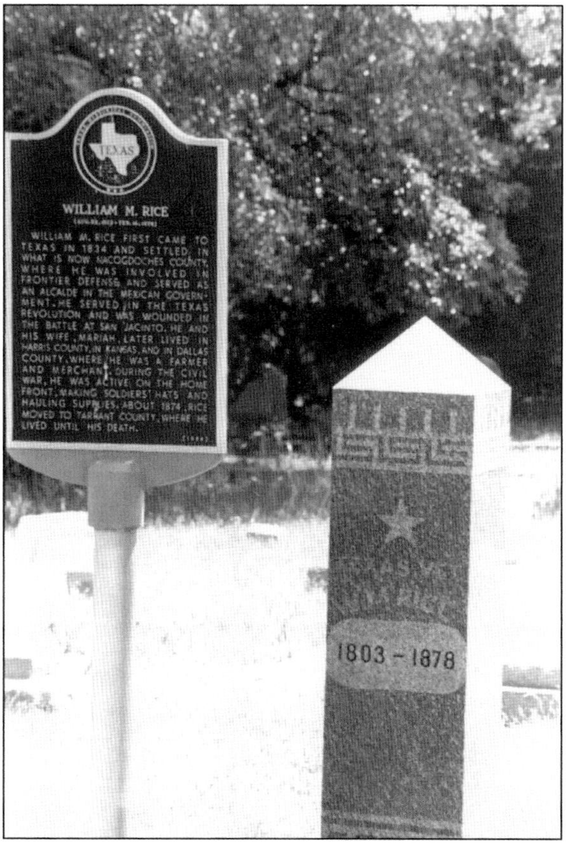


The William M. Rice Historical Marker is seen close-up at left. Below, members of the Rice family pose at the dedication of the marker in 1984. The marker is in Ash Creek Cemetery, where Rice lies buried. He is the only person buried in Tarrant County who fought in the Texas Revolution of 1835–1836. The marker states, "William M. Rice first came to Texas in 1834 and settled in what is now Nacogdoches County, where he was involved in frontier defenses and served as an alcalde in the Mexican government. He served in the Texas Revolution and was wounded in the Battle at San Jacinto. He and his wife, Mariah later lived in Harris County, in Kansas, and in Dallas County, where he was a farmer and merchant. During the Civil War, he was active on the home front, making soldiers' hats and hauling supplies. About 1874, Rice moved to Tarrant County, where he lived until his death."

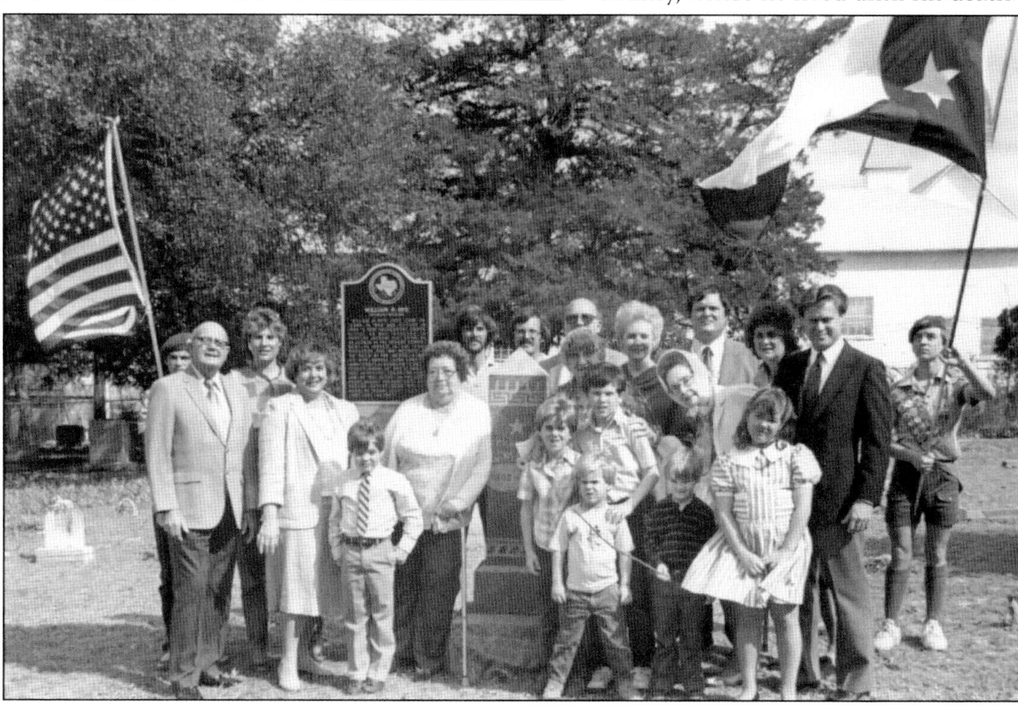

This marker states, "The Silver Creek Methodist Church was organized on Nov. 15, 1900, and by the following year area residents had completed work on this frame sanctuary. The building site had been deeded to the congregation by Farmers Joseph Gillis Steele and Thomas Nelson Clayton. The sanctuary also served as a community center for the surrounding rural area. Regular worship services were held here until 1967."

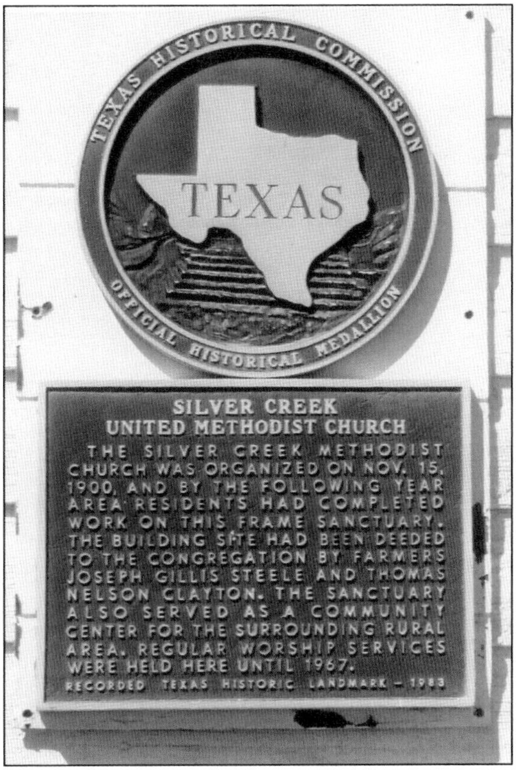


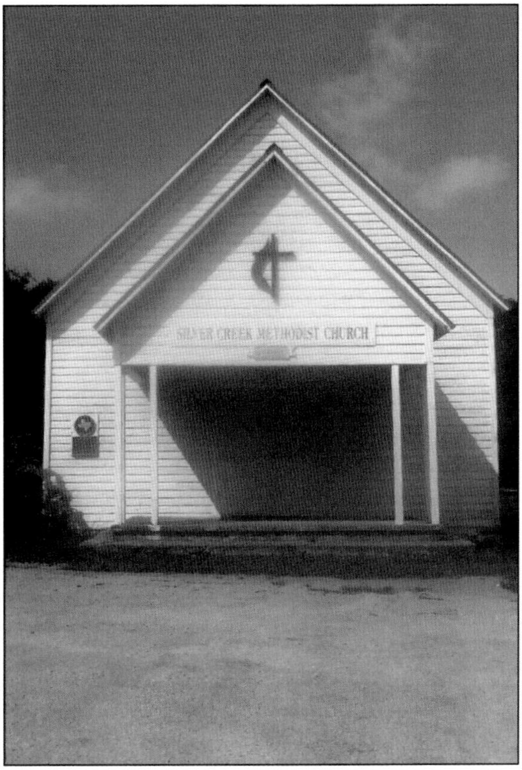


Silver Creek United Methodist Church's original building is one of the oldest houses of worship in Parker County. Even though there is a new sanctuary and surrounding buildings, the little white 1901 church house is still standing after 111 years. The marker hangs on the outside of the building at 2200 Church Road and was dedicated in 1983.

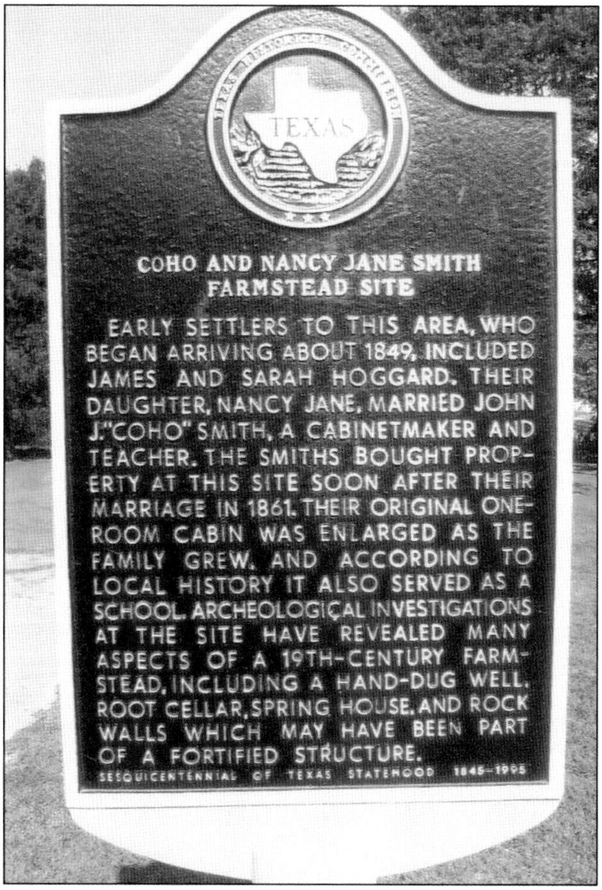


The marker states, "Early settlers to this area, who began arriving about 1849, included James and Sarah Hoggard. Their daughter, Nancy Jane, married John J. 'Coho' Smith, a cabinetmaker and teacher. The Smiths bought property at this site soon after their marriage in 1861. Their original one-room cabin was enlarged as the family grew, and according to local history it also served as a school. Archeological investigations at the site have revealed many aspects of a 19th-century farmstead, including a hand-dug well, root cellar, springhouse, and rock walls which may have been part of a fortified structure."

This outdoor display case and adjacent historical marker stand at the 18th hole of Cross Timbers Golf Course, which is owned by the City of Azle. The site of the Coho and Nancy Jane Smith family home was located in what is now golf course property and has been recognized by the permanent marker. Also on the site is a unique rock-lined well.

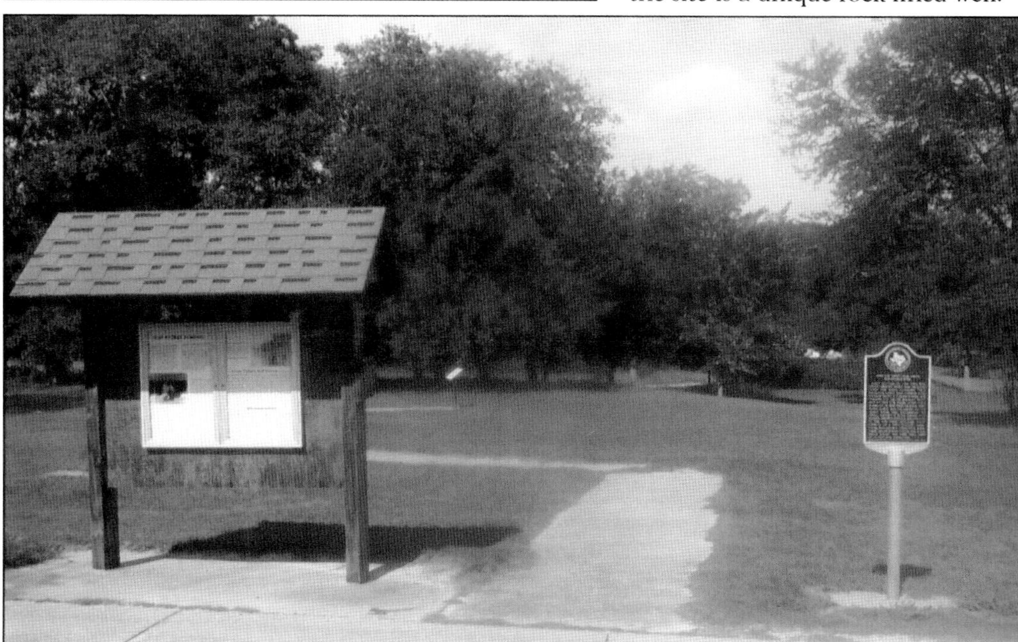

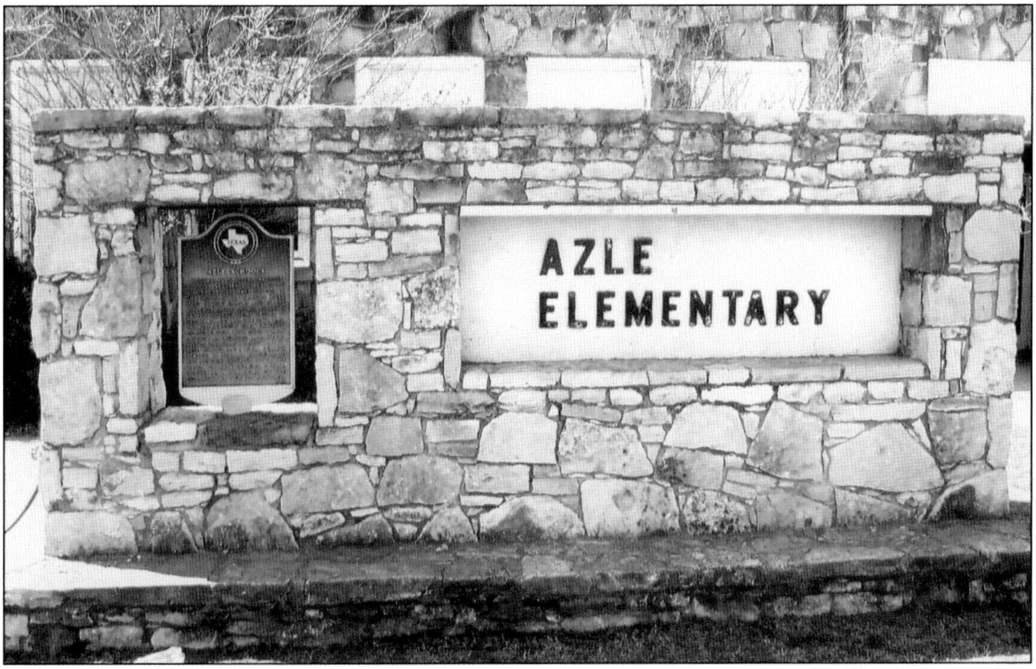


Of the numerous historical markers in Azle, this one honoring the Azle schools on this site has the best display. The Azle Independent School District encapsulated both the marker and the name of the present school on the site in a permanent rock home.

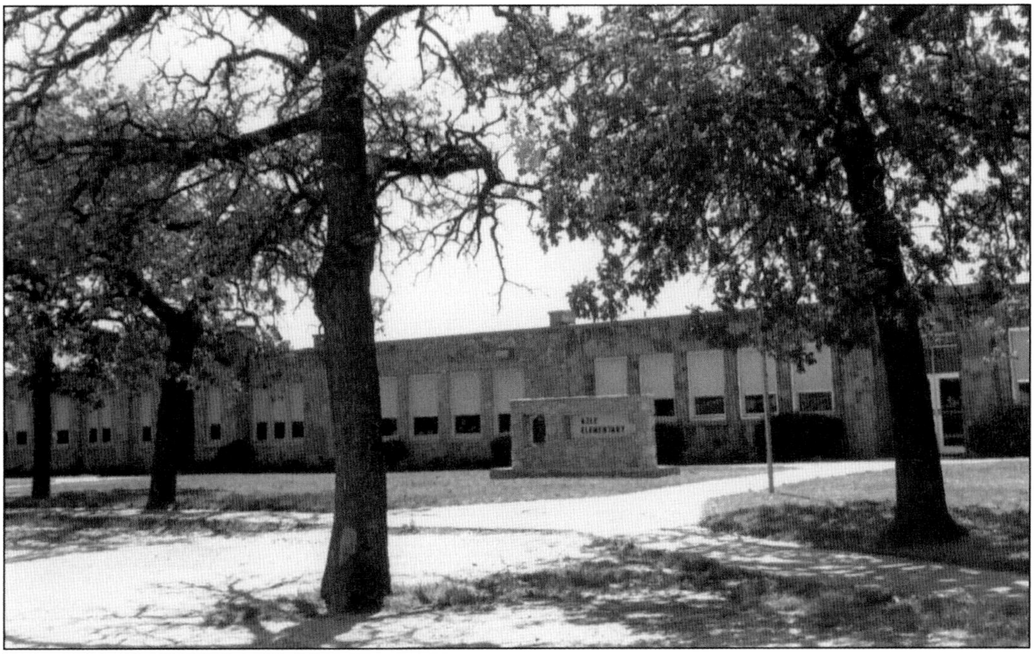

Nestled among shade trees, this rock structure, completed in 1939, is on the site of the earlier Red Brick School. In fact, the lower floor of the earlier school was once attached at the back of the present Azle Elementary. The Rock School is the oldest building still in use as a school in the Azle Independent School District.

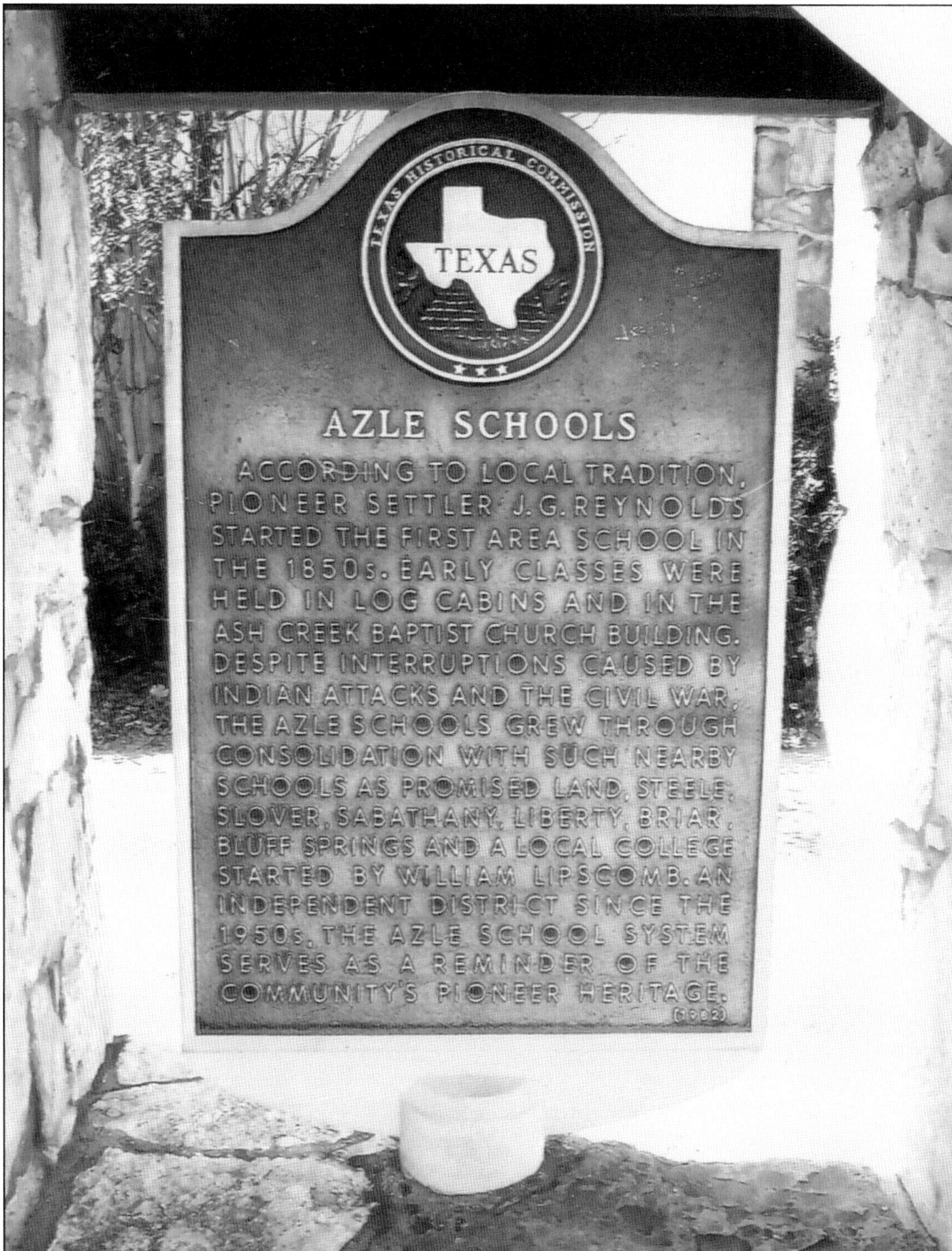


This marker states, "According to local tradition, pioneer settler J.G. Reynolds started the first area school in the 1850s. Early classes were held in log cabins and in the Ash Creek Baptist Church building. Despite interruptions caused by Indian attacks and the Civil War, the Azle schools grew through consolidation with such nearby schools as Promised Land, Steele, Slover, Sabathany, Liberty, Briar, Bluff Spring, and a local college started by William Lipscomb. An independent district since the 1950s, the Azle School System serves as a reminder of the community's pioneer heritage."

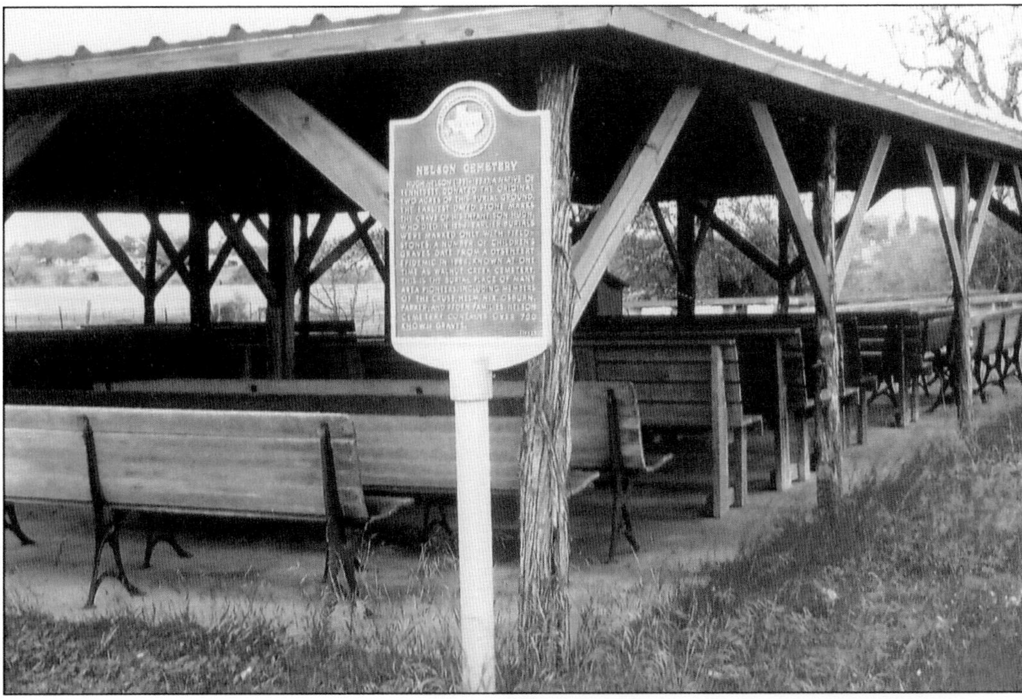

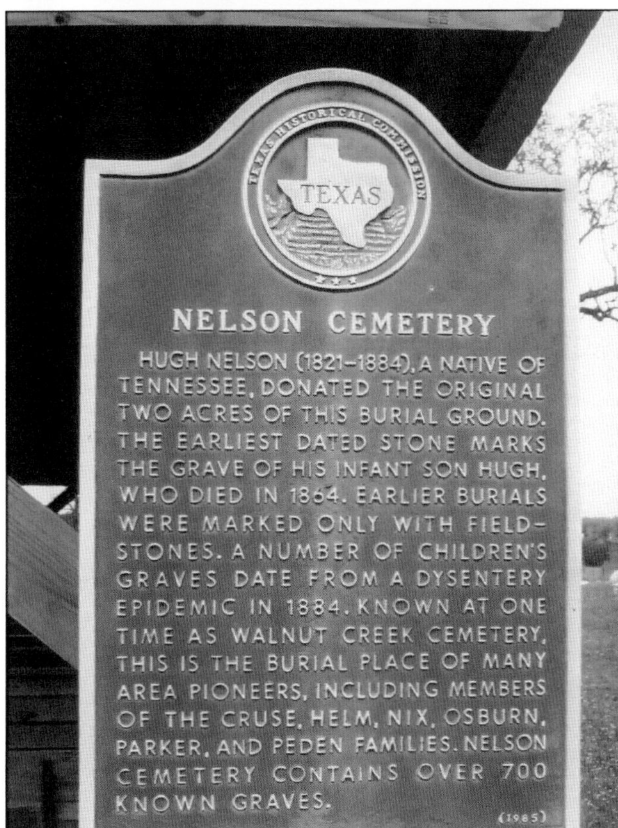


Many early Azle pioneer families are buried in the original two acres that were donated by Hugh Nelson Sr. for a cemetery around 1882. The marker is located beside the covered arbor in the cemetery on Nelson Road, about 3.5 miles northwest of Azle. The Nelson Cemetery marker was dedicated in 1985. The marker states, "Hugh Nelson (1821–1884), a native of Tennessee, donated the original two acres of this burial ground. The earliest dated stone marks the grave of his infant son Hugh, who died in 1864. Earlier burials were marked only with field stones. A number of children's graves date from a dysentery epidemic in 1884. Known at one time as Walnut Creek Cemetery, this is the burial place of many area pioneers, including members of the Cruse, Helm, Nix, Osburn, Parker, and Peden families. Nelson Cemetery contains over 700 known graves."

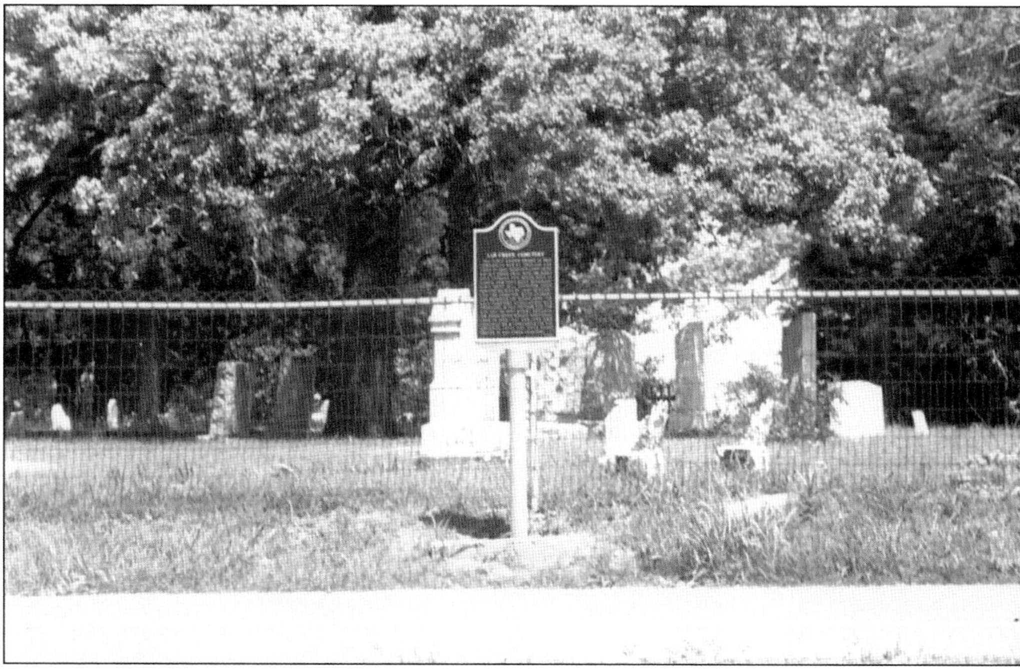

Ash Creek Cemetery lies behind Ash Creek Baptist Church. Many of the church's original 48 charter members are buried here. Dr. James Azle Steward, after whom Azle is named, donated the first acre of land and is buried in the cemetery. The historical marker was dedicated in 1985 along the front fence.

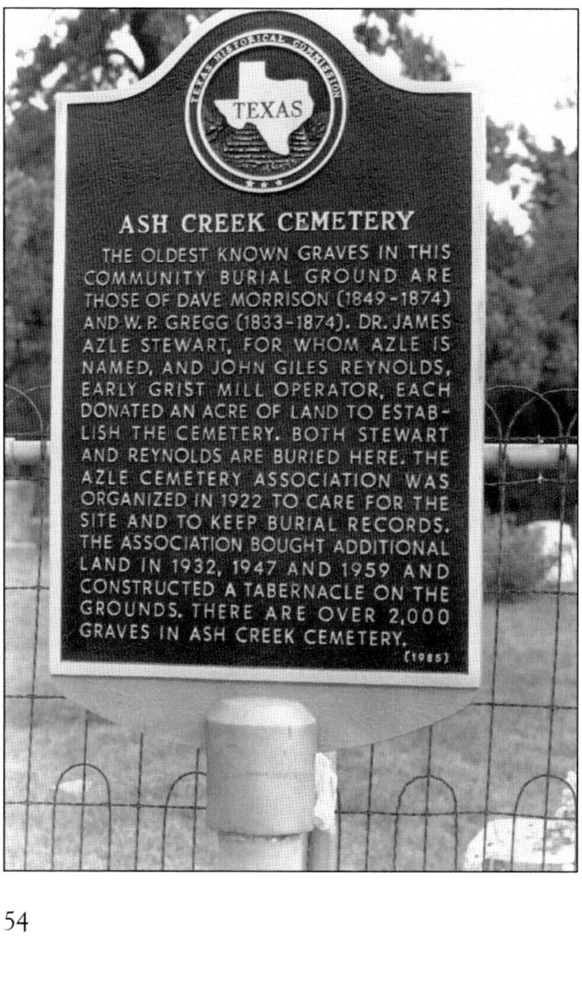


The marker states, "The oldest known graves in this community burial ground are those of Dave Morrison (1849–1874) and W.R. Gregg (1833–1874). Dr. James Azle Steward and John Giles Reynolds, early gristmill operator, each donated an acre of land to establish the cemetery. Both Steward and Reynolds are buried here. The Azle Cemetery Association was organized in 1922 to care for the site and to keep burial records. The Association bought additional land in 1932, 1947, and 1959 and constructed a tabernacle on the grounds. There are over 2,000 graves in Ash Creek Cemetery."

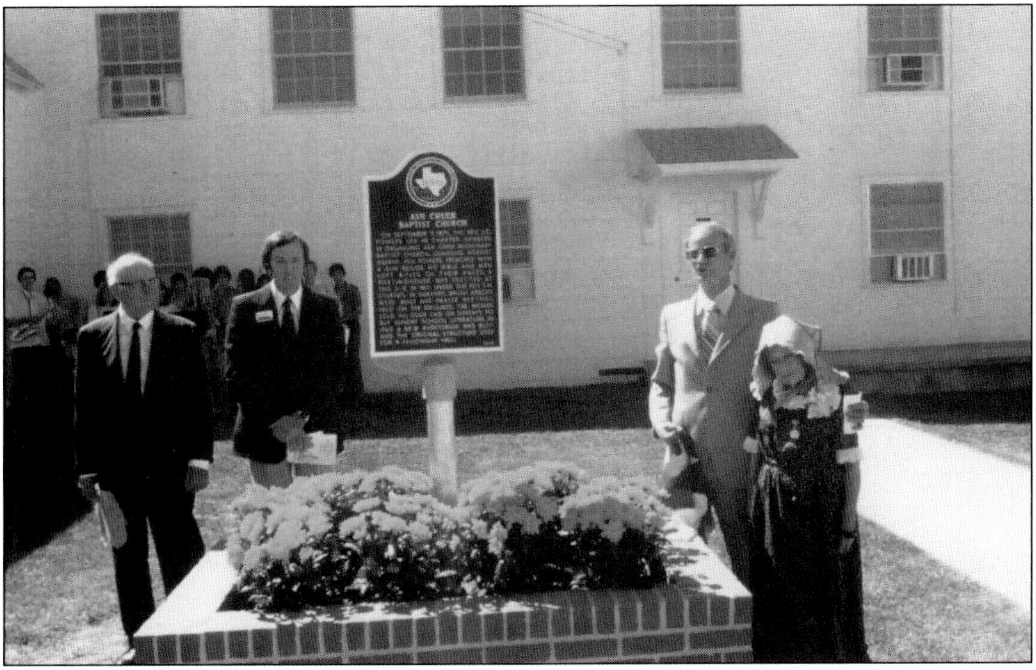

B.J. Clark, the president of the Azle Historical Museum Society at the time, assists Blanche Scrimshire as they unveil a new historical marker for the Ash Creek Baptist Church (300 South Stewart Street). The church officials stand to the left. Scrimshire was a granddaughter of Azle's first permanent settler, John Giles Reynolds.

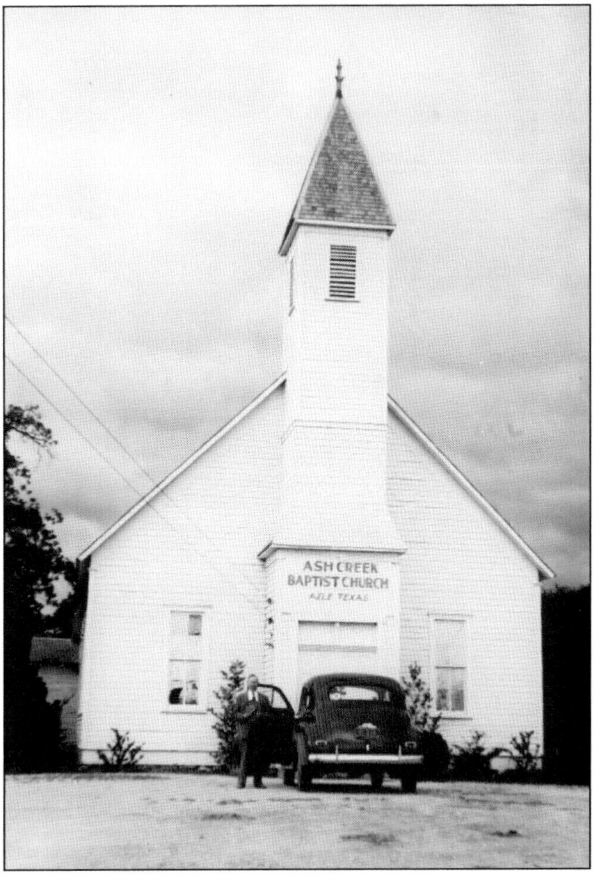


This marker pictured above states, "On September 9, 1871, the Rev. J. C. Powers led 48 charter members in organizing Ash Creek Missionary Baptist Church. Guarding against Indians, Rev. Powers preached with a gun beside his Bible, and men kept rifles on their knees. A meetinghouse was erected at this site in 1891 under the Rev. T.H. Sturges. In summers, brush arbors were built, and prayer meetings held on the grounds. The women sold all eggs laid on Sundays to buy Sunday School literature. In 1967 a new auditorium was built, and the original structure used for a fellowship hall." At right is the church in 1939 with Rev. C.R. Bullock.

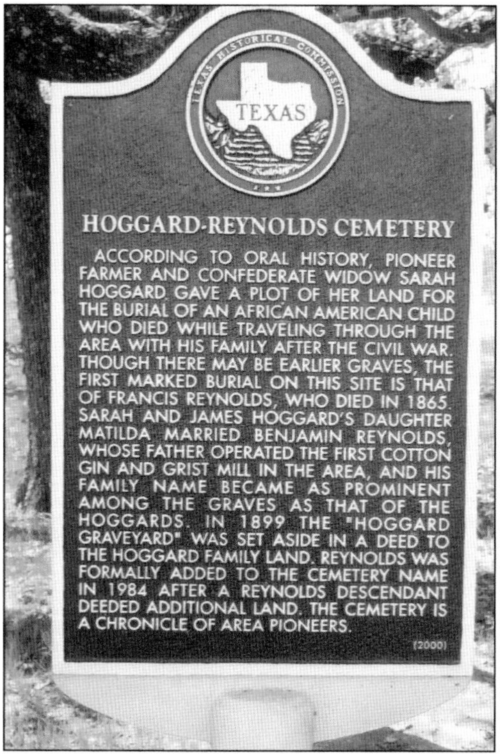


This marker states, "According to oral history, pioneer farmer and Confederate widow Sarah Hoggard gave a plot of her land for the burial of an African American child who died while traveling through the area with his family after the Civil War. Though there may be earlier graves, the first marked burial on this site is that of Francis Reynolds, who died in 1865. Sarah and James Hoggard's daughter Matilda married Benjamin Reynolds, whose father operated the first cotton gin and grist mill in the area, and his family name became as prominent among the graves as that of the Hoggards. In 1899, the 'Hoggard Graveyard' was set aside in a deed to the Hoggard family land. Reynolds was formally added to the cemetery name in 1984 after a Reynolds descendant deeded additional land. The cemetery is a chronicle of area pioneers."

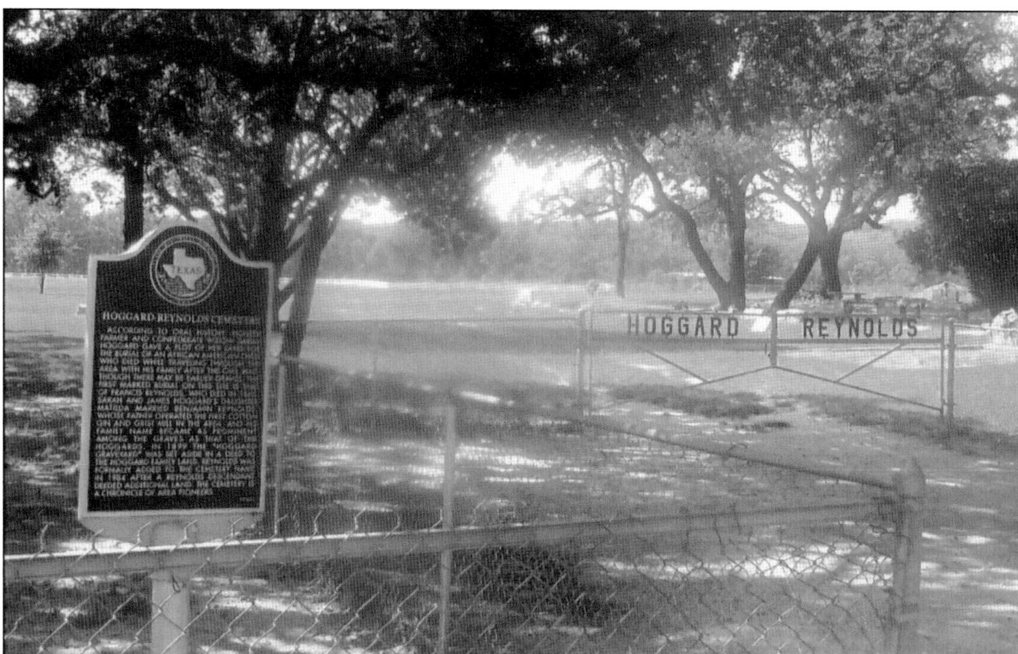


The Hoggard-Reynolds Cemetery is located at 851 South Stewart Street, and the marker, erected in 2000, stands to the left of the entrance. There are presently around 220 marked graves in the private family cemetery. There are also uncarved stone markers that may predate the first marker in 1865 or were placed there during the same early time period.

This marker states, "This congregation grew from worship services conducted here in the 1880s on land donated by Dr. Azle Stewart (*sic*), for whom the town was named. Organized in 1890, the fellowship met under a brush arbor until 1893, when the first sanctuary was completed. The earliest youth organization for the church was the Christian Endeavor, started about 1904. Members of that group established the first public library for Azle in the home of Valera Huster. Additions were later made to the original structure and a new sanctuary was built in 1974."

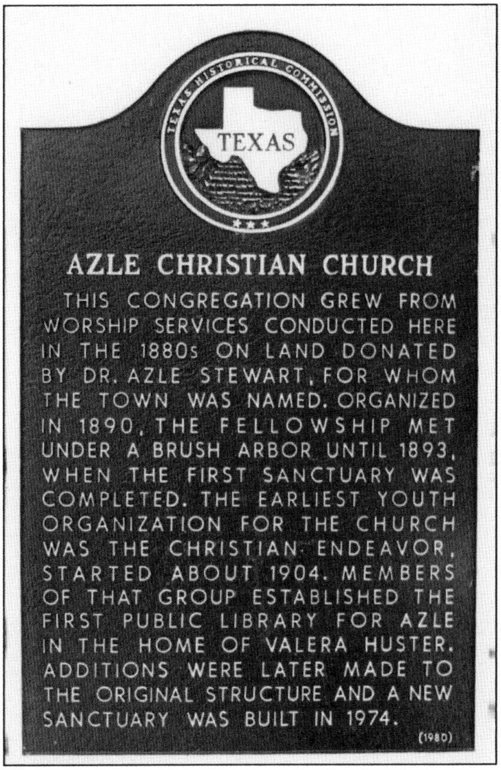


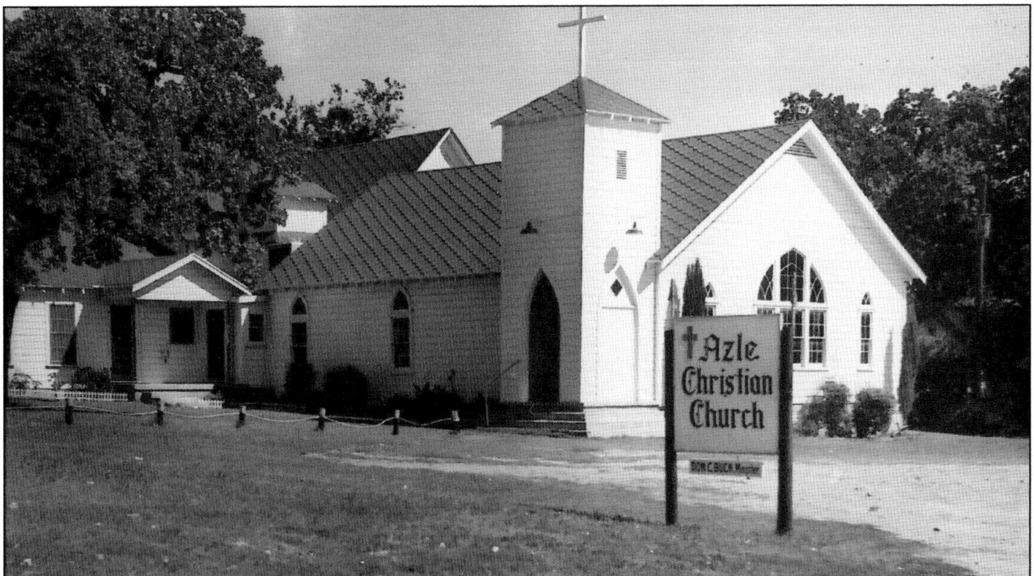


Azle Christian Church (Disciples of Christ), at 117 Church Street, grew from 14 charter members in 1890. The original church house was built in 1893 on land donated by Dr. James Azle Steward, whose wife, Mary, was a charter member. Later, it was used as a fellowship hall when a new sanctuary was completed in 1950. This photograph was taken in 1954. In the church's current building program, they have made provisions to restore the 1893 building that was moved to the back of the church property. The marker, dedicated in 1980, is located in front of the church.

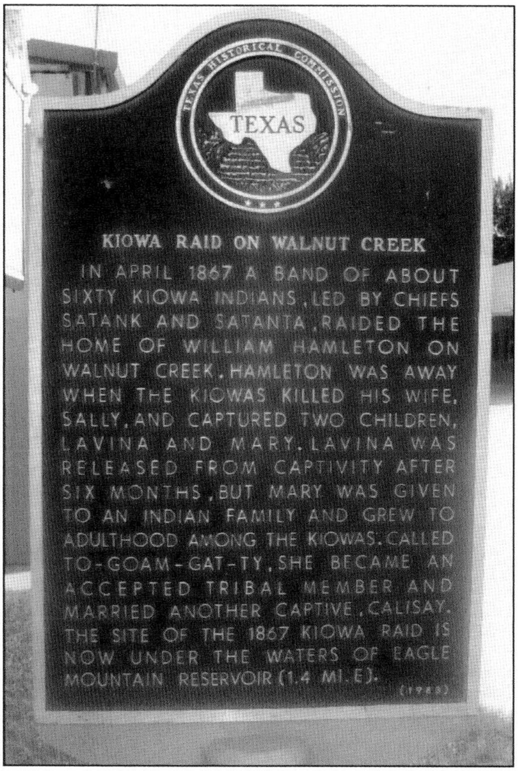


The marker states, "In April 1867 a band of about sixty Kiowa Indians, led by Chiefs Satank and Satanta, raided the home of William Hamleton on Walnut Creek. Hamleton was away when the Kiowas killed his wife, Sally, and captured two children Lavina and Mary. Lavina was released from captivity after six months, but Mary was given to an Indian family and grew to adulthood among the Kiowas. Called To-Goam-Gat-ty, she became an accepted tribal member and married another captive, Calisay. The site of the 1867 Kiowa raid is now under the waters of Eagle Mountain Reservoir (1.4 Mi. E)."

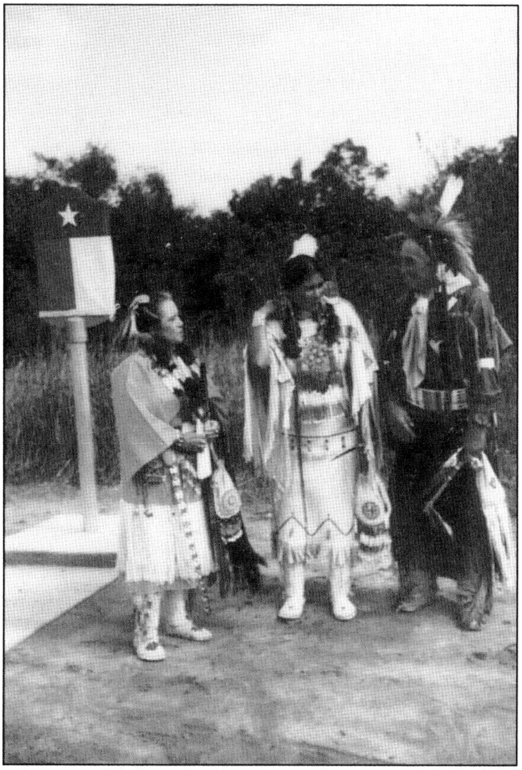

These Kiowa Indians, seen here in their native costumes, were present at the historical marker dedication in 1984. George Tahbone of Fort Worth is a descendant of the kidnapped Mary Hamleton. The Kiowa Raid marker was dedicated to the memory of the early pioneers, especially the Hamleton family, whose home was raided and whose members were killed or carried away. The marker was placed on FM 730 N since the original site was submerged in Eagle Mountain Lake.

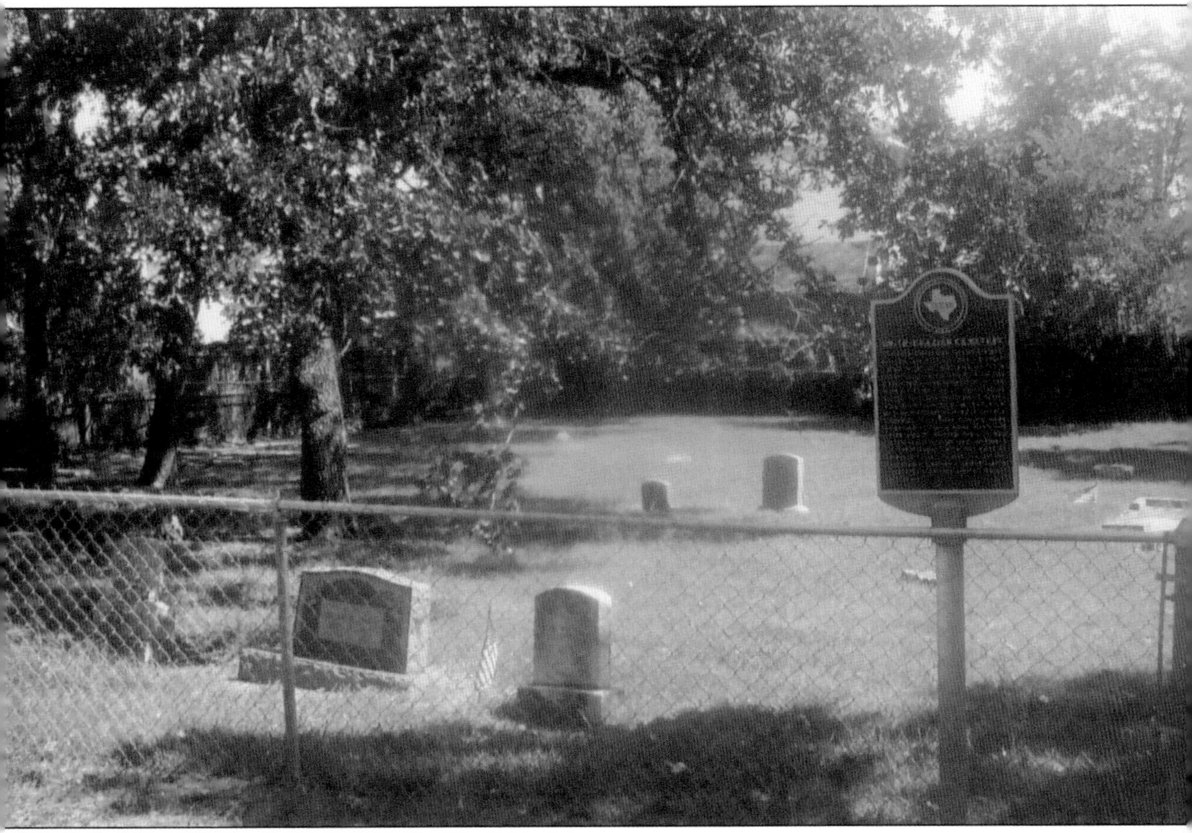

The Smith-Frazier Cemetery marker honors the founders and descendants of the Azle African American community. The burial ground has been in use since at least 1877. The marker stands at the gate of the cemetery, located in the 300 block of South Ash Avenue, and was erected in 1983.

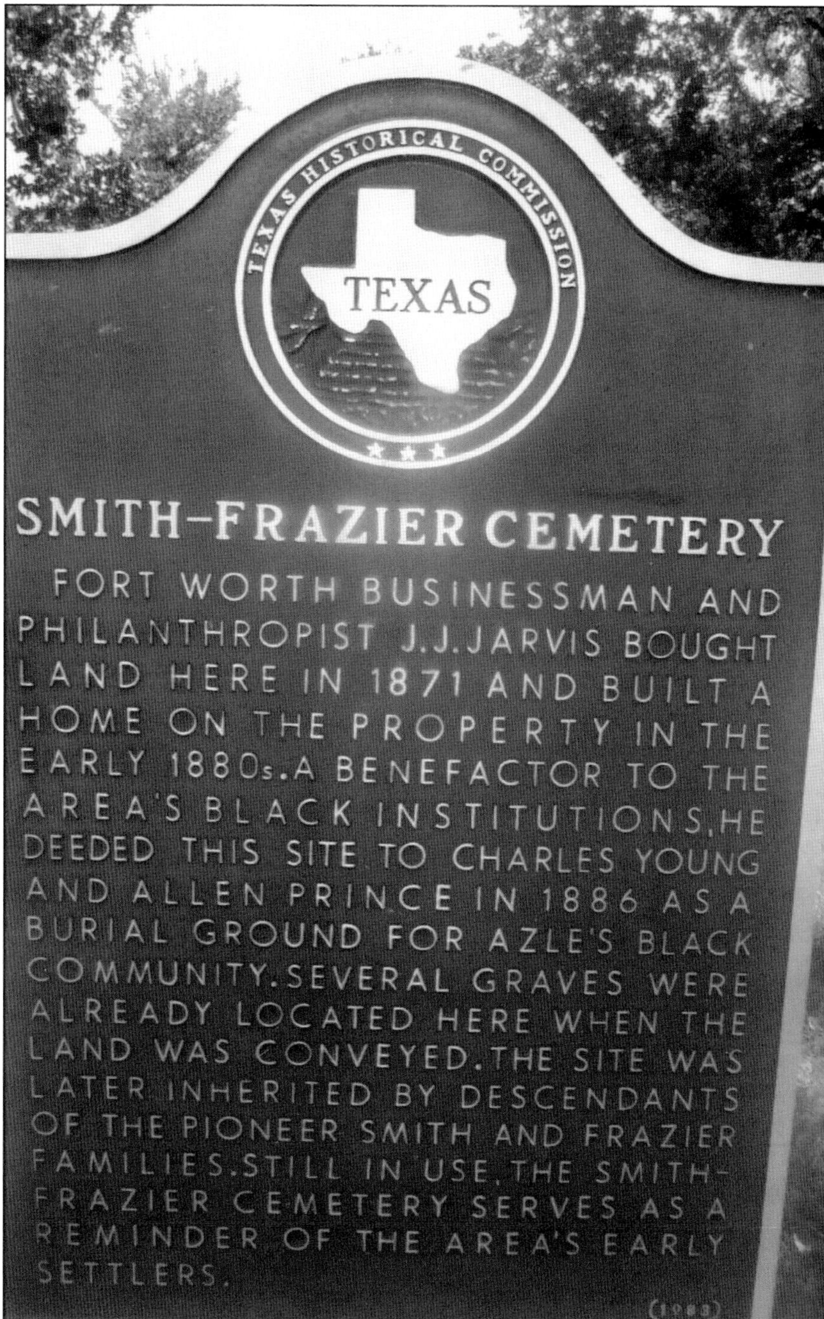


This marker states, "Fort Worth businessman and philanthropist J.J. Jarvis bought land here in 1871 and built a home on the property in the early 1880s. A benefactor to the area's black institutions, he deeded this site to Charles Young and Allen Prince in 1886 as a burial ground for Azle's black community. Several graves were already located here when the land was conveyed. The site was later inherited by descendants of the pioneer Smith and Frazier families. Still in use, the Smith-Frazier Cemetery serves as a reminder of the area's early settlers."

# *Four*

# BUSINESSES

The first general store in Azle was thought to be owned by a man named Moore in the 1860s, when the settlers called this small outpost of civilization Mooresville. Moore later sold the store to Henry Miller and Dan Woods. Joseph Fowler then bought the store and ran it for more than 30 years. W.N. McDonald, Horace Grigsby, and W.B. Scrimshire, and his son Floyd also had general stores in early Azle.

This growing town, with one short main street about two blocks long, also had a blacksmith, gristmill, cotton gin, drugstore, saloon, gunsmith, millinery shop, barbershop, watch repairman, and furniture maker. The buildings were not painted and there was nothing beautiful about them, but the town had a sort of ruggedness that bespoke of the character of the pioneers. The town depended on the settlers in its midst to provide all services and help of any kind. There was no need to travel beyond the little settlement for anything.

An article in the April 1975 *Azle News* encouraged citizens to keep an eye on Azle's growth, and grown it has. No one in the 1860s could have known that there would be more than 650 businesses in the 2011–2012 telephone book. The Azle Area Chamber of Commerce boasts more than 300 members. The article credited this growth to things like Carswell Air Force Base, General Dynamics (Lockheed Martin) contracts, completion of Loop 820, Eagle Mountain Lake recreation facilities, and Azle's excellent education system, but it also pointed out that locals, with their tough pioneer legacy, were proud to see their town grow.

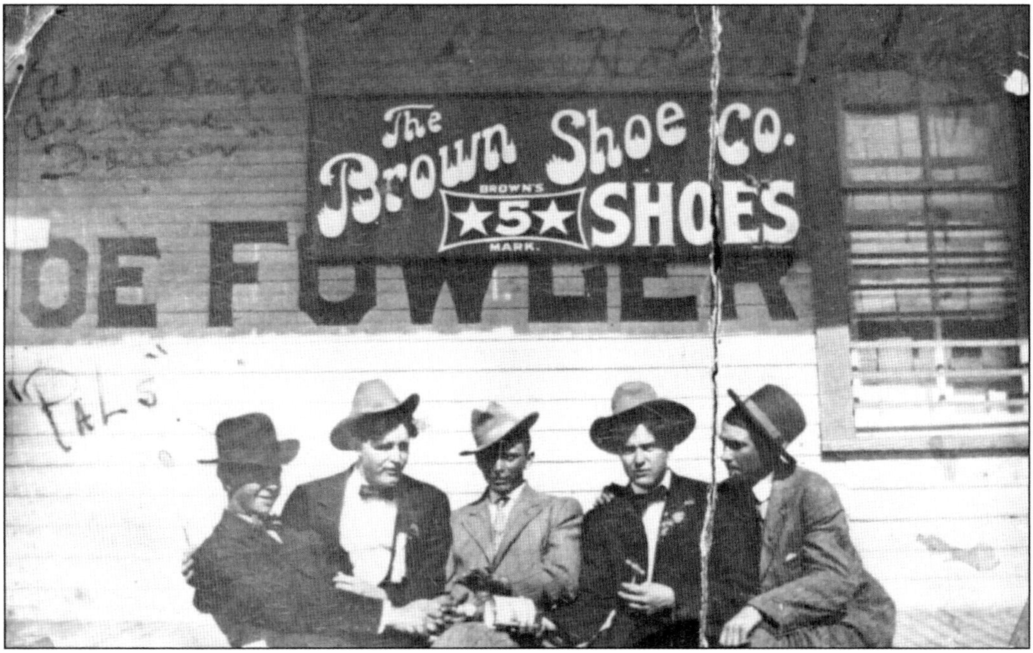


Five dapper gentlemen ham it up in front of Joe Fowler's Store in the early 1900s. Azle was called Fowler's Store until a post office was established in 1881. Shown from left to right are Robert Walker, of the Walker family who owned Walker Drug Store; Minor Kirby; Charlie Gipson; Will Kirby, Minor's brother; and John Holmes, the father of Marshall Holmes.

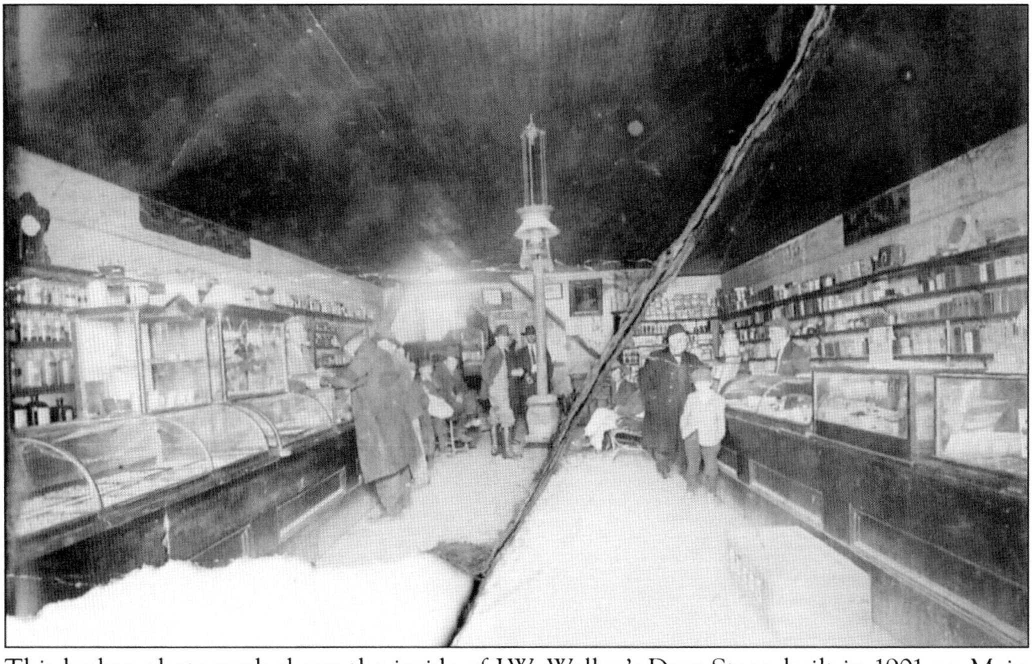

This broken photograph shows the inside of J.W. Walker's Drug Store, built in 1901 on Main Street. The Walker family operated the drugstore for 40 years before selling it to J.B. and Byra Stribling. The Azle Historical Museum recently received this treasured photograph from Walker's descendants. (Courtesy of Charlotte Betts, Carol Malone, and Cynthia Bailey.)

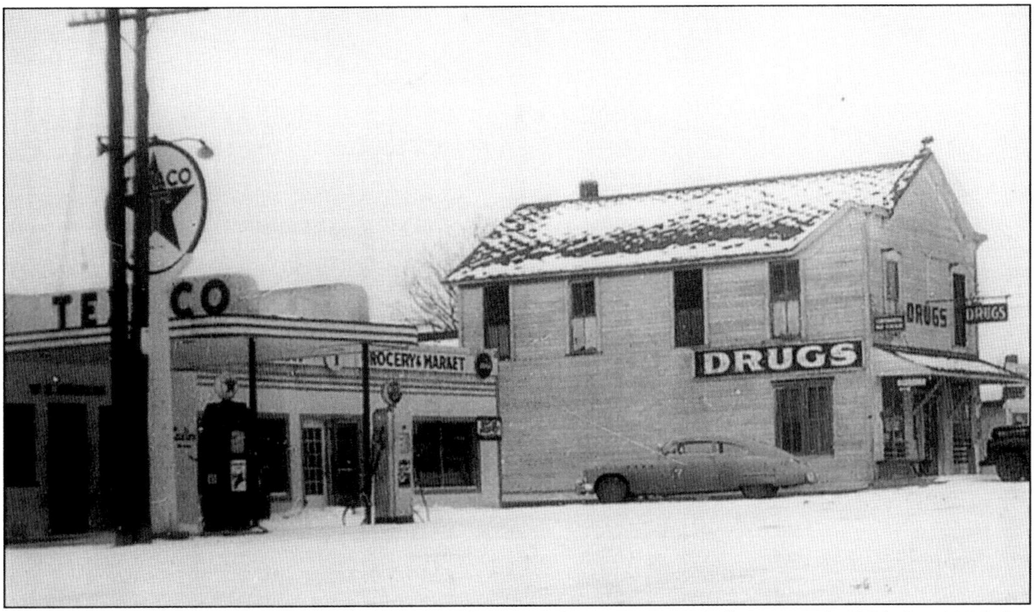


Lewis Thomas Wigfall Reynolds opened the first drugstore in Azle around 1880. In 1888, he sold it to J.W. Walker, who ran it until it burned in 1900, at which point he built this two-story building at 117 West Main Street. J.B. and Byra Woody Stribling purchased the drugstore in 1932. After the Striblings bought the store, they installed a Delco system of electricity and had the first lights in Azle. It was rented to Milton Tompkins in 1961 and then to Paul Worthen and Frank Couch in 1963 for their C and W Electronics. Paul and Kathryn Worthen bought the building in 1978. The historic landmark was sold to Shibby Holdings, LLC, in April 2012. Also in the above photograph, on the left, is W.E. Shields Jr. Cash Grocery, which opened in 1949. Shields operated the store until 1952. Byra and J. B. Stribling are shown below.

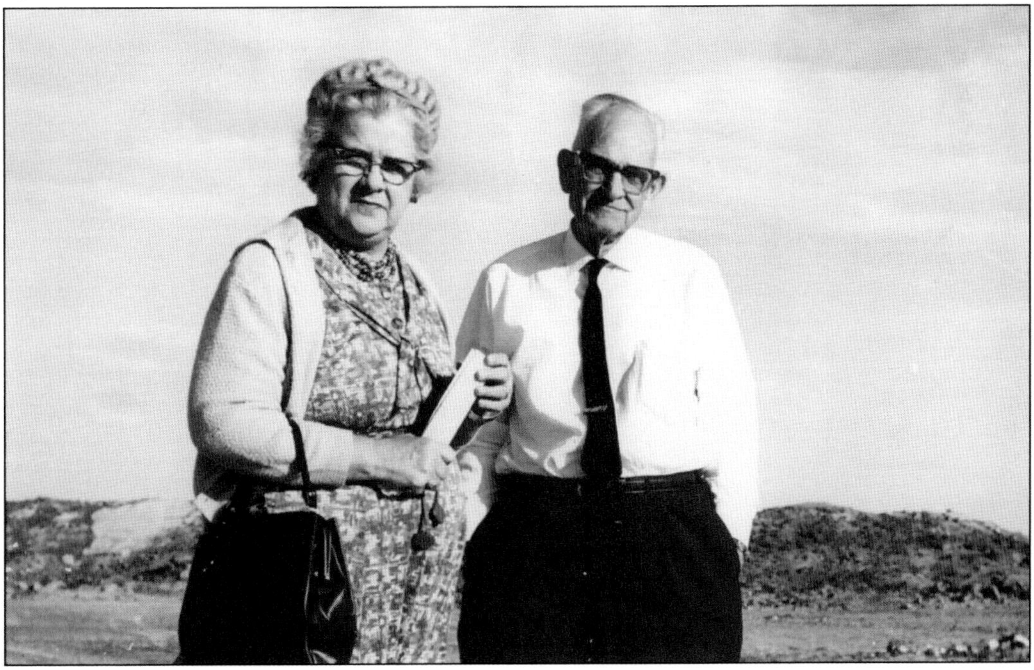

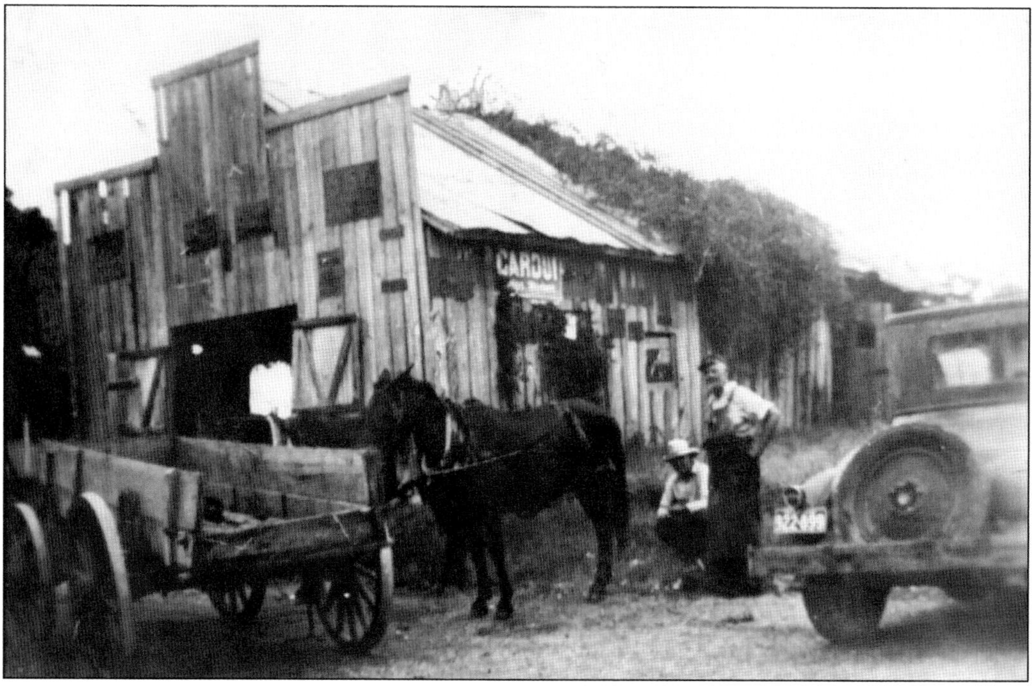


The John Parker blacksmith shop was located on Main Street in early 1900. Parker is seen here in front of the shop servicing the old and the new. His father, Andy Parker, was Azle's first blacksmith, and people said he never saw a horse he could not fit with shoes.

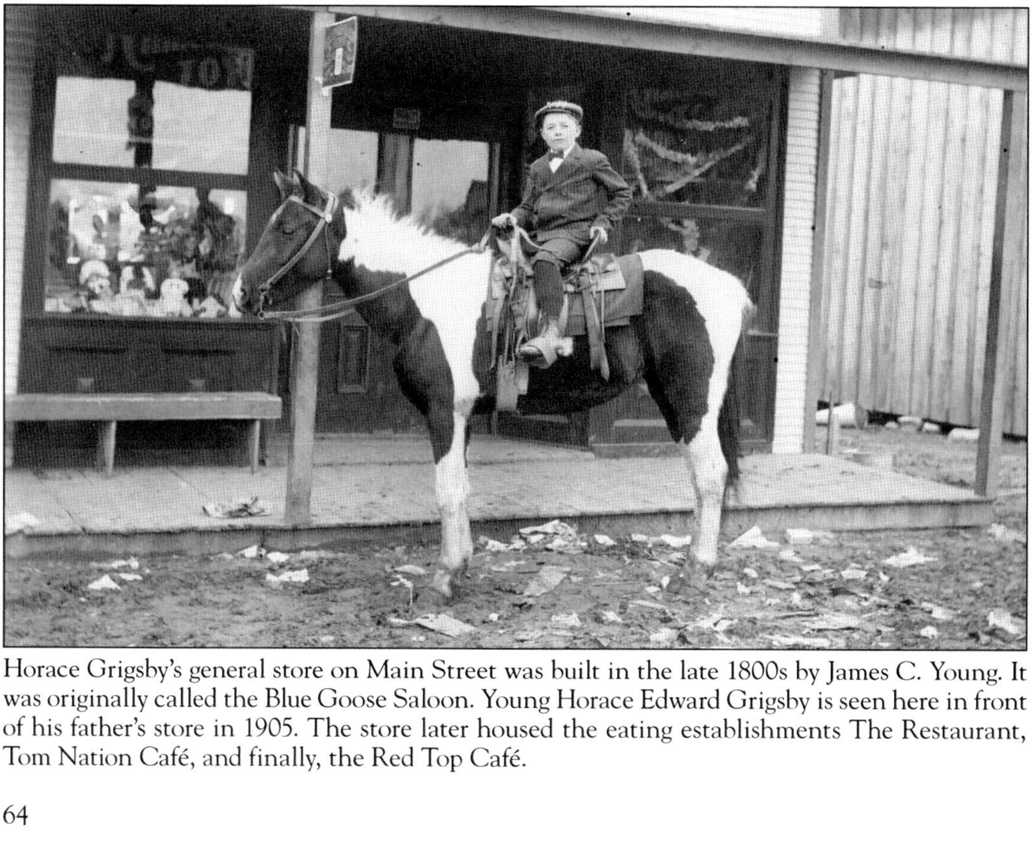

Horace Grigsby's general store on Main Street was built in the late 1800s by James C. Young. It was originally called the Blue Goose Saloon. Young Horace Edward Grigsby is seen here in front of his father's store in 1905. The store later housed the eating establishments The Restaurant, Tom Nation Café, and finally, the Red Top Café.

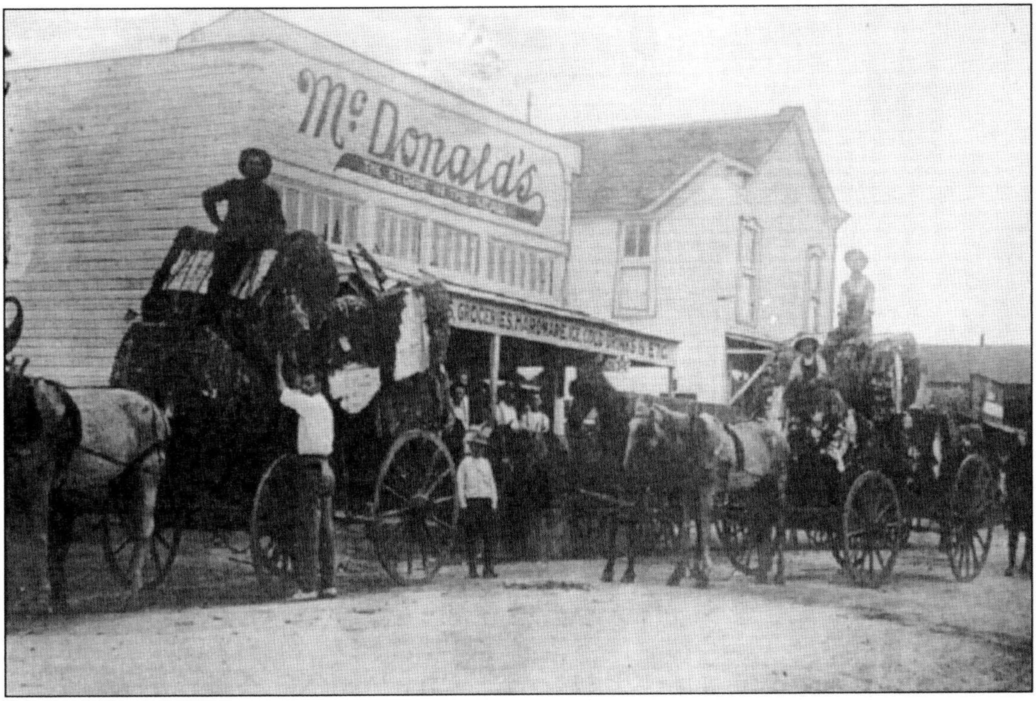


William Newton McDonald built his first general store in 1906 next door to the Walker drugstore on Main Street. He built a new store directly across the street around 1920. He also owned two cotton gins and was Azle's second postmaster. He bought cottonseed from the farmers and took it to Fort Worth. The wagons always left from in front of his store, as seen here.

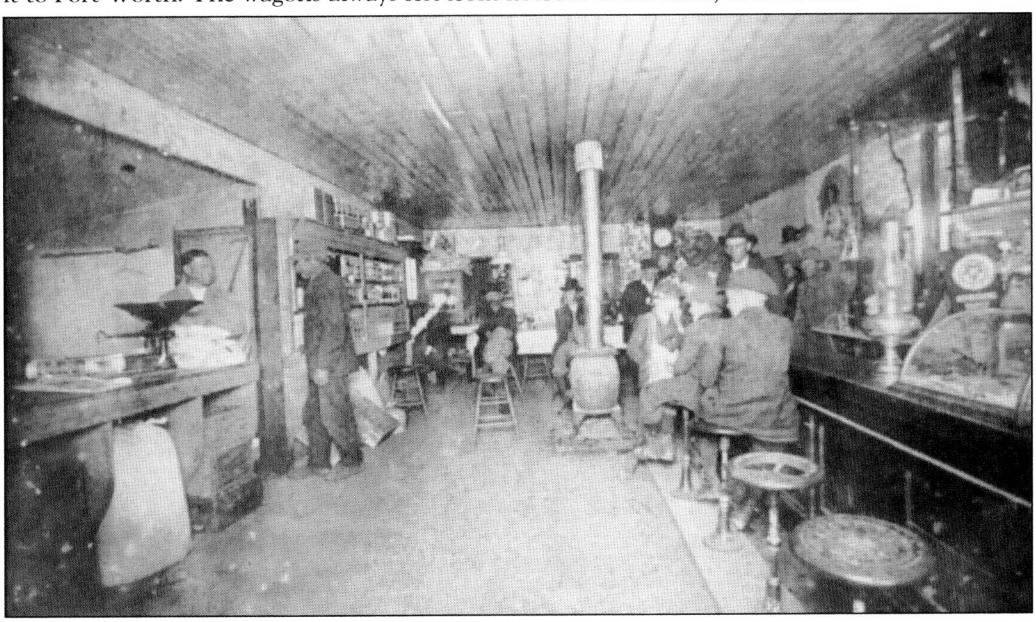

Tom Nation's Store and Café was an early-1900s gathering place in Azle. It was located at 125 West Main Street and was called the Red Top Café from the 1940s through the 1960s. On the left talking to the clerk is T.H. Nation Sr., the grandfather of Jim Bob Nation. On the right facing the front is Charlie Gipson, the son of W.T. Gipson.

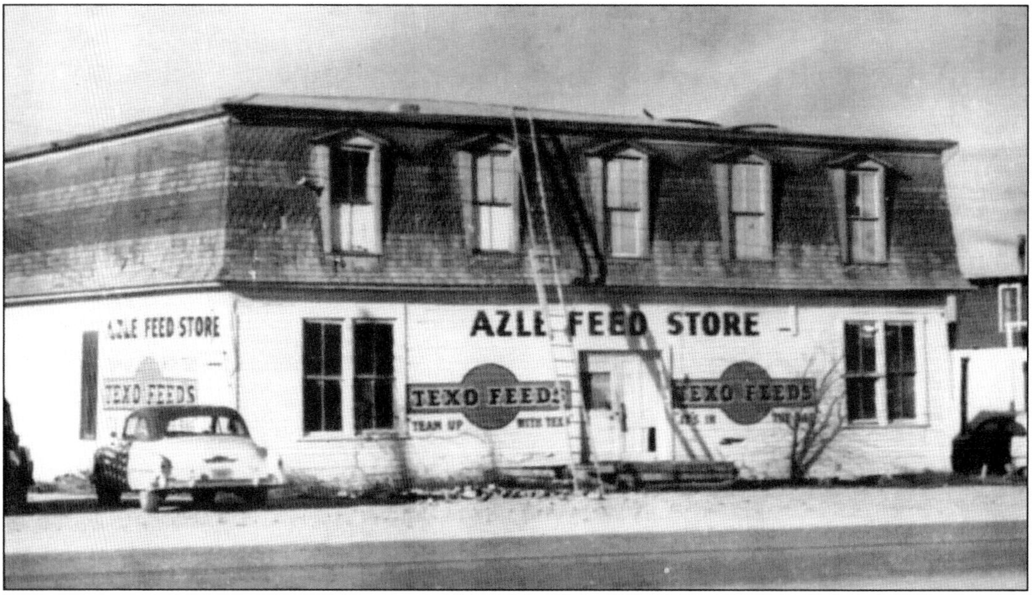


Weldon Beasley's Azle Feed Store was originally Joe Fowler's General Store and was built about 1892 on the corner of Main and Church Streets. In 1936, the Masons, who owned the building at this time, had it moved to 257 West Main Street. Beasley operated his store on the bottom floor between 1936 and 1954. The building was torn down, and the Masonic Lodge was built at this location in 1954.

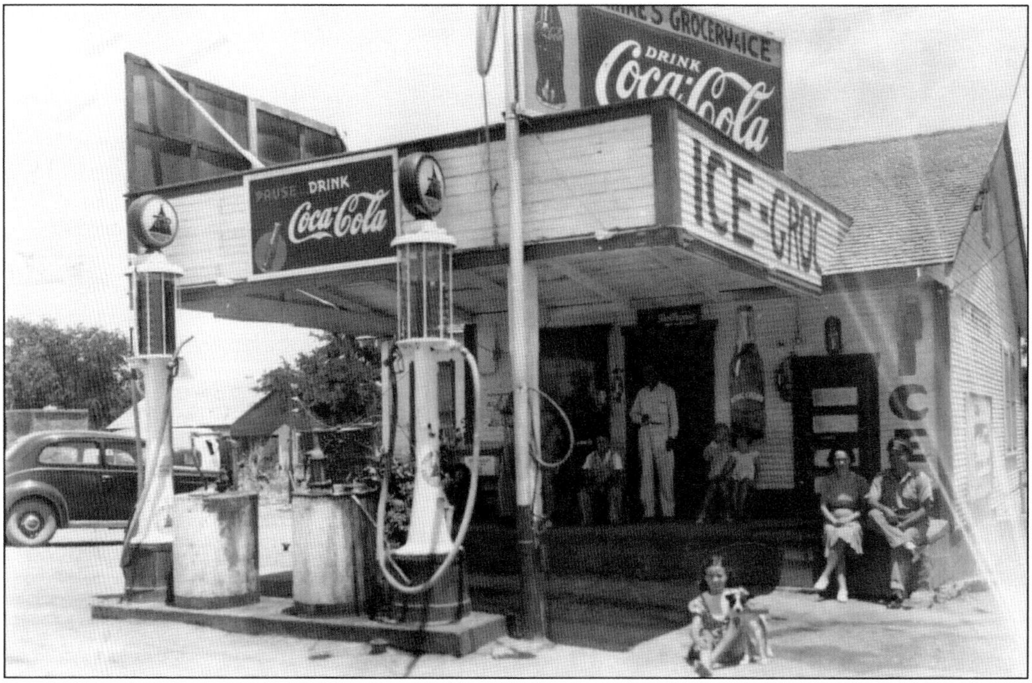


Admire's Grocery and Ice was one of the many businesses on Main Street in the 1930s, on the corner of Main and North Stewart Streets. Here, customers enjoy icy soft drinks under the gas station's overhang. The eight year old in the foreground is Jeanine "Tiny" Admire Irby posing with her dog, Spot. (Courtesy of Jeanine Admire Irby.)

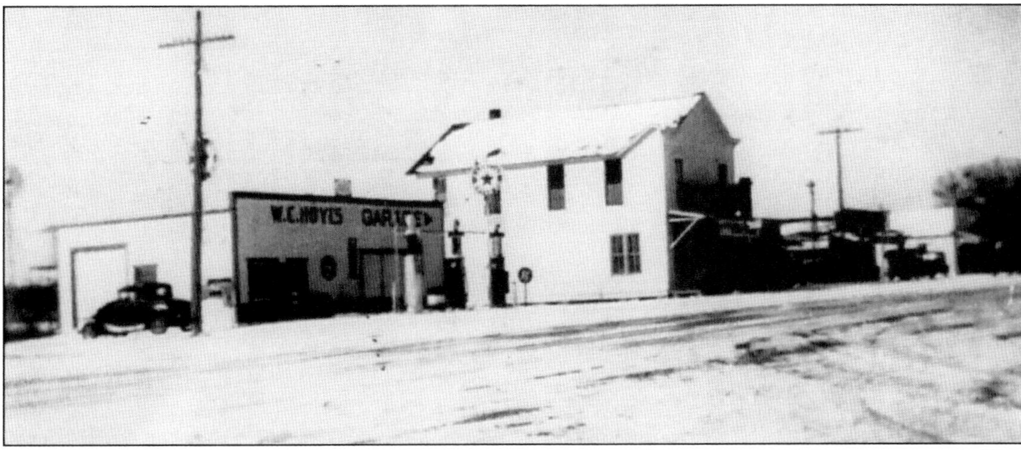


W.C. "Cy" and Ella Hoyl's family came to Azle in 1934 and opened Hoyl's Garage at 113 West Main Street. The Hoyls were the parents of Trudy Head Trammell, who had one of the first beauty shops in Azle. This 1935 photograph shows, from left to right, Hoyl's Garage, the two-story Stribling drugstore, Tom Nation Café, and the Azle post office.

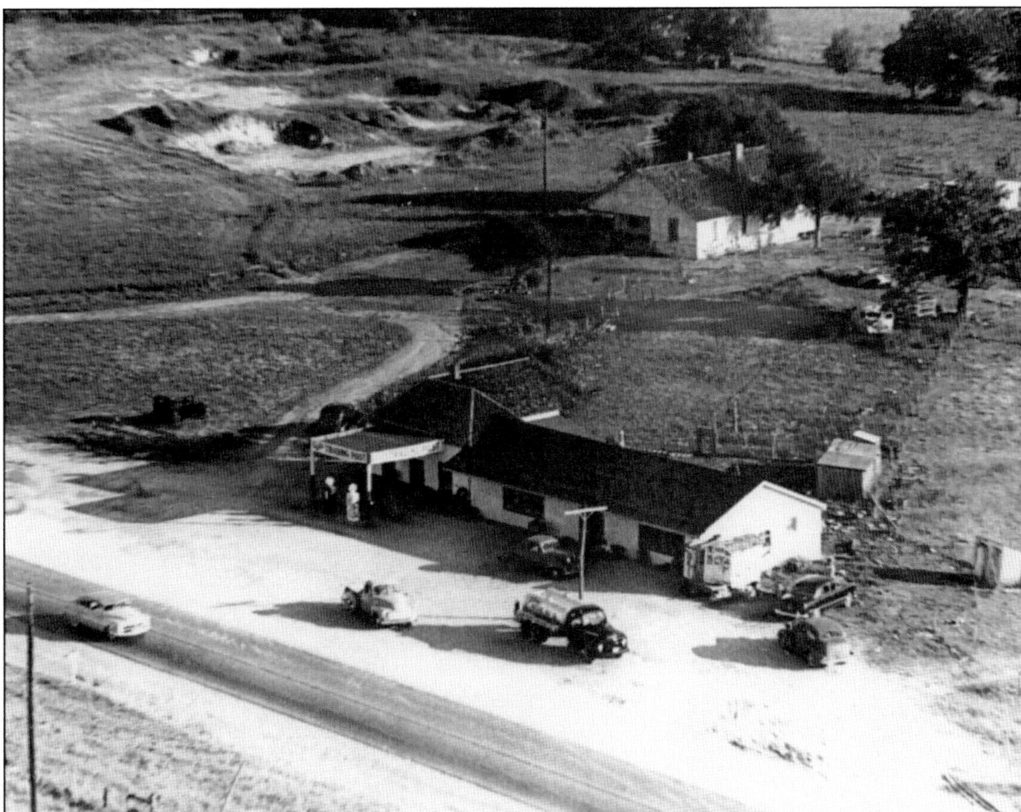

C.J. and Lucille Langston built the Azle Trading Post around 1943 on Highway 199 north of Azle. The family lived in the house behind the store. The building burned in 1963 and was not rebuilt. Their son Donald built the Trading Post Barbeque in 1988 at the original site of his parents' store. After Donald retired, his son Mark built a new restaurant west of there that opened in May 2007.

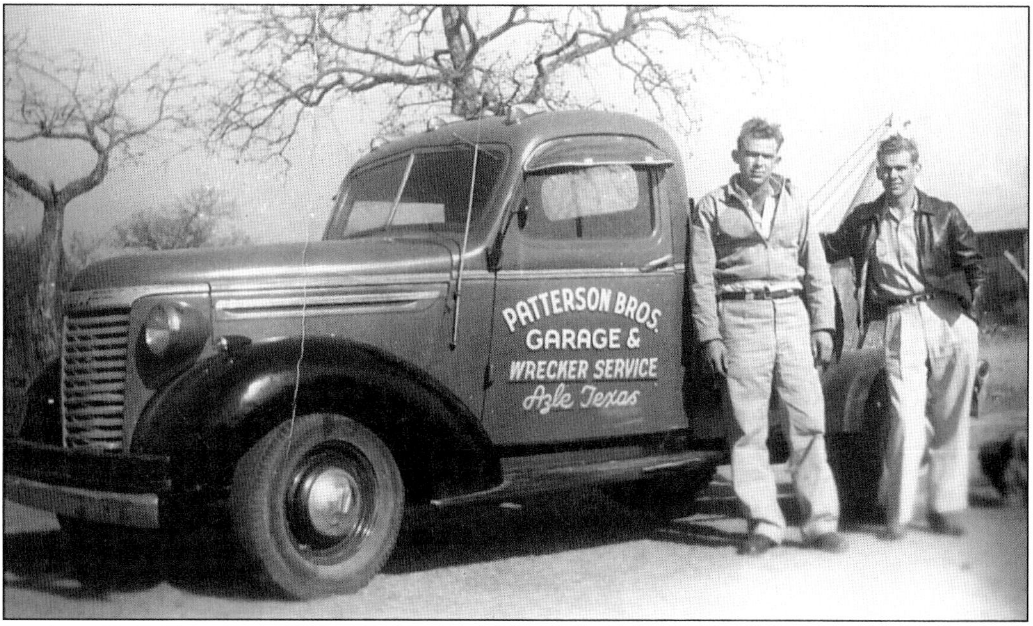


Brothers J.T. (left) and Butch Patterson went into the car repair business in 1947, opening Patterson Brothers Garage and Wrecker Service on Highway 199 south of Azle. Butch has since been partnered with others in the auto repair and parts business but sold out in 1995 and built Ash Creek Self Storage on West Main Street. Butch Patterson may hold the title of longest-running businessman in Azle—he's been at it for 65 years.

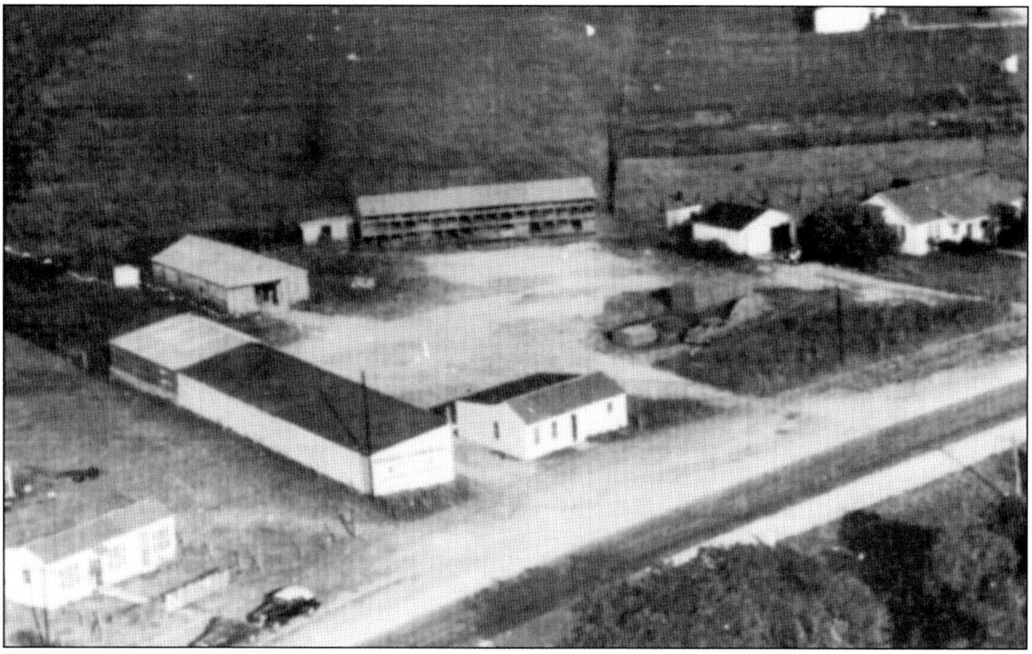

In 1949, J.R. Emanuel bought this Main Street lumberyard from Roy Andrews, who had established it four years earlier. As Emanuel Lumber Company, it expanded to include home construction and hardware supplies. Emanuel's daughter Betty and her husband, Ken Haas, ran the business from 1976 until it closed in 2003.

W.T. Gipson owned and operated this syrup-cooking business at his home in early 1900. The juice from sugarcane was squeezed out on a press, which was turned by a horse. The juice was then piped to this vat, where it was cooked into syrup. W.T. was the father of early Azle postmasters Mamie Gipson McCurdy and Elsie Gipson Parker.

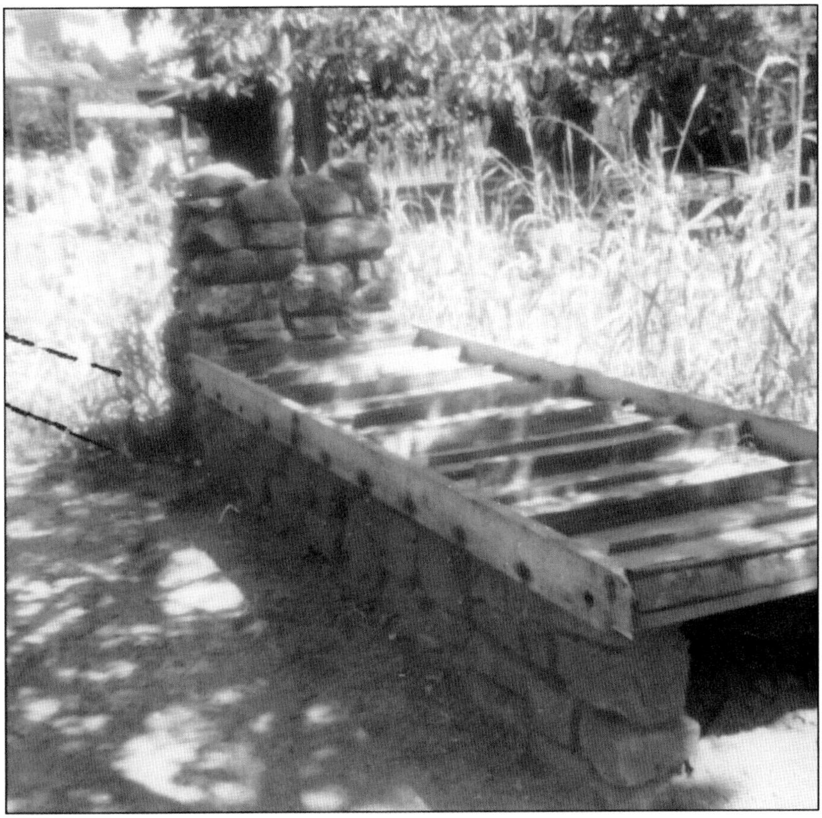

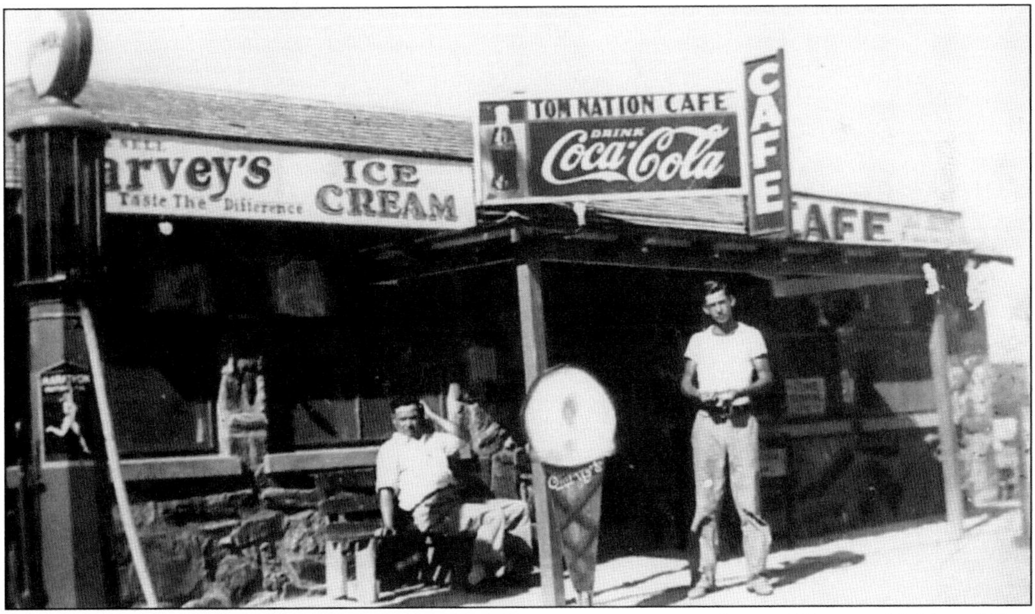


T.H. "Tom" Nation (left) and his son Jim Bob Nation are seen in front of Nation Café on West Main Street around 1938. The café was originally the Blue Goose Saloon and was built in the late 1800s. It was later named the Red Top Café and was a very popular eatery with Azle citizens and truckers traveling on Highway 199.

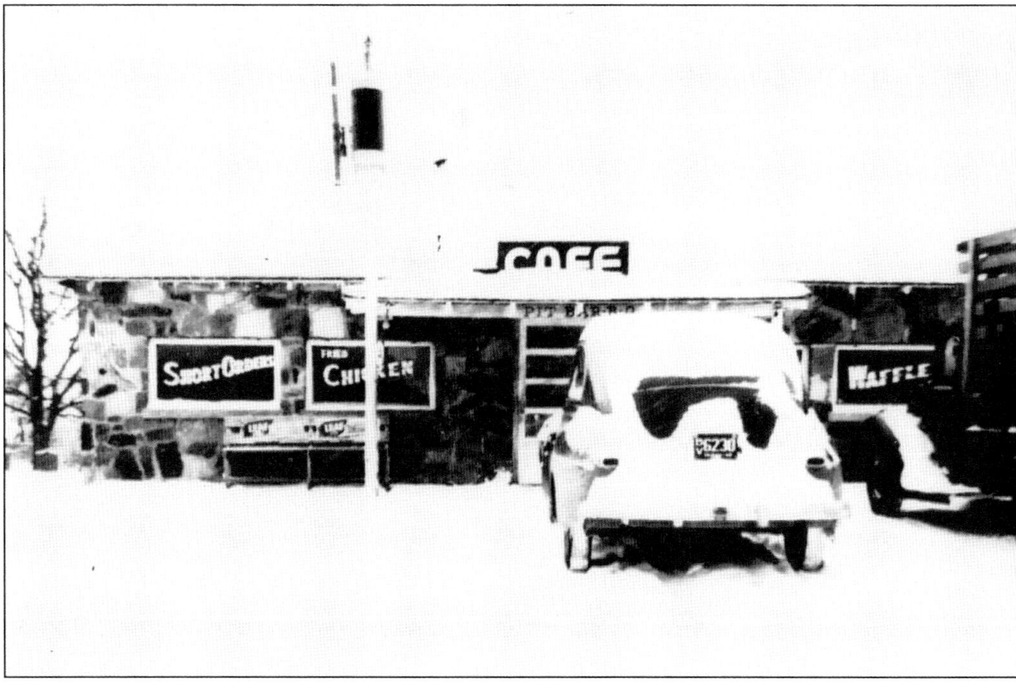


Azle's famed Red Top Café was given its name by owner Eral Yates in 1940. Before that, it was the Tom Nation Café. It became well known nationwide as truckers traveled through Azle and stopped at the 24-hour café. The Red Top Café ran from 1940 until 1966. After other businesses occupied the building, it was vacant for a time and was demolished in 1972.

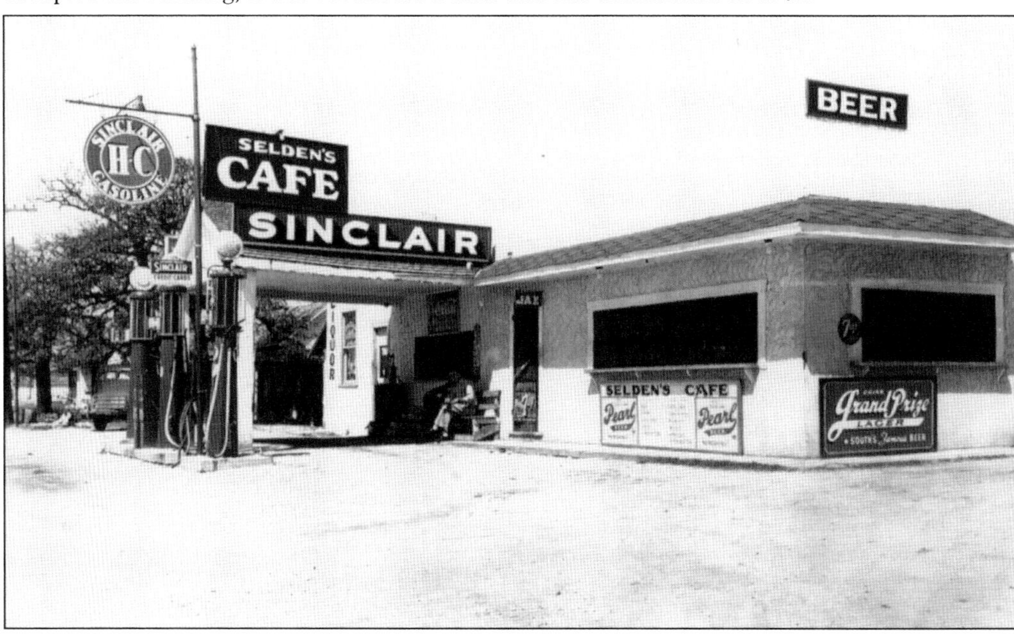


W.E. and Johnnie Selden opened their café and service station in 1936 on West Main Street. Today, it is occupied by Bransom Real Estate and Allstate Insurance. The Selden family's rock home next door was built about the same time, and their daughter Nancy Selden Foster still lives there. W.E. Selden is seen here sitting in front of the service station.

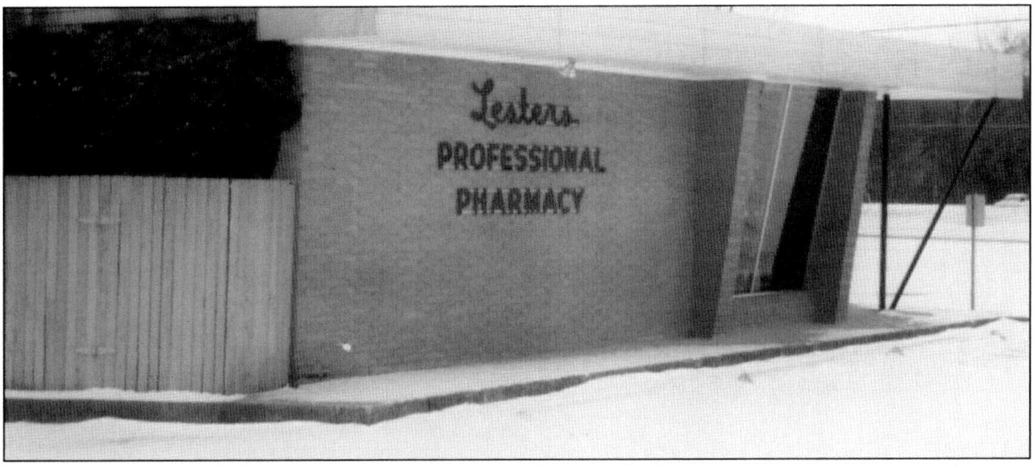


T.D. "Kelly" and Iola Lester opened Lester's Professional Pharmacy in 1954 along with their daughter Imogene and her husband, "Sandy" Standefer. It was first located at the Azle Clinic and Hospital but was moved to 100 Denver Trail in 1961. After Kelly's death in 1967, the Standefers operated the pharmacy. Their only child, Thomas, joined them in 1983 as a registered pharmacist. Lester's Pharmacy closed in March 1997.

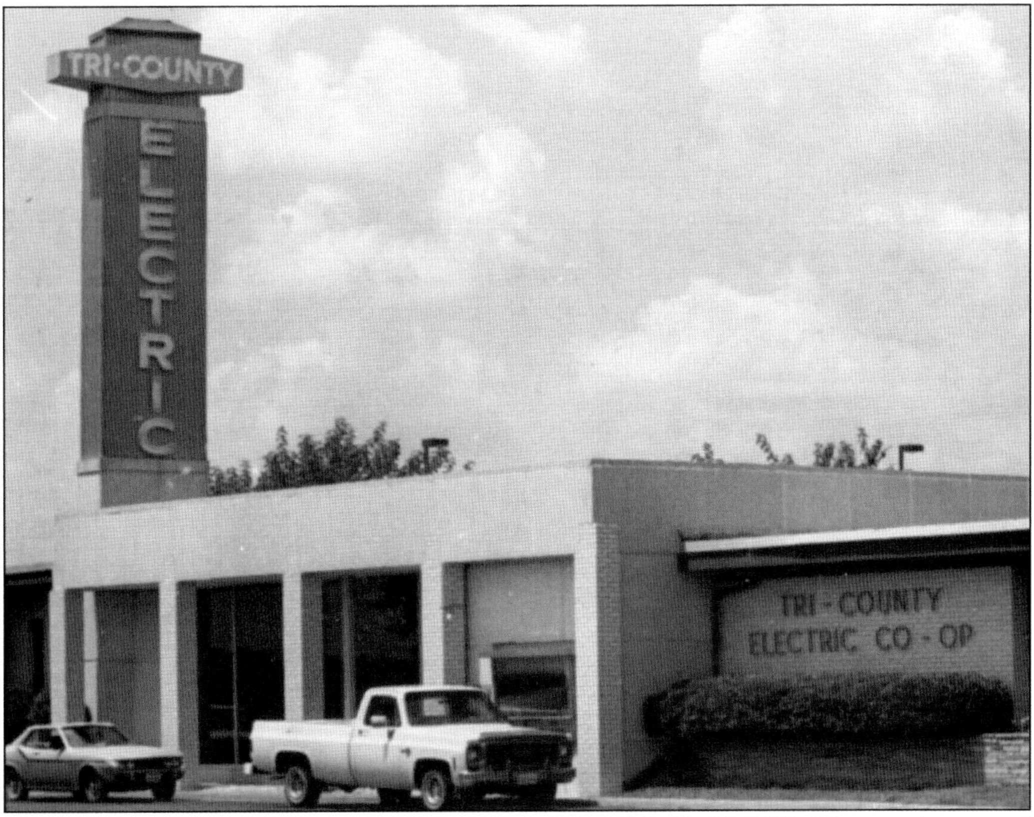


Tri-County Electric Cooperative, Inc. was organized on March 20, 1939. The member-owned co-op serves customers in 16 counties with district offices in Azle, Fort Worth, Granbury, and Seymour. The co-op built a headquarters building at 413 West Main Street around 1940. In 1964, the co-op office was moved to its current location at 600 Northwest Parkway, seen here.

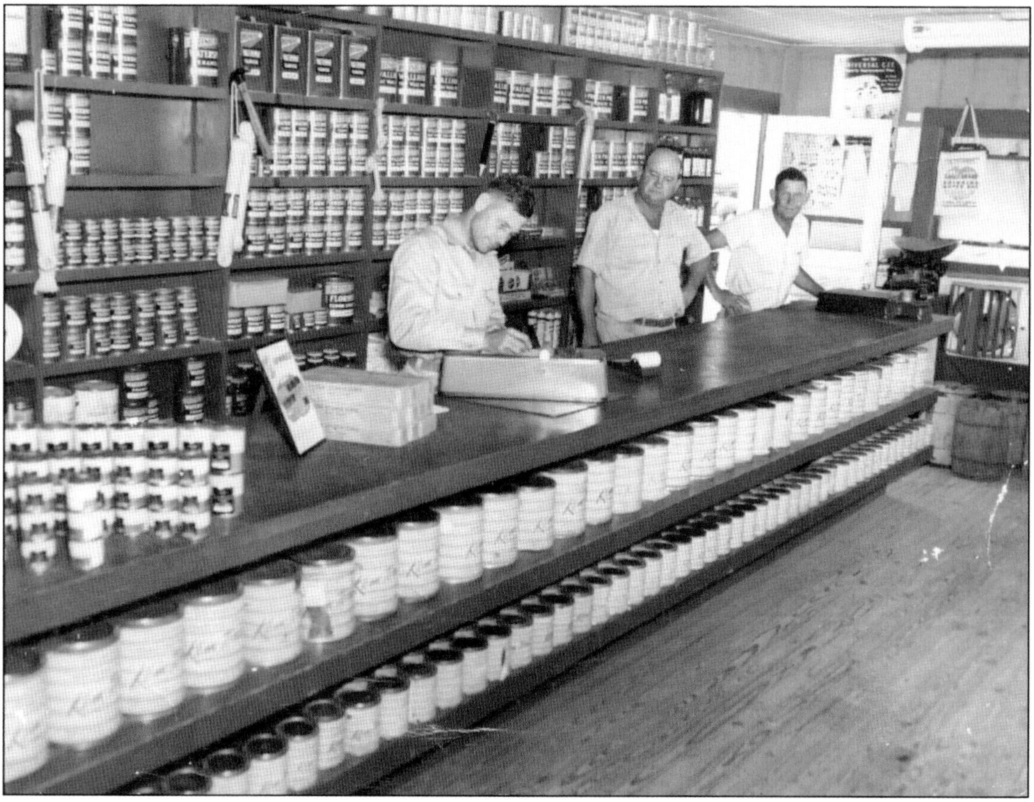

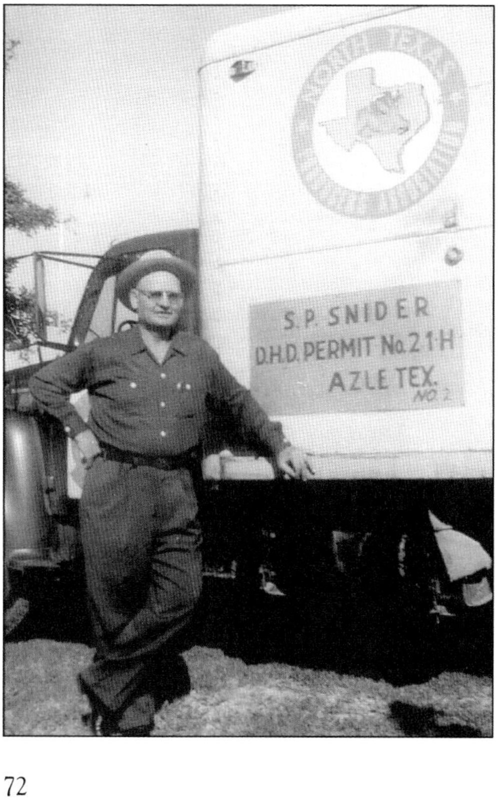


Charlie Dunlap and David Hawes bought the Trinity Lumber Company at 112 East Main Street in 1946, renaming it Eagle Mountain Lumber Company. Dunlap operated the business until 1971. A well-known and respected businessman, Dunlap was easily recognized around town in his yellow truck with "There Goes Charlie" printed over the back window. This 1946 photograph shows Charlie Dunlap (left) and employees Ewing Robinson (middle) and Arthur Smith.

Before refrigerated trucks, S.P. Snider used big blocks of ice to keep milk cans cold on the way to Metzger's Milk in Dallas. He owned four trucks that picked up milk from dairies in the Azle area from 1933 to 1956. Snider drove for the North Texas Producers Association for about three years before he retired. This photograph was taken in 1958.

Hampton's Store, owned by Flossie and Wade Hampton, is fondly remembered by generations of Rock School students. Their first store was on Main Street from 1920 until 1936. In 1937, the store moved next to Azle Elementary School. Eventually, it closed in 1965. This 1949 photograph shows, from left to right, Juanita Phillips, Lois Hill, and Nancy Selden in the doorway. Jessie Waggoner is standing on a friend's shoulders.

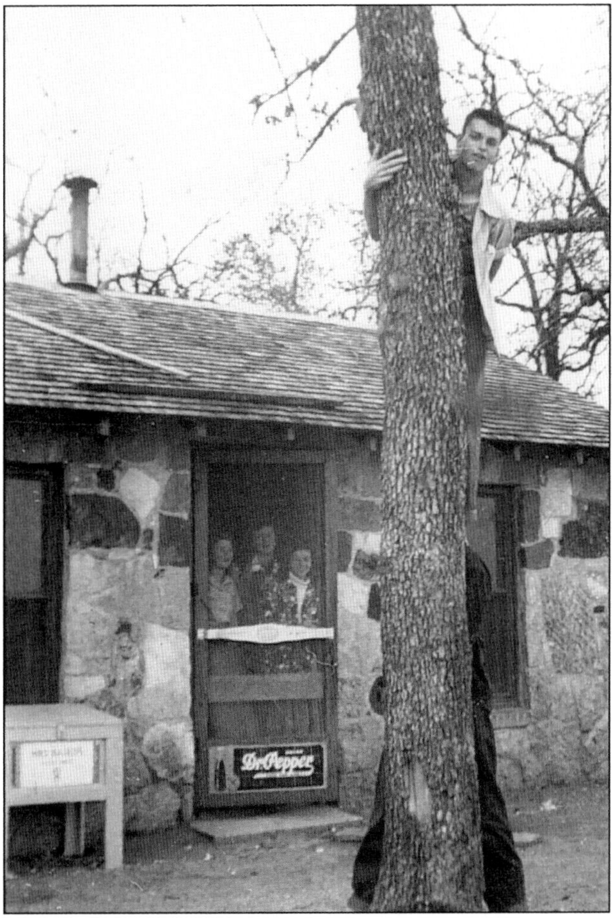


J. Mansel Steele and Sidney Miller operated Miller and Steele Grocery and Market and Texaco station in the 1940s, at 113 West Main Street, where Southern Belle Restaurant stands today. They bought Hoyl's Garage and remodeled the building by closing-in the large garage door.

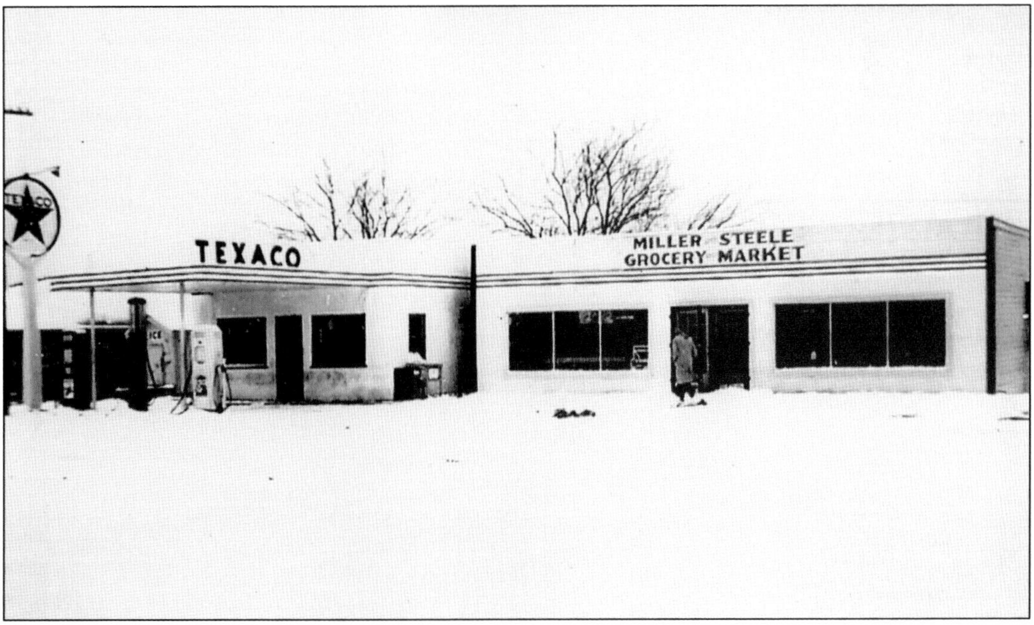

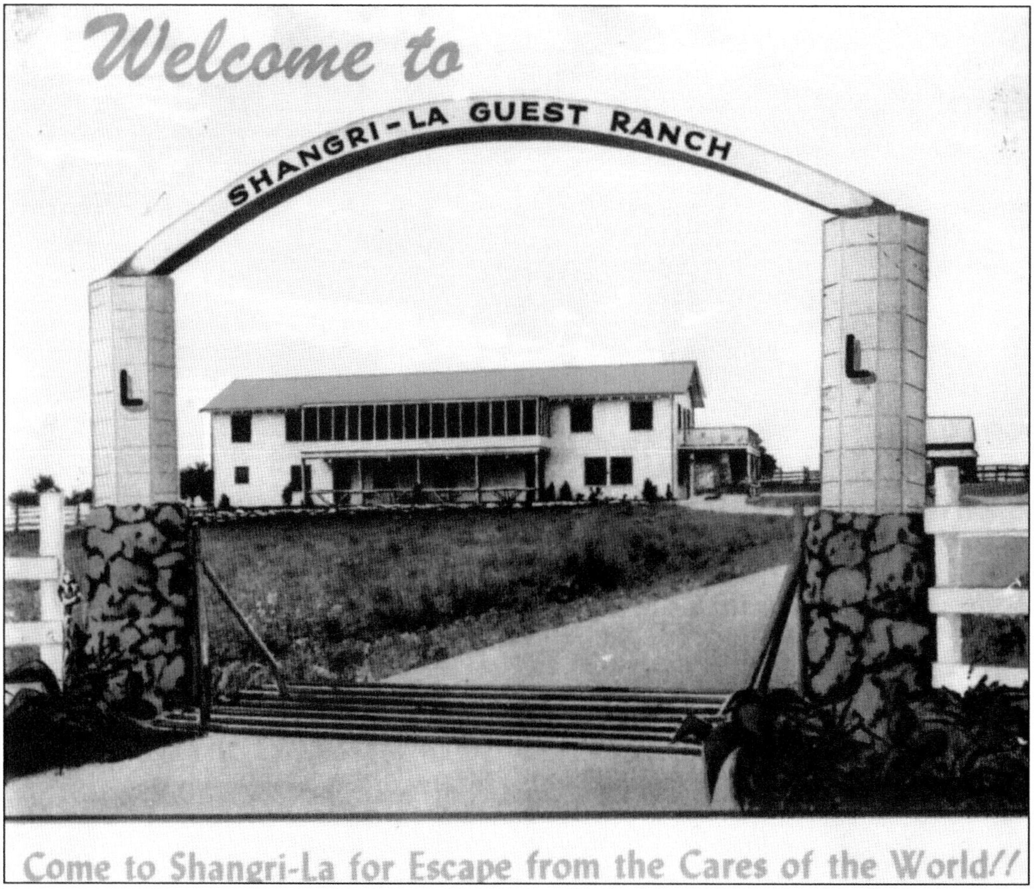


Shangri-La Guest Ranch, a Western-themed resort, was located seven miles west of Azle on FM 730 South. Walter Lane of Fort Worth built the ranch about 1945, which featured a swimming pool, horseback riding, buggy rides, dancing, fishing, lodging, and home-style cooking. It was enjoyed by families and high school students for about 20 years. (Courtesy of Delbert Dake, Sr.)

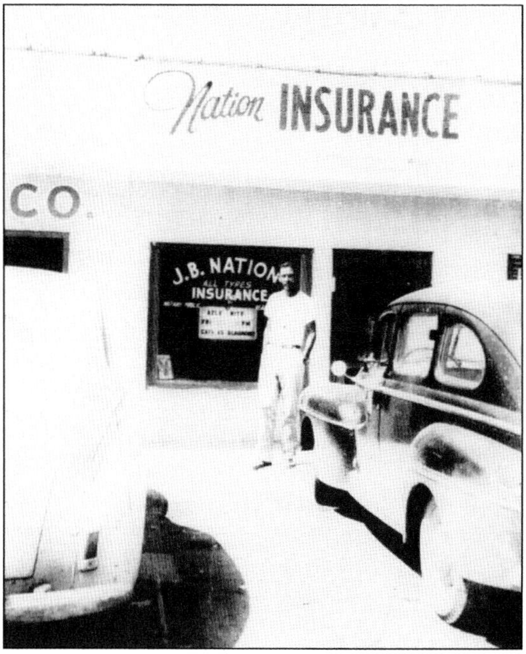


Jim Bob and Beryl Nation began Jim Bob Nation Insurance Agency in 1949 at 133 West Main Street and then moved across the street in the 1970s, next door to the present-day Rural Gas Supply. Nation often advertised the Fort Worth Cats baseball games in the front window of the agency.

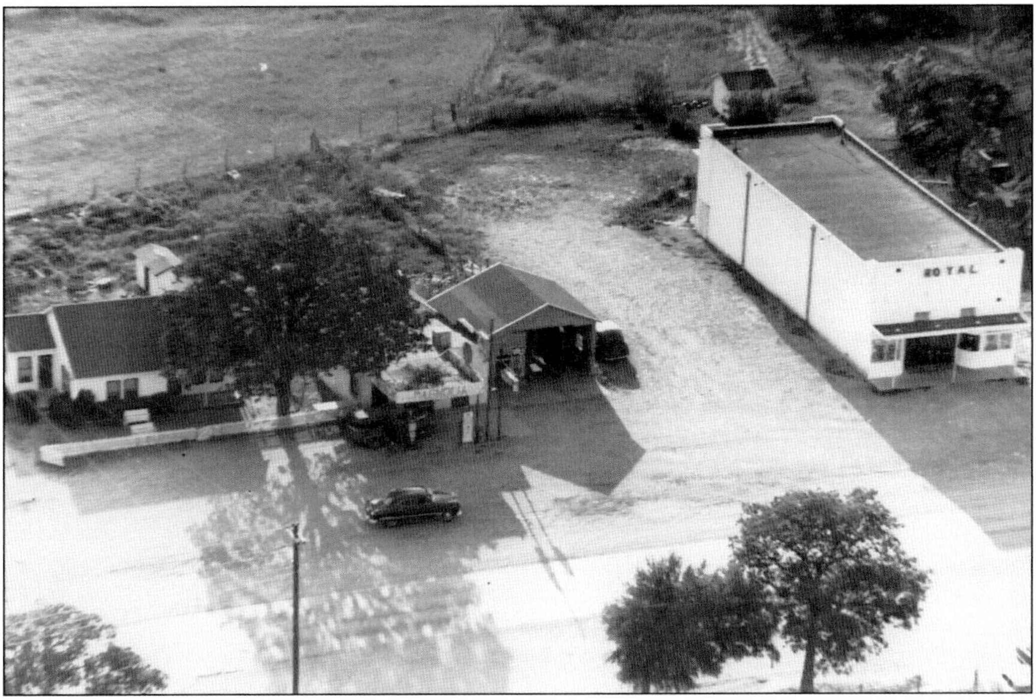


Azle's only indoor theater was the Royal Theater, at 233 West Main Street. It was opened by Roy and Louise Nation Wood around 1946. Also in this photograph is the Magnolia Service Station and the home of Douglas Phillips. The large tree in the Phillipses' front yard was once part of the playground at Azle's fourth schoolhouse around 1892.

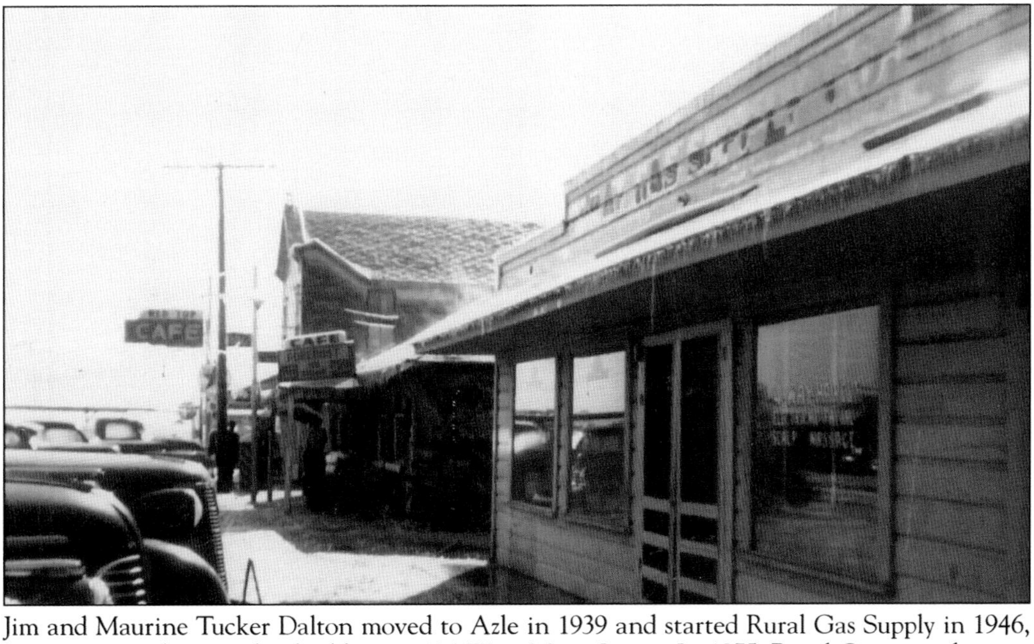


Jim and Maurine Tucker Dalton moved to Azle in 1939 and started Rural Gas Supply in 1946, beginning in this wooden building at 126 West Main Street. In 1975, Rural Gas moved across the street to its present location at 140 West Main Street. The Dalton's daughter Peggy owns and operates the business today with her husband, Jackie Carpenter, and their sons Jim and John.

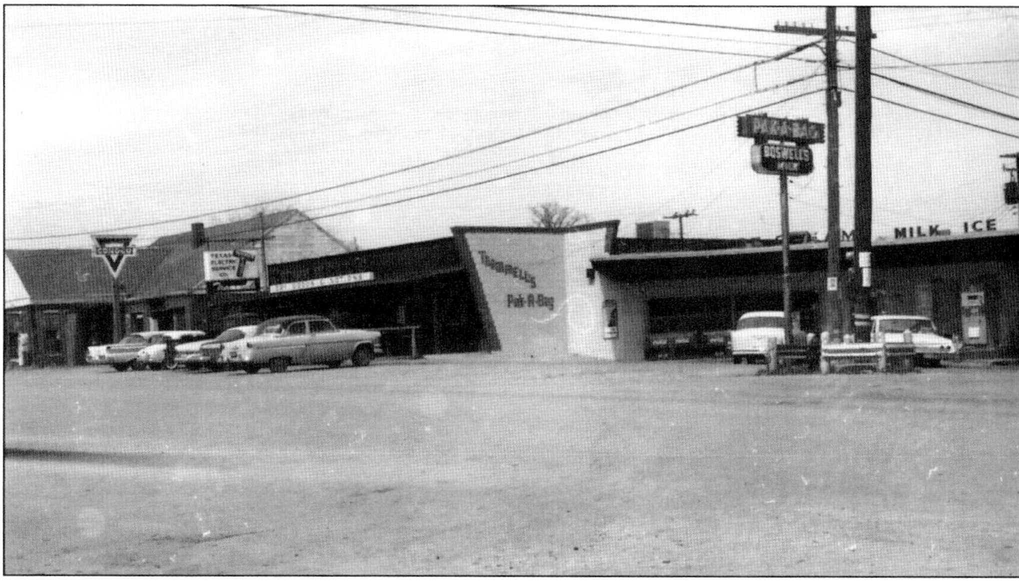


Travis and Vancil Trammell purchased land on Main Street where Dunn and Elam Real Estate is now located. Trammell Brothers Grocery and Market opened in a small frame building in May 1940. When World War II came around, the brothers left the store in the hands of their parents, W.E. and Grace Trammell, and Vancil's wife, Audrey. After they returned in 1946, they moved across the street into a modern building of concrete and opened Azle's first supermarket. A department store and ready-to-wear store were added in 1952 but later converted into Trammell's Village Restaurant in 1964. After much soul-searching, the decision was made to close the grocery store, and Trammell's Flying T Gallery opened there in September 1977. Below, Travis (left) and Vancil Trammell sit in the Flying T Gallery in 1985.

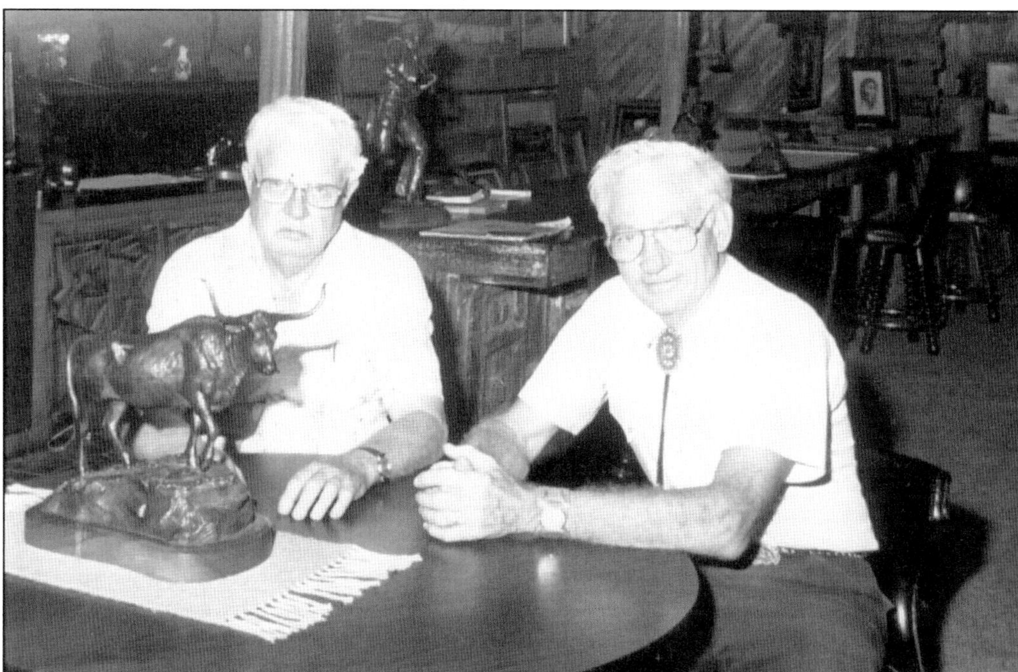

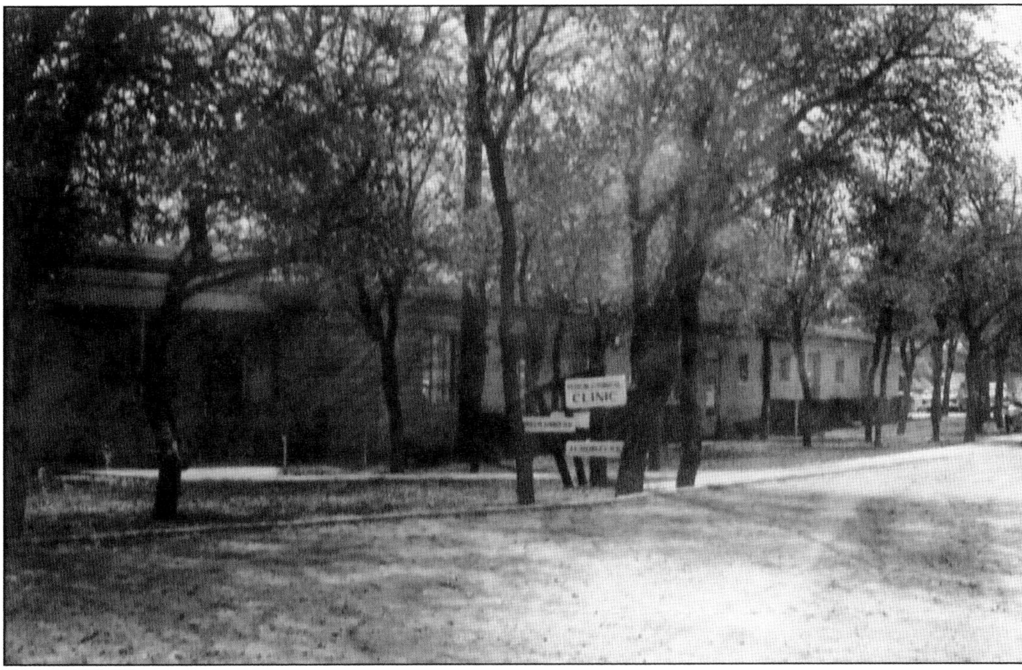


James Emanuel, T.D. Lester, and Dr. W.B. McLeroy formed E.L.M. Construction Corporation for the purpose of building a clinic and hospital in Azle. The clinic opened in March 1954 and the hospital opened in May. Dr. James Savage bought the clinic and the hospital, located at 112 Denver Trail, in 1961.

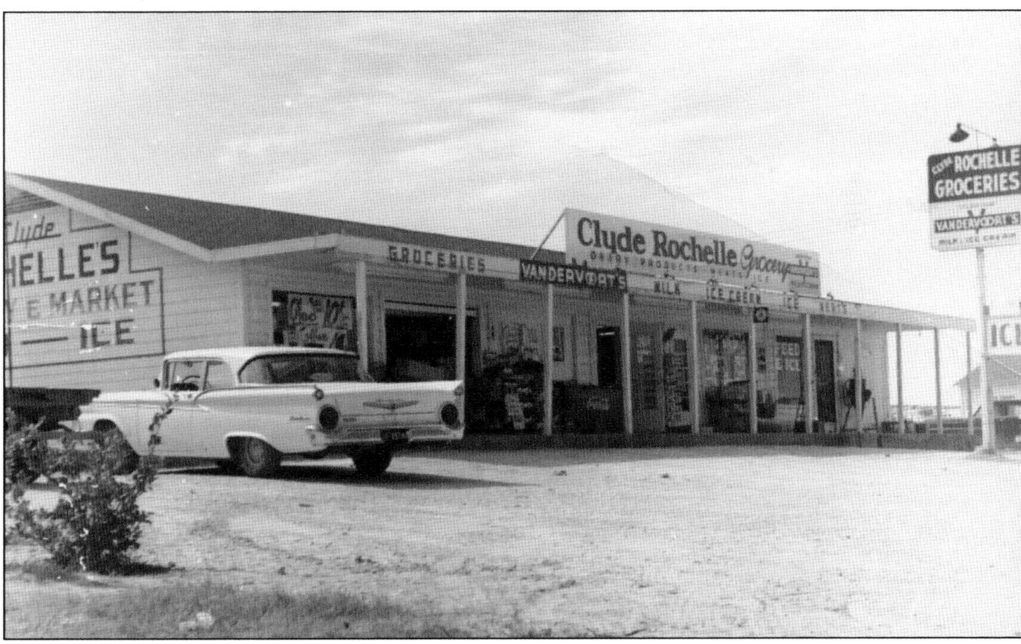


Clyde and Marguerite Rochelle built a frame building on Highway 199 in 1954 after taking down a barbed-wire fence and clearing off the corn stalks. They opened Clyde Rochelle Grocery and operated it for eight years, living behind it for five of them. A desire to get back into the real estate business, which they had been in before moving to Azle, caused them to sell the store in 1962.

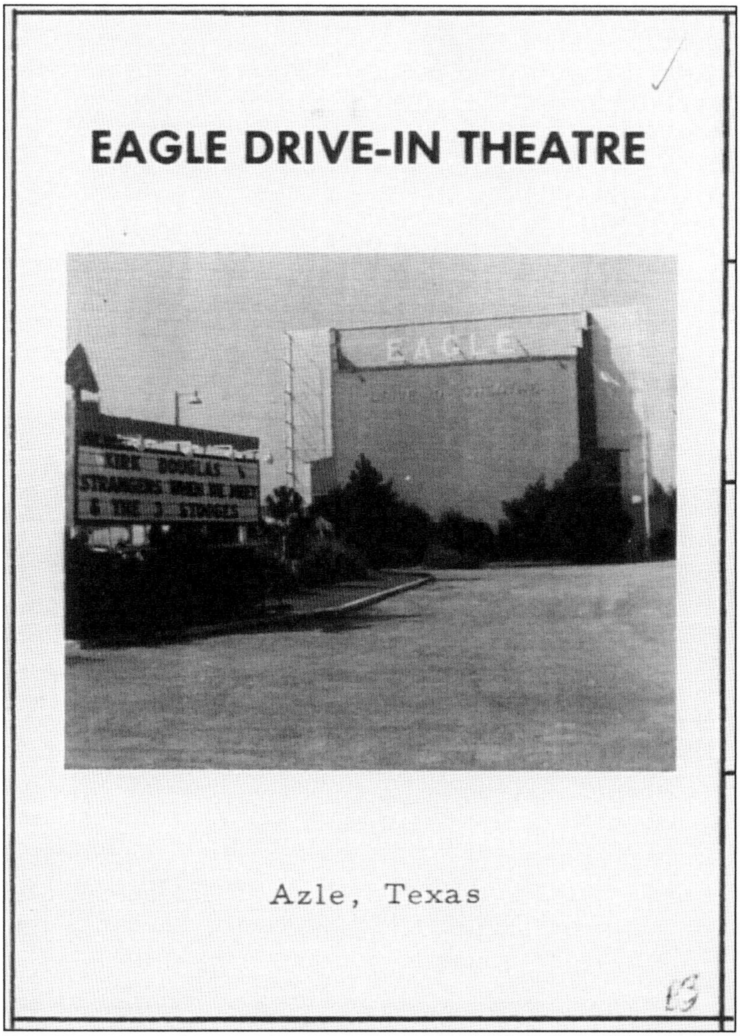


The Eagle Drive-In Theatre was built around 1952 by Jack and Jo Watson at 812 Highway 199, south of Azle. They sold it to Dwayne and Beverly Gates in 1968. It closed in 1983 and was eventually torn down. In 1962, when this photograph was taken, *Strangers When We Meet*, starring Kirk Douglas, was playing.

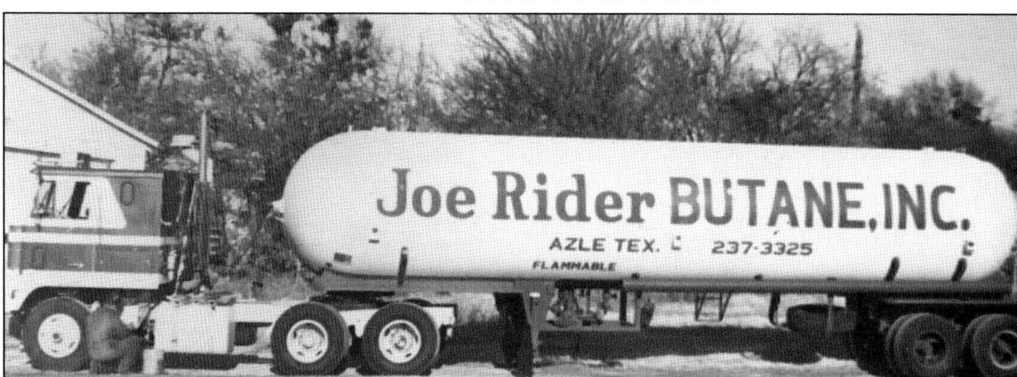


Joe Rider Propane, Inc., has been a staple business in Azle since 1954. The first office was in Lucia Ione and Joe V. Rider Sr.'s garage. Their son Joe V. Rider Jr. built an office in front of his parents' home at 7808 Jacksboro Highway in 1976. He and his wife, Jean, ran the business until his death in 1977. Today, it is run by their son Jeff and his wife, Michelle.

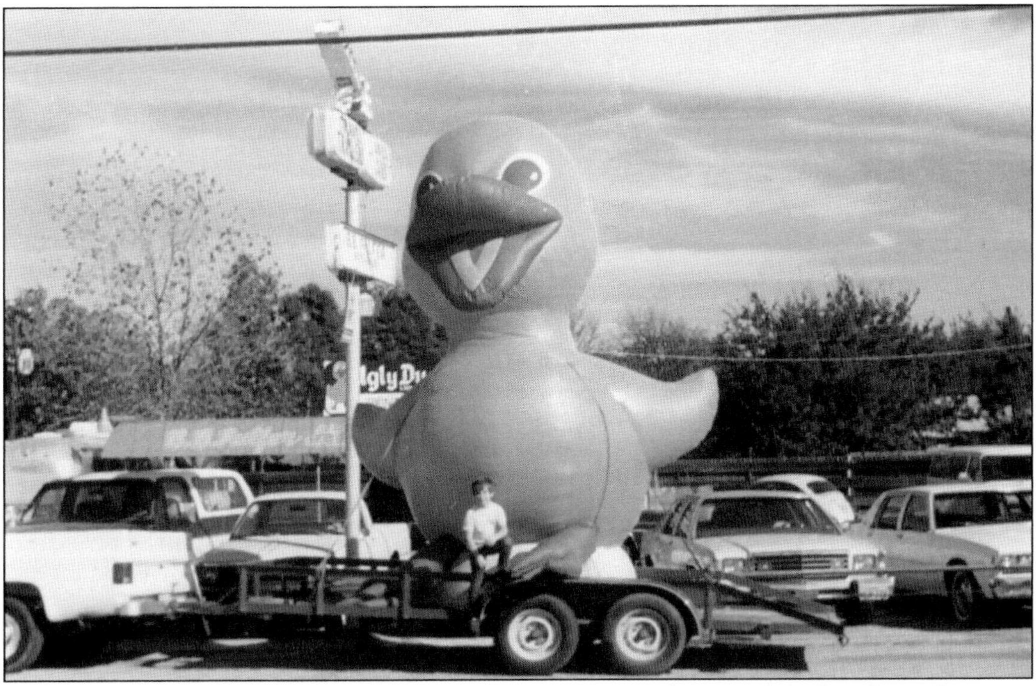


B.B. Fulfer's Garage began in 1958 on Main Street. In 1961, he moved farther down the street next to the Masonic Lodge and added car sales. After closing the garage in 1970, he opened Fulfer's Auto Sales at 1109 Southeast Parkway. Later, in 1984, Fulfer provided Azle with its first rent-a-car business when he added Ugly Duckling Rent-a-Car. He closed down in 1995 after 37 years in business.

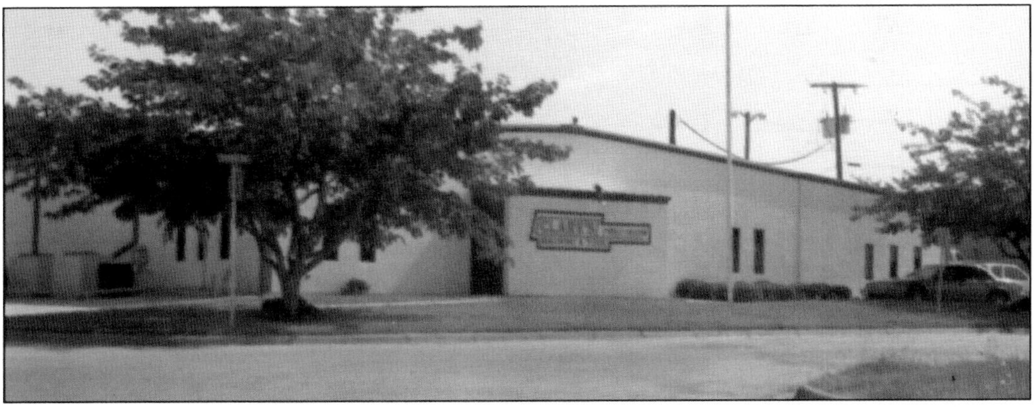

In 1967, B.J. Clark started repairing guns as a hobby in his backyard. A hobby turned into a business, and in 1970, he opened Clark's Gun and Ammo four miles north of the Lake Worth Bridge. In 1977, Clark entered the manufacturing business fabricating small precision tools. The gun business was phased out and Clark's Precision Machine and Tool moved into a new facility at 636 Profit Street in 1981.

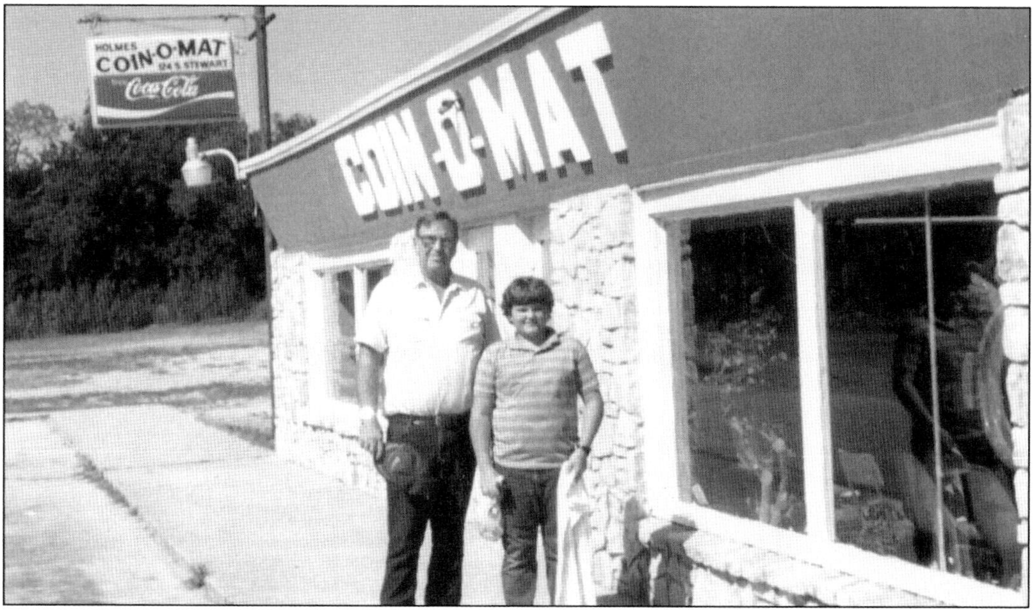


Marshall and Vonnie Holmes began the Coin-O-Mat Laundry at 124 South Stewart Street in 1961. One Friday night in 1963, Holmes and a friend brought their guitars to the Laundromat, and soon, other musicians started showing up for a weekly jam they named the Azle Opry. The jams continued and drew a large crowd, so in the early 1990s, Holmes removed the machines, added a stage and rows of chairs, and secured a house band. Featured on *4 Country Reporter*, *PM Magazine*, and *Real People*, the Azle Opry is still going strong every Friday night starting at 7:00 p.m. and is free to the public. Standing in front of the Coin-O-Mat are Marshall Holmes (left) and his nephew Michael Holmes. Marshall is seen below in 1967. (Courtesy of Vonnie and Marshall Holmes.)

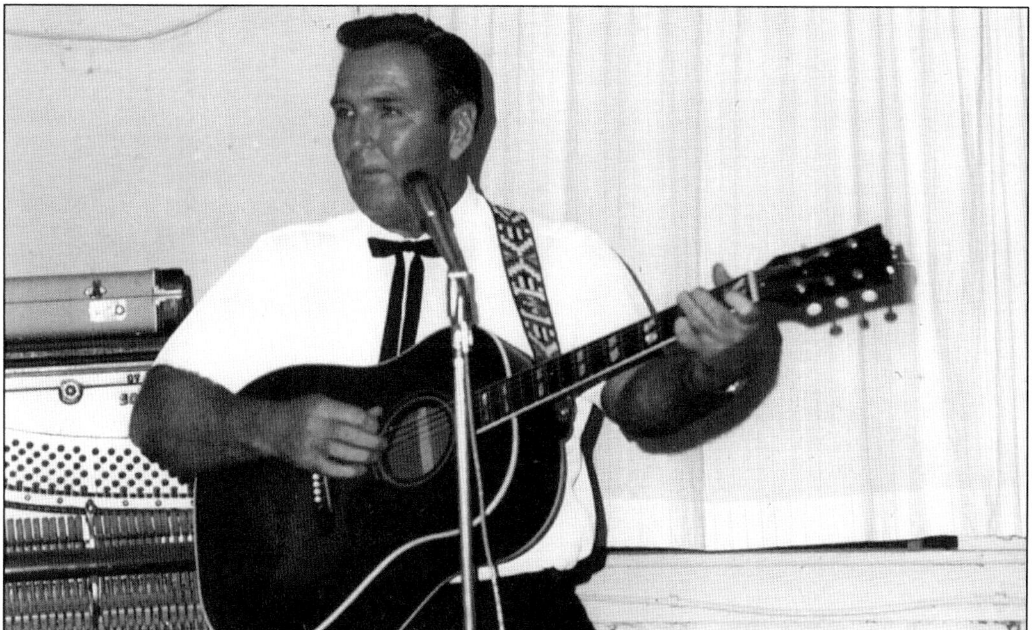

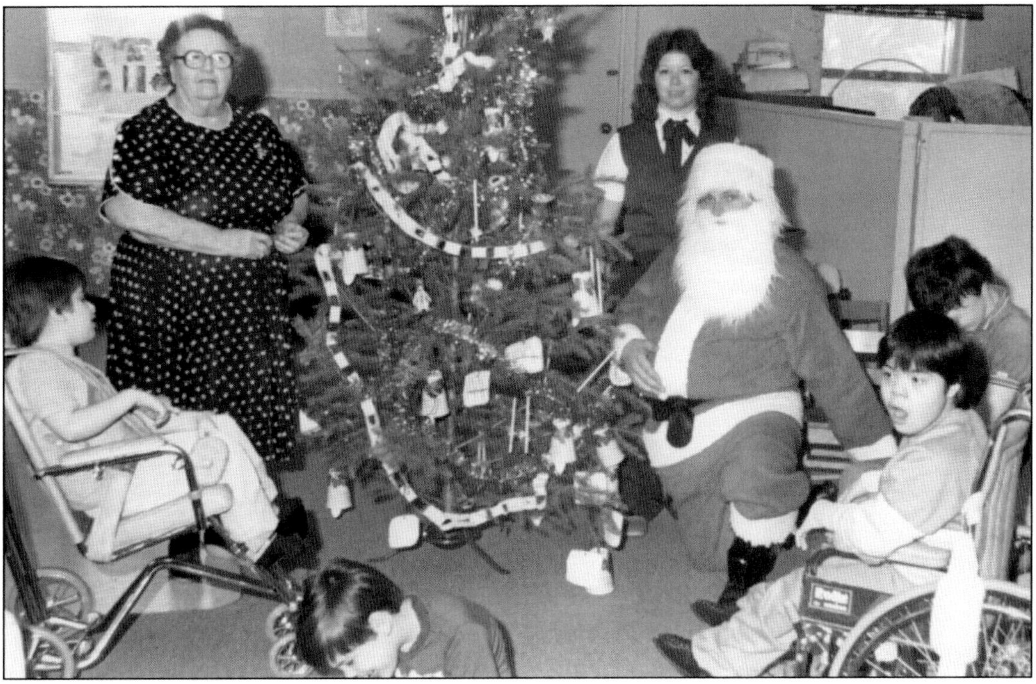

Mamie Jewell Jefferson opened her home for handicapped children in 1961, and it was licensed as a child caring institution in 1969. The Jefferson's Home for Children was for children who were severely delayed in development and unable to walk independently. The home closed in January 2000 after Jefferson's death in 1998. This photograph shows Jefferson (left), with some of the children, a volunteer, and Santa Claus.

The Azle State Bank had its grand opening on January 7, 1961, at 401 Northwest Parkway. Arvel W. Boyd organized the bank and was the first president. Joe M. Bonfield bought the bank in 1966 and built a larger bank at 150 Industrial Avenue. Tucker B. Teutsch bought controlling interest in 1975. The Teutsch family sold the bank in 1981 to Compass Bank. Today, it is owned by BBVA Compass.

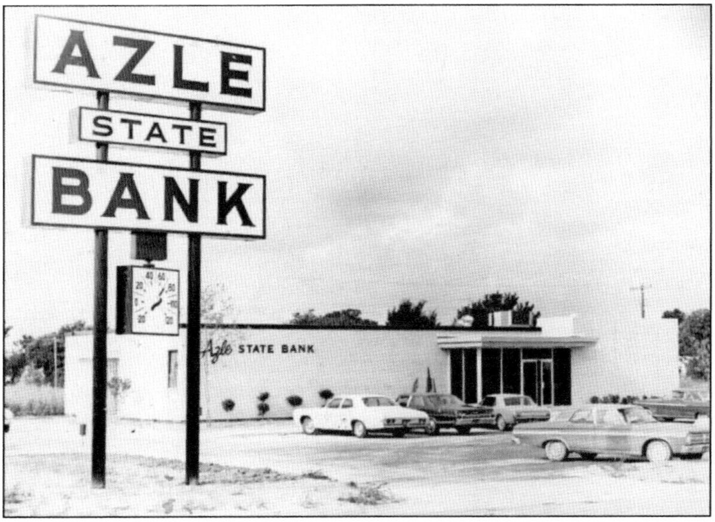

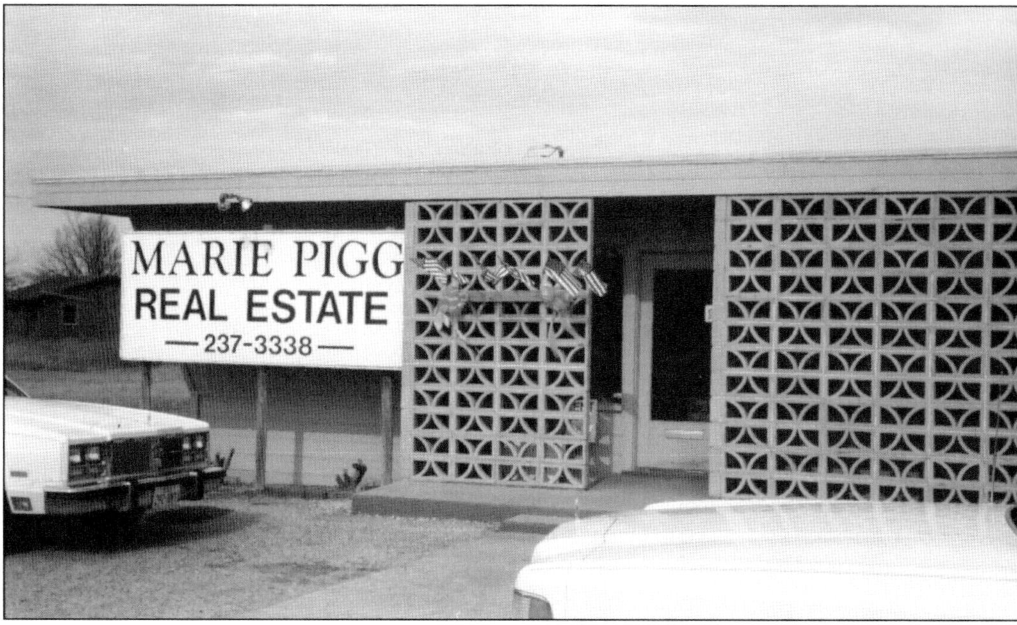


Marie Pigg opened her real estate office in 1969 at 1401 Southeast Parkway after working at Real Estate Exchange for 33 years. Her daughter-in-law Elise joined her at that time. Elise and her husband, Billy Pigg, continued the business after Marie's death in 1995 with the help of their daughter Bonnie and her husband, Bill Erter. A new office building was dedicated in 2002 at 1341 Southeast Parkway.

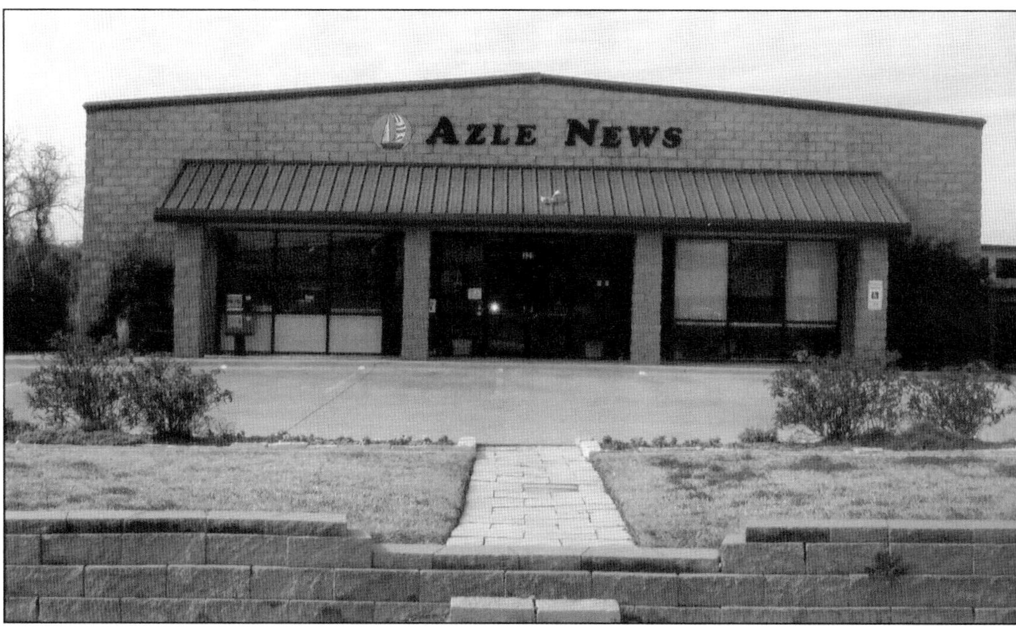


The current *Azle News*, located at 321 West Main Street, evolved from a long line of local newspapers dating back to 1887. From the handwritten *Boomerang* to today's coverage of 4,500 subscribers, the *Azle News* is an award-winning weekly publication. It is owned by Azle Tri-County Advertiser, Inc. Kim Ware took over as publisher in January 2012 after Bob Buckel held the reigns for nearly 25 years.

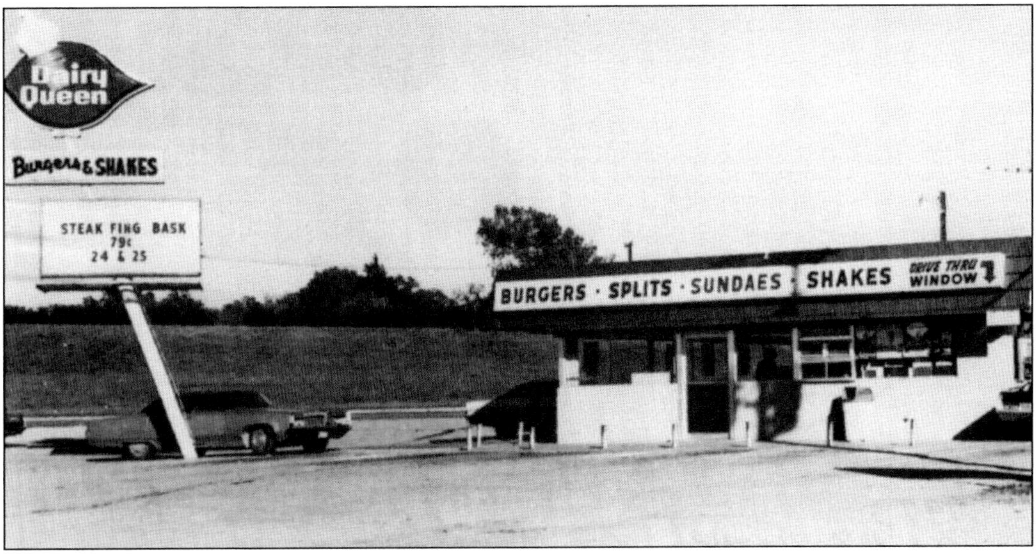


The Azle Dairy Queen was opened in December 1965 by O.D. Smalley. It is located at 164 Industrial Avenue and is owned by William Hall. It is one of the few area Dairy Queens still open and remains one of the busiest eating establishments in Azle. This 1973 photograph shows a Steak Finger Basket selling for only 79¢.

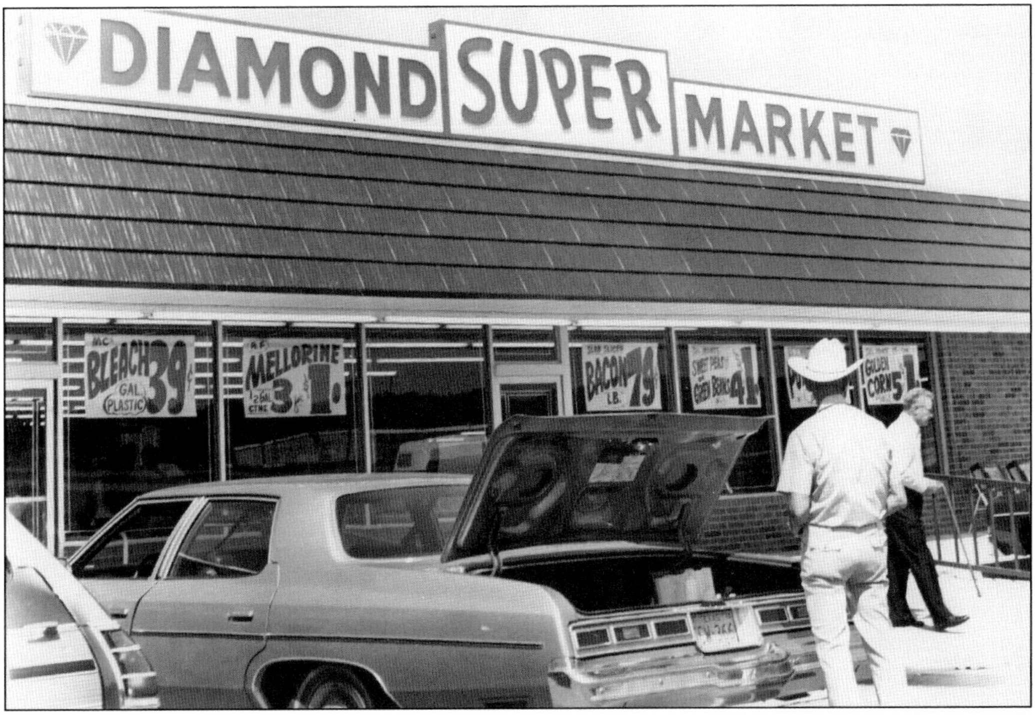


Azle's Diamond Supermarket opened in 1972 at 605 Northwest Parkway. Owners Albert, Paul, and Jerry Smith's parents opened their first store in 1926, the Diamond Hill Market. The Azle store closed in 2002, but Diamond Supermarket, Inc., still owns eight Diamond and three Metro stores in Texas. Jerry's daughter Lisa Geer runs the business today.

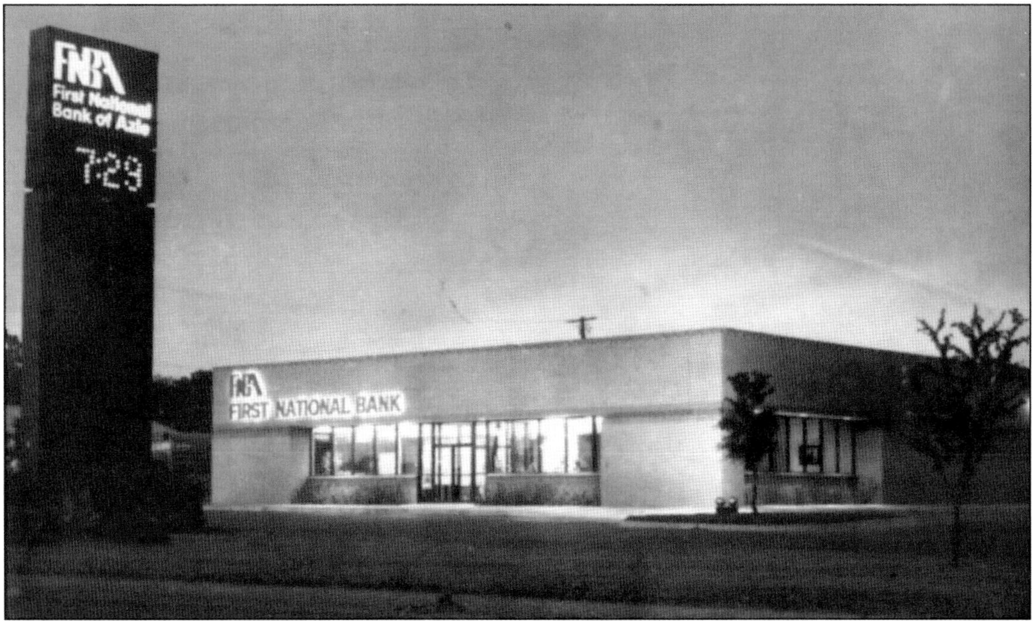


Weatherford Bancshares, Inc., filed application for the First National Bank of Azle, and the building, at 316 Northwest Parkway, opened on October 26, 1981. The bank was sold to Larry Calhoun in 1982, and since then has been sold and renamed several more times. It became First Texas Bank in 1993 and First Bank in 1996. The Dinsdale family of Nebraska bought the bank in 2008 and renamed it Pinnacle Bank.

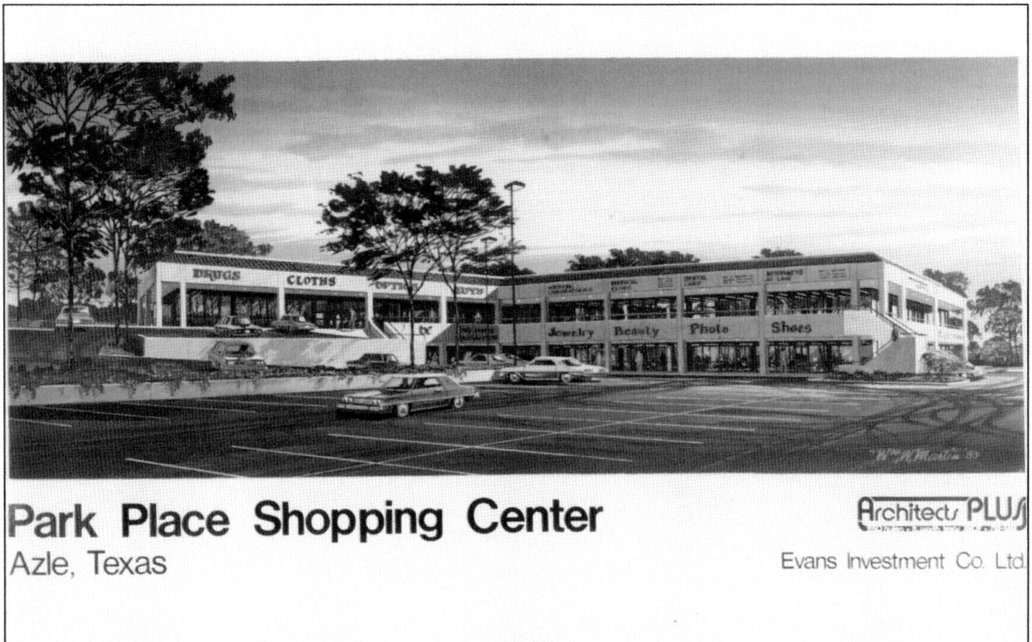


Construction of the Park Place Shopping Center on the corner of the Highway 199 service road and North Stewart Street began in May 1983. It was built on two levels by Evans Investment Company of Azle. Radio Shack, at 168 Park Place, has been the principal store since it opened.

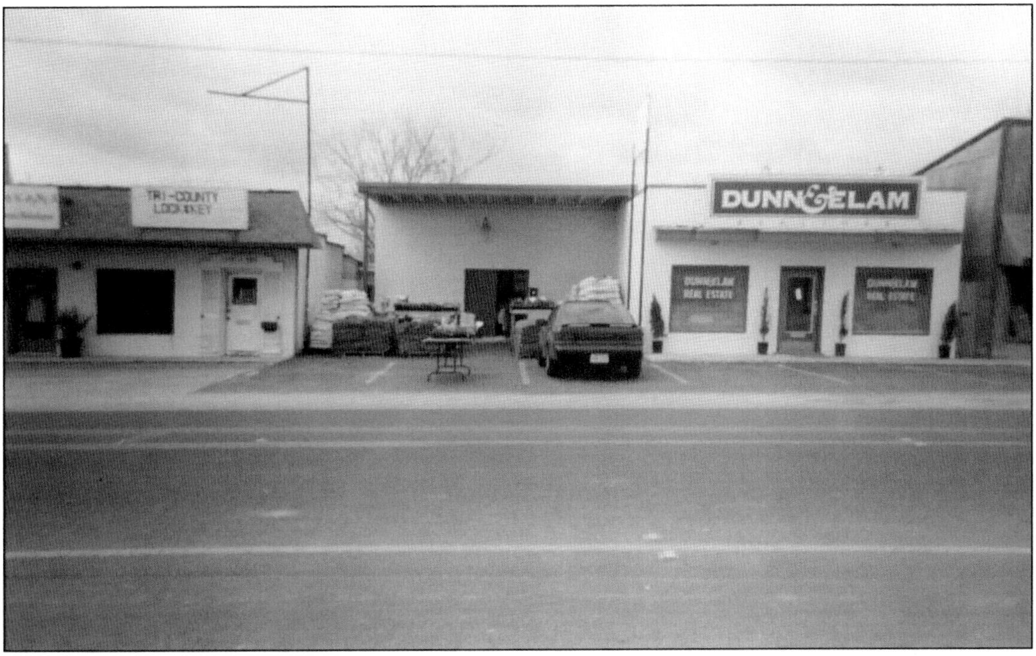


Elaine Dunn and Olivia Elam opened Dunn and Elam Real Estate in 1993. The agency is located at 141 West Main Street, which was built in 1953 and housed the Azle post office until 1971. Dunn bought out Elam's half in 1999 and was joined in business by her husband, Henson Dunn, at that time. Their daughter Leah Dunn purchased everything in 2005 and is the sole owner of the business today.

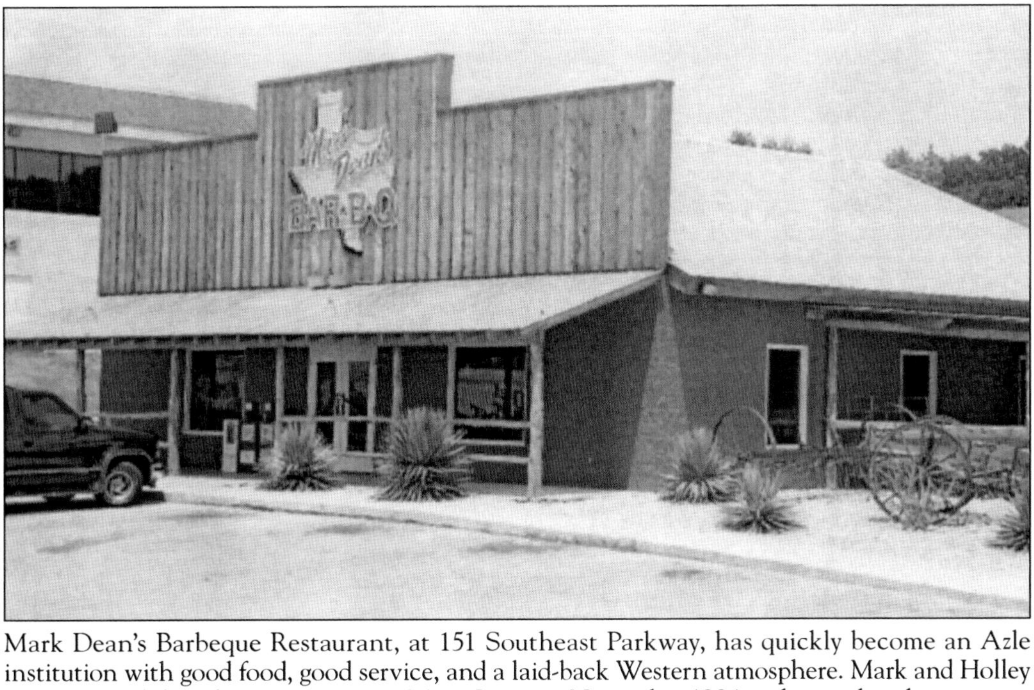


Mark Dean's Barbeque Restaurant, at 151 Southeast Parkway, has quickly become an Azle institution with good food, good service, and a laid-back Western atmosphere. Mark and Holley Dean opened their first restaurant on Main Street in November 1994 and moved to their present location in April 1996.

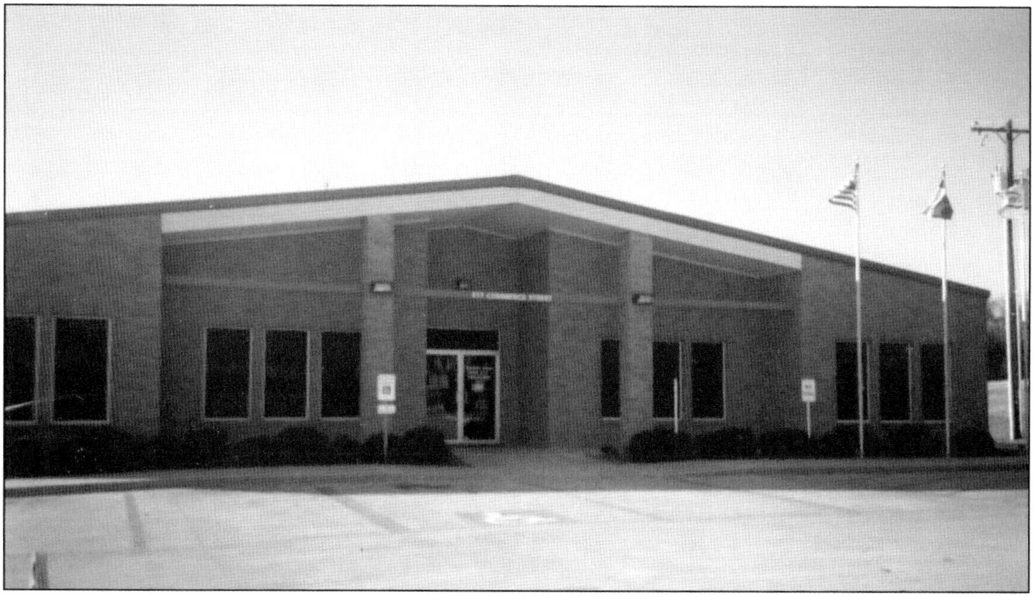

Located at 317 Commerce Street, the Community Caring Center provides food, clothing, household items, and help with bills to needy families in Azle. Funding comes from private donations, club and organization fundraisers, local church and school support, the gift shop, matched grants, and the Azle Fun Run. Joe Lieb, the executive director, holds the only paid position; all others are volunteers.

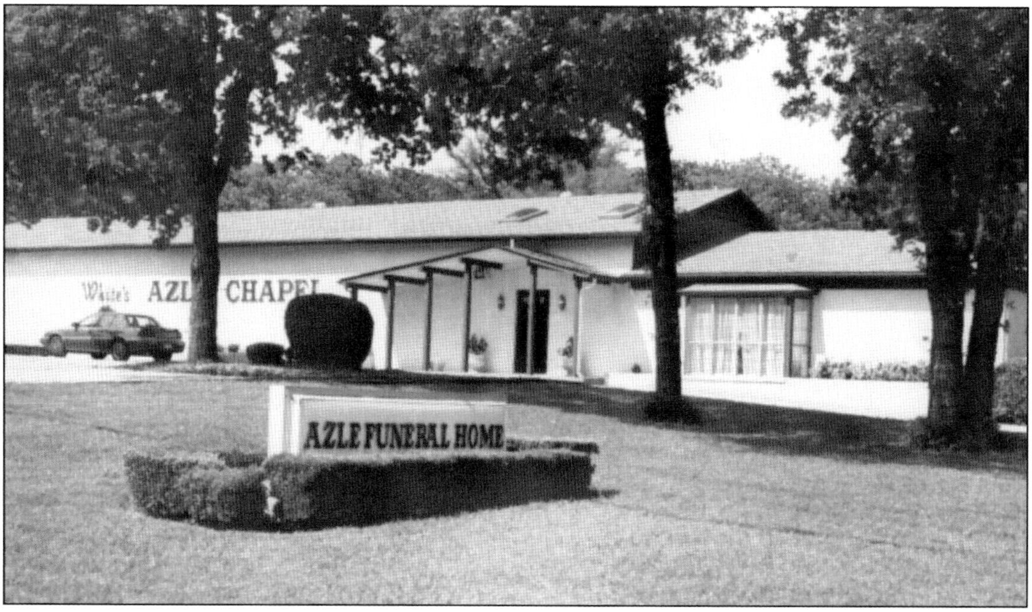


White's Funeral Home, at 105 Denver Trail, was originally named Azle Community Funeral Home. Azle citizens bought shares to finance it and it opened in 1953. Webber and Mary Farris bought it in 1957. Longtime mayor C.Y. Rone came to Azle in 1960 to manage the funeral home, purchasing it in 1966. White's Funeral Home bought it in 1986.

# *Five*

# Organizations

Azle has always had individuals who stepped up to help the community with projects in the schools and churches, but over time, people realized that something more was needed to unite the town and that every citizen needed to take part in the way his or her world was shaped. Thus, organizations and clubs to better the community started to develop.

The first organization in Azle was the Masons, who received their charter in 1884. The Masons have grown to have 215 lodge members over their more than 120 years. Another early organization was the Azle School Parent Teachers Association, which had its first meeting in April 1930 and continues today.

The Azle Civic League was first organized in the early 1930s with Faris Ross as the first president. He brought many notable speakers, such as Texas governor James Allred, to the little town of Azle, which had only 250 citizens at the time. The Azle Garden Club was organized in 1947 with 46 charter members. One of the garden club's first projects was to work with the Azle Civic League to raise funds for the organization of a volunteer fire department, buy a $4,800 fire truck, and build a firehouse, which was completed in 1951.

Some forgotten and nonactive organizations are the Home Demonstration Club, organized in August 1935; the Mary Anderson Music Club, started in 1954; the Circle Bridge Club, organized in 1954; the Aztex Saddle Club, started in 1962; the Aztex Rifle and Pistol Club; and the Azle Racquet and Tennis Club.

Today's organizations and clubs are numerous and varied, but they all fulfill the requirements those early citizens had in mind: improving the quality of life in the community, uniting the town, and making the community enjoyable for everyone.

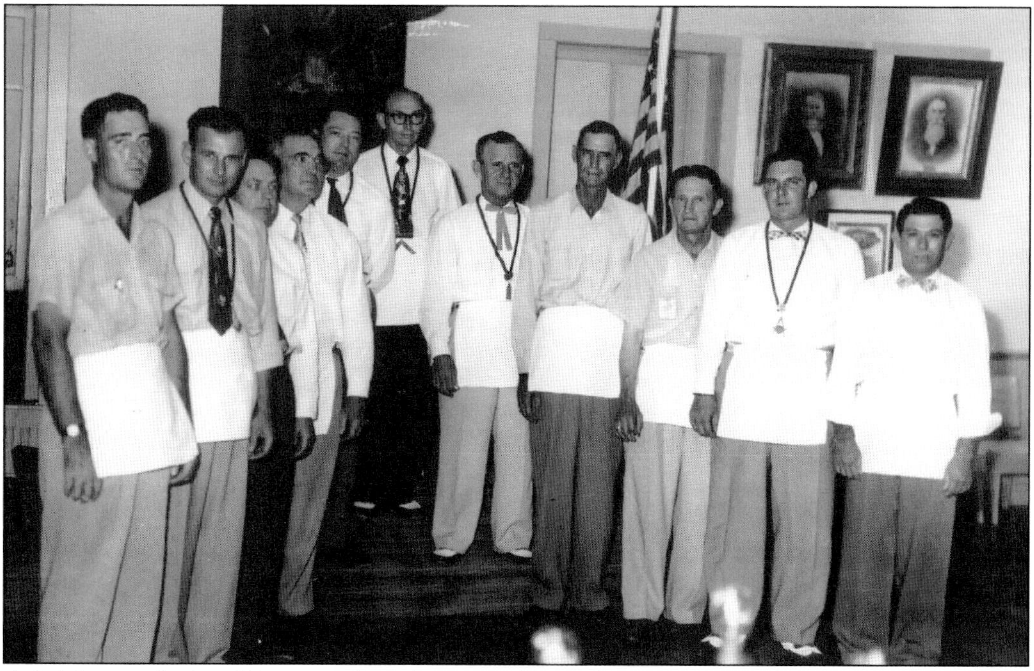

Azle Masonic Lodge 601 received its charter on December 12, 1884, and formed the lodge with W.W. Wiley as the first master. Members purchased the second floor of Joe Fowler's general store around 1892 for their meeting place. They bought the remainder of the building in 1936. The Masons moved the entire structure down the street, and it was in use until the present building was built in 1954. These lodge members in 1953–1954 were, from left to right, Edwin Ross, M.R. "Tutor" Winnett, R.B. Springfield, Willie Speer, Roy Williams, Fred Nation, F.E. "Curly" Wallace, Slim Smethers, Joe Reynolds, John Reynolds, and Carl Rightmer. The Azle Masonic Lodge 601, at 257 West Main Street, is shown below as it looks today.

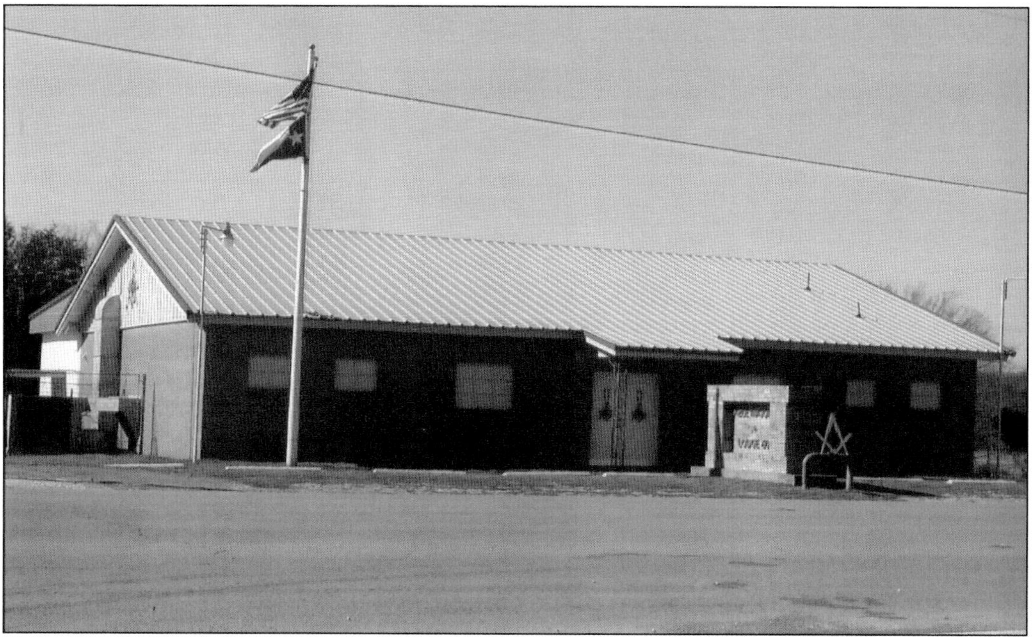

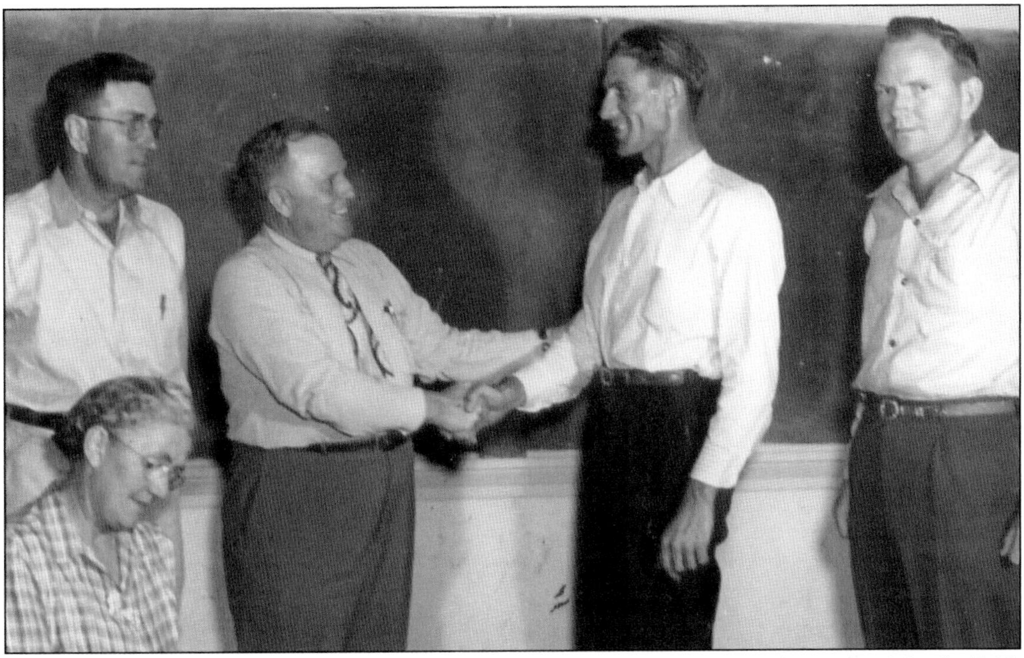

The Azle Methodist Church received a charter to form Boy Scout Troop No. 46 in March 1946. Joe W. Scott was the Scoutmaster and A.D. Bell and Byrne C. Moody were assistant Scoutmasters. This photograph was taken in 1948–1949, when the Scouts were reorganized. From left to right are Roger Hiett; Joe Driskell, from the Fort Worth Scout office; A.D. Bell; and Herbert Holmes. (Courtesy of Carolyn Bell Stevens.)

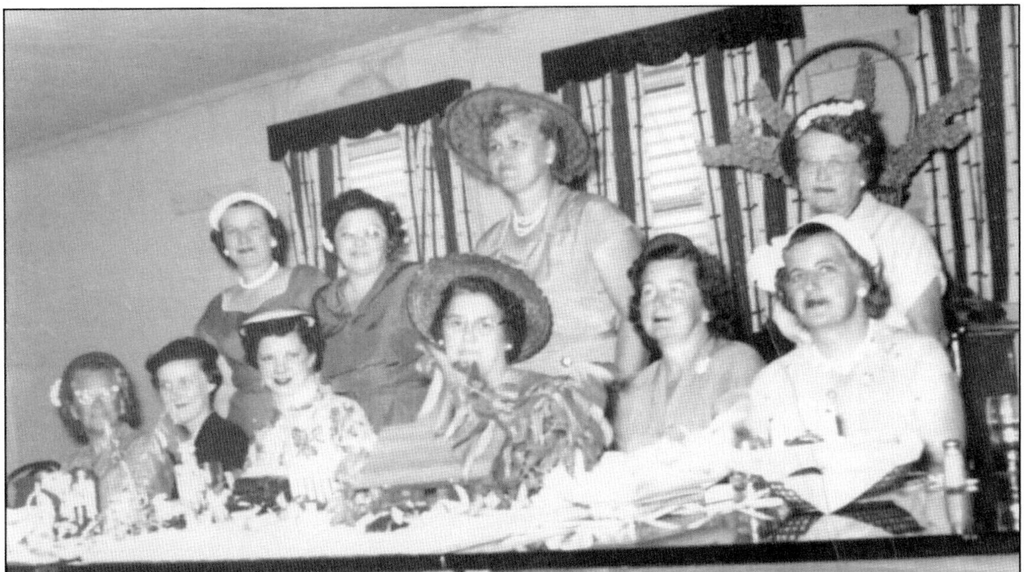

The Azle Garden Club was organized on June 9, 1947, with 46 charter members. Their first project was to erect a memorial at Ash Creek Cemetery in honor of Dr. James Azle Steward, Azle's namesake. The members seen in this 1954 photograph are, from left to right, (first row) Odessa Emanuel, Mary Stine, Jo Nichols, Byra Stribling, Mildred Wilson, and Lucille Young; (second row) Connie Pickens, Inez Powell, Helen Beard, and Blanche Scrimshire.

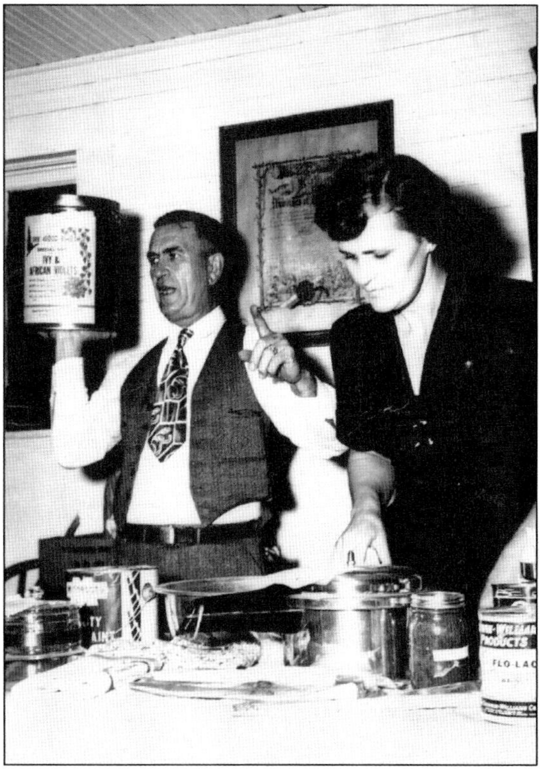

Lewie Berry auctions a can of special soil for Ivy and African Violets with the help of Helen Warn Beard at the Azle Civic League meeting in 1948. The auction was to raise money for Azle's first fire truck, volunteer fire department, and firehouse. The civic league organized in the 1930s to take an active part in the way the town was shaped.

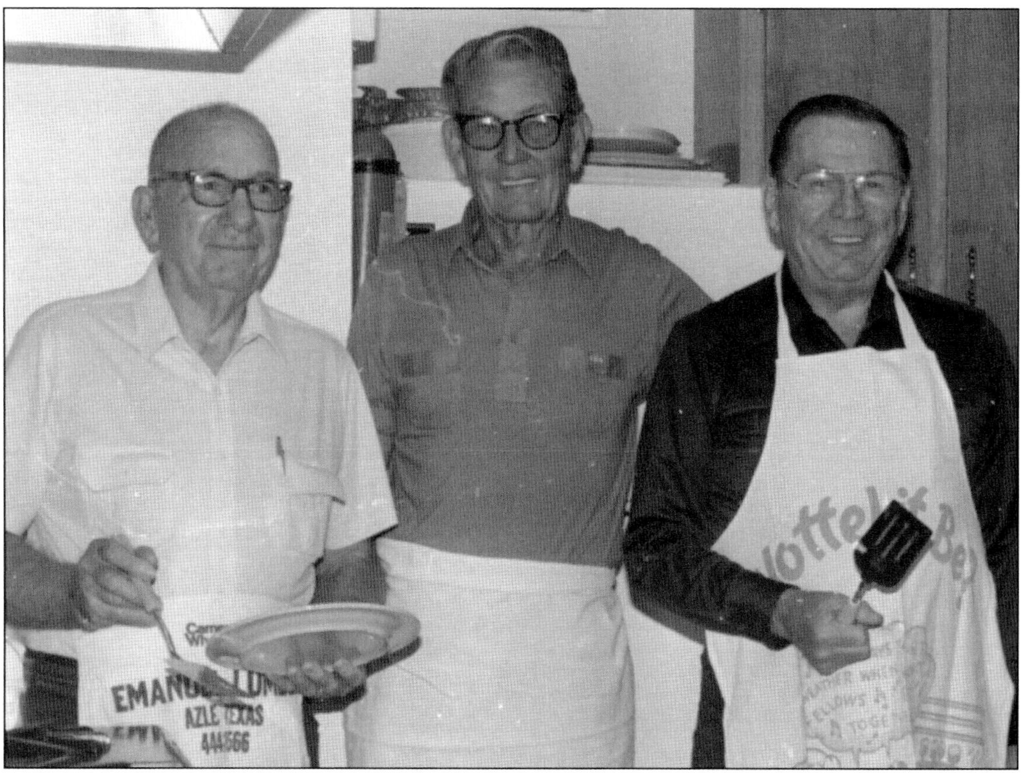


Ready to flip flapjacks for the Azle Lions Club pancake supper in 1990 are, from left to right, Johnny Ammons, Jim Bob Nation, and Ray Fisher. The proceeds went toward projects such as eye exams and glasses for needy children. The Lions Club received its charter in 1950 with 29 charter members.

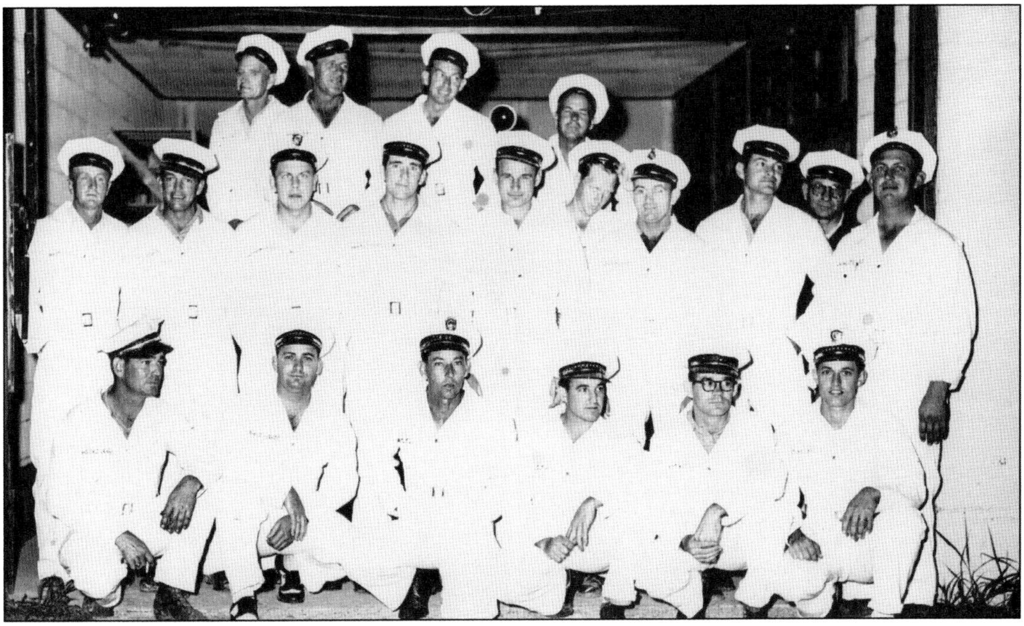

Members of Azle's first organized volunteer fire department in 1951 are, from left to right, (first row) Jake Collins, Waymon Martin, Jim Bob Nation, Ray Beeman, Jay Woody Stribling, and Elbert Lancaster; (second row) Edsel Newsom, Rudolph Looper, Kenneth Reynolds, Harry Cutshall, Tutor Winnett, Billy Bob Ingram, Byrne C. Moody, Allison Reed, Charlie Dunlap, and Alfred Reynolds; (third row) Carl Ingram, Curly Wallace, Ed Lewis, and Steve Anderson.

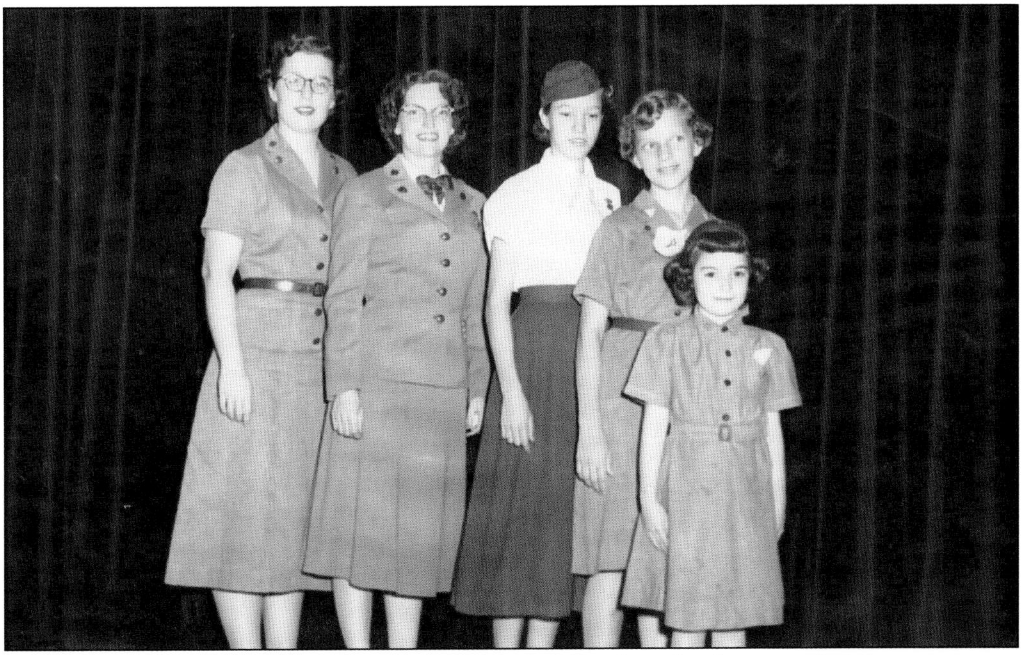

In the fall of 1952, a group of mothers in Azle decided that their daughters needed the experiences being a Girl Scout could offer. Three troops were registered with the Circle T Council in April 1953. Modeling the new Girl Scout uniforms in 1955 are, from left to right, Betty Rowland, Alice Geeslin, Barbara Trammell, Peggy Dalton, and Martha Sue Tucker.

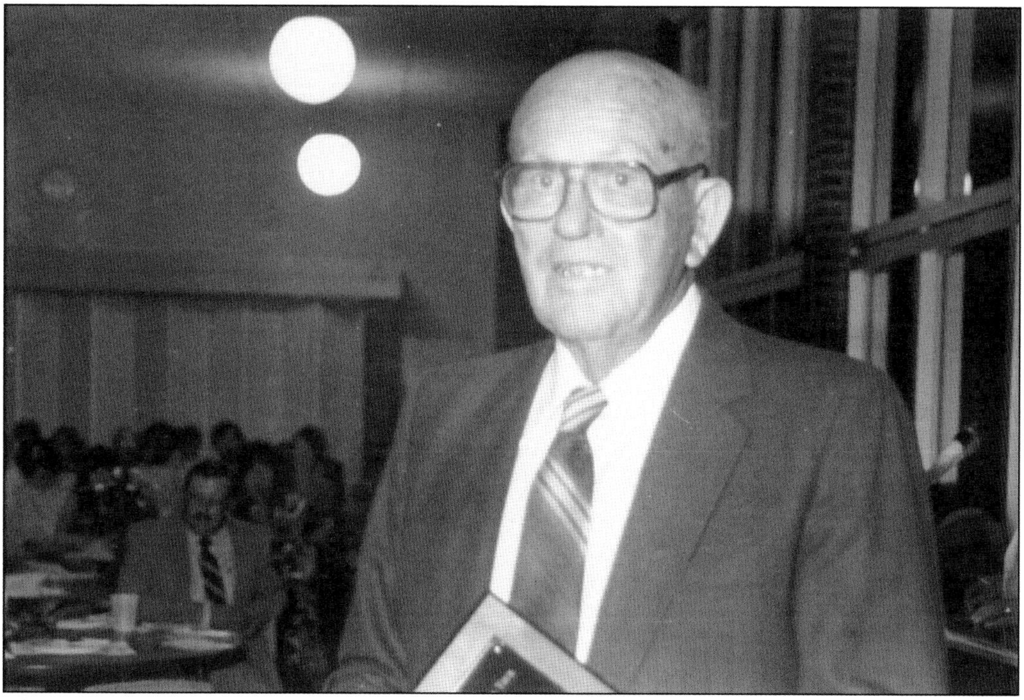

The organizational meeting of the Azle Chamber of Commerce was held in February 1959. It organized to encourage existing businesses, to assist new ones, and to promote the welfare of all area citizens. The photograph shows the chamber's first president, Ray Finney, who was also one of the first directors of Azle State Bank when it was organized in 1960.

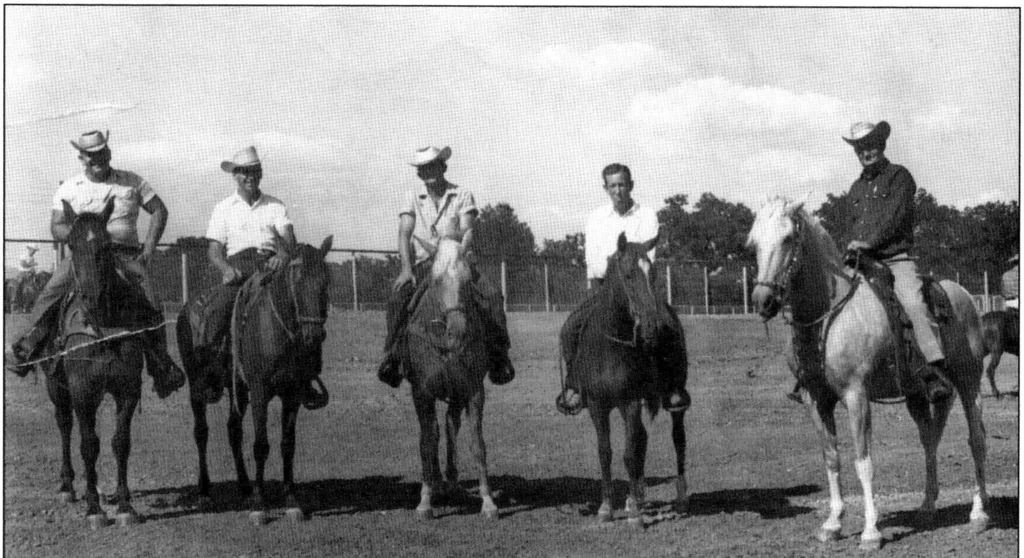

The Aztex Saddle Club was formed in 1962 to provide support for the local livestock activities of the Future Farmers of America. The club built a rodeo arena on Park Street and held annual junior rodeos. The club shared funds from its activities with groups such as orphanages, fire departments, service groups, and college scholarship funds. Seen from left to right are Lay Mullins, Butch Patterson, Thomas O'Rear, Charles Rowden, and Hack Markum.

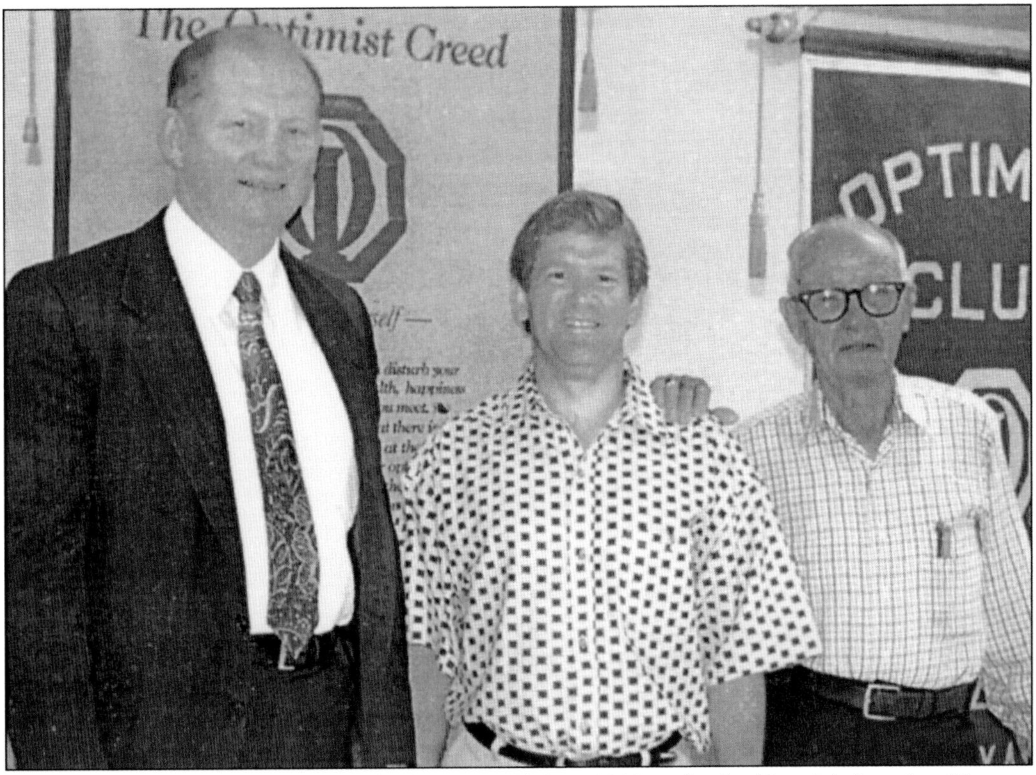


Jack Scott, the president of the Azle Optimist Club in 1997, is flanked by club founders Henson Dunn (left) and Guy Harrell. Harrell enlisted Dunn and King David Cox's help to form the club in 1979. It was not difficult to sell the 36 new members on the idea of a "Friend of Youth" and the belief in dedicating talents to serving the youth and the community.

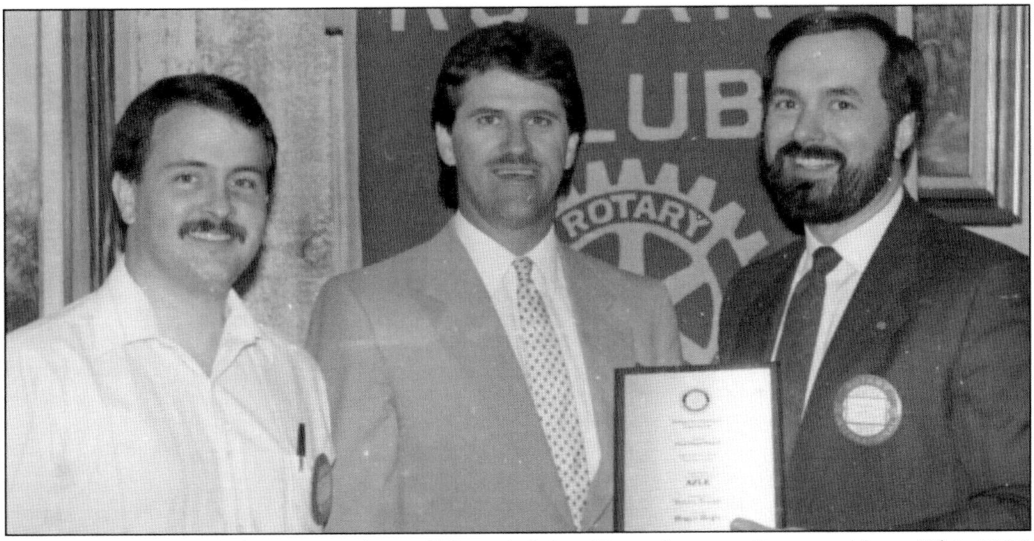


The Azle Rotary Club organized in 1979 with John Teutsch as its first president. This 1990 photograph shows members (from left to right) Bob Buckel, Hogye Hogle, and Gary Stone receiving one of the Rotary's many honors. The Rotary Club motto is "Service Above Self." The name of the club derived from the early practice of rotating meeting places among members' offices.

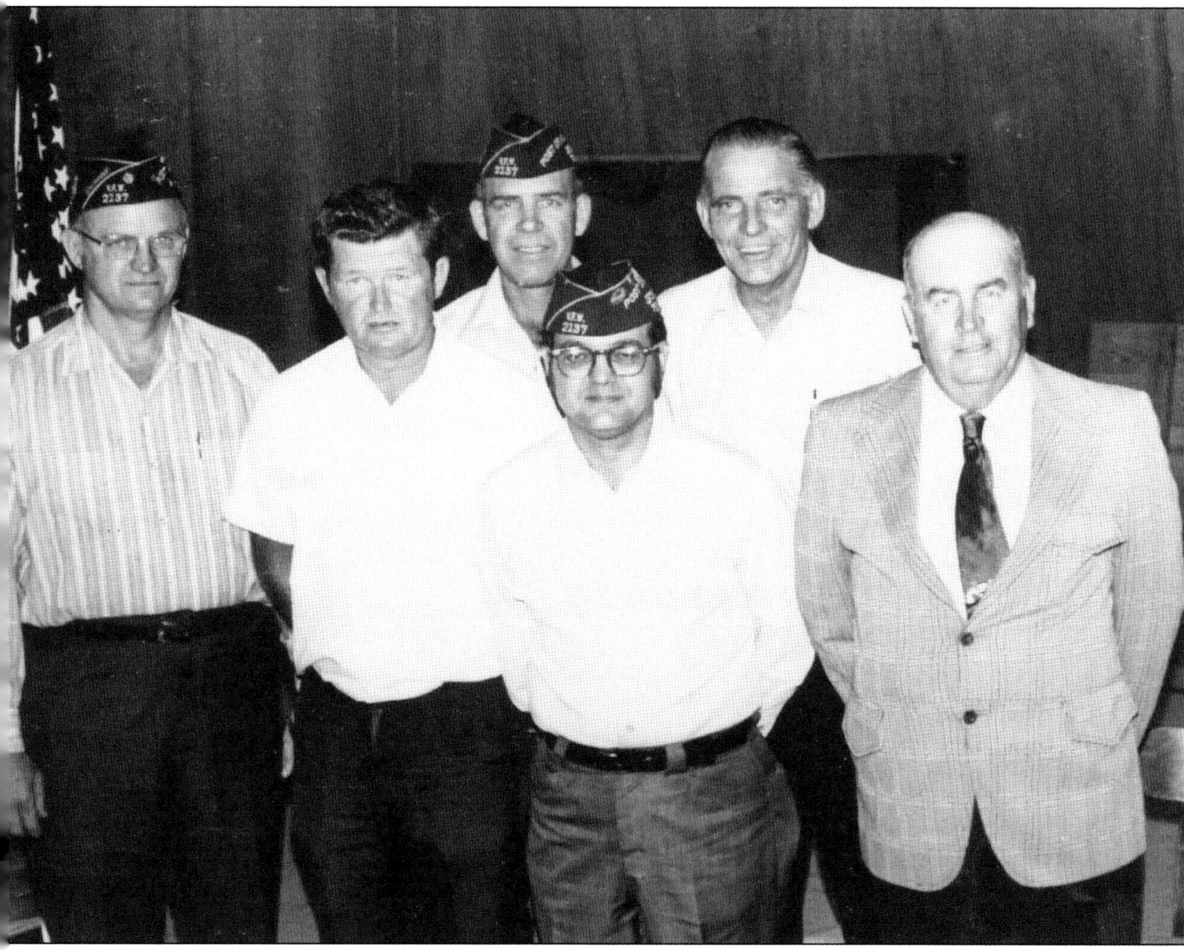

In 1972, Azle's Veterans of Foreign Wars Post 2137 included officers, from left to right, (first row) Bill Zeigler, quartermaster; Dennis Elam Jr., vice commander; Charles Chick, post commander; and Ford Hearell, chaplain; (second row) Charles Lindsey, senior vice commander; and Elmer Brown, judge advocate. The VFW hall is located at 11875 FM 730 North.

# *Six*

# People and Events

Memories are made through the people and events in everyday life, and Azle has had its share. Azle boosters came with the first wagonload of people. Land was bought by early settlers and then given away to provide the community with churches, schools, cemeteries, and places to live.

Citizens were concerned not only about their own families but also about everyone else's. The building of community facilities and programs for the young and old was done by individuals who saw the needs of a growing town and worked together with others to make them happen. Early settlers in the Fowler, Steward, Reynolds, and McDonald families set the standard for the leaders today.

Some early events in Azle were the programs presented by the literacy society in 1891 at Azle College and its grand picnic with entertainment in 1892. The picnic was rained out, but the society presented music, skits, tableaus, and a speech by Sen. J.J. Jarvis, who once owned land in Azle and was one of its biggest benefactors. Old-timers told of the Fourth of July picnics in the early 1900s with free barbecue and homemade ice cream—the first ice cream eaten by area children.

There were also Old Confederate Reunions, Children's Day at Ash Creek Baptist Church, and fish fries at the Jefferson Crossing on the west fork of the Trinity River. Often, there was a lemonade stand and Arthur Jackson would call, "Come and get it, ice cold lemonade, made in the shade, stirred with a spade." Azle's first community fair was held in October 1935, with Will Younger as the general manager. A parade down Main Street kicked off the celebration. Corbet Jackson had an exhibit that contained 54 different farm products, ranging from sweet potato candy to butter. The current fall fair is called the "Sting Fling."

Azle would not be the city it is today without the special events put on by clubs and organizations and the people who have worked so hard to make a difference. Look around; they are everywhere.

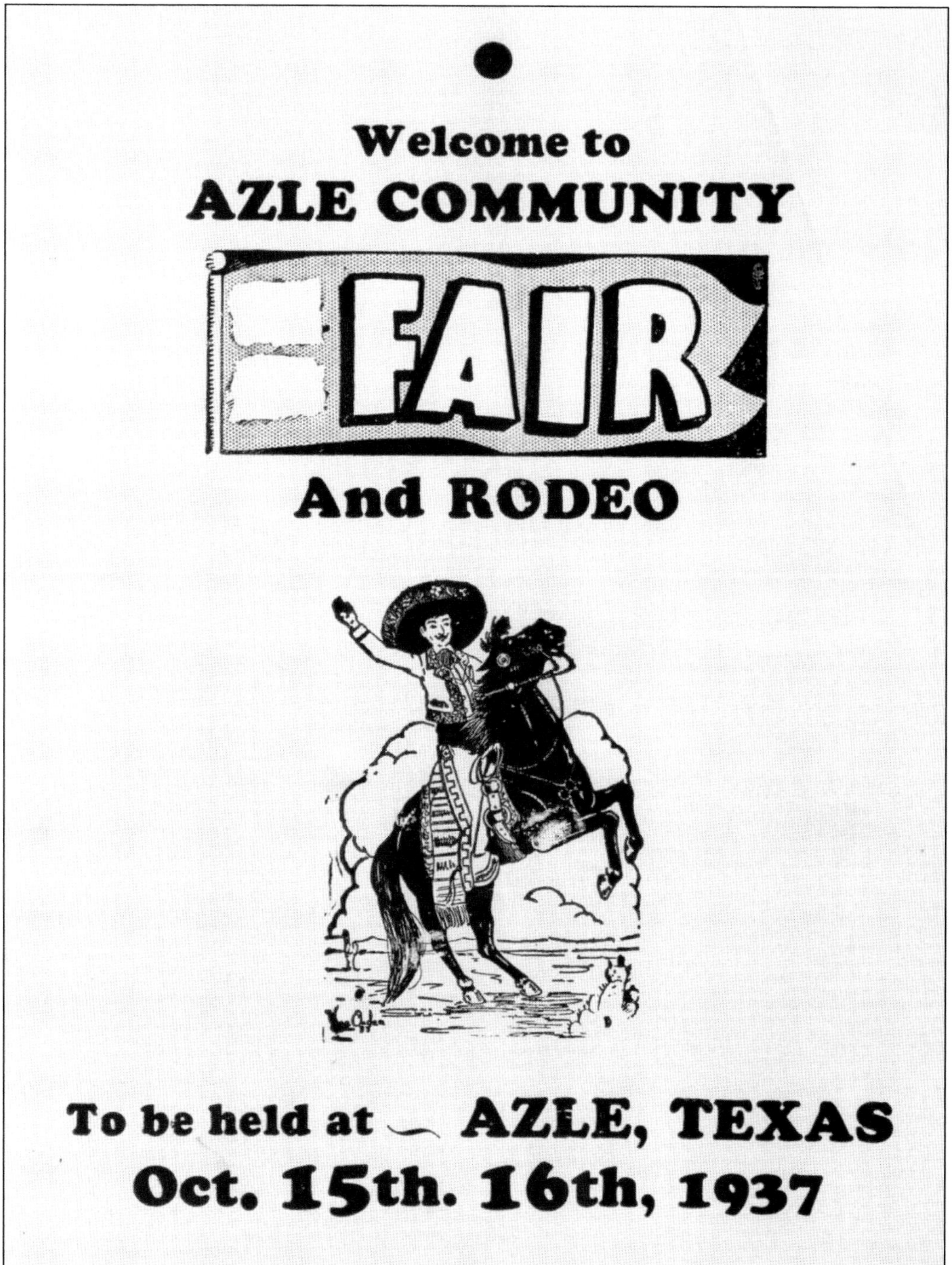


The 1937 Azle community fair was held under the direction of Roger Hiett, Faris Ross, H.L. Barber, and Blanche Scrimshire. It featured dirigible rides over Eagle Mountain Lake, parachute jumps, circus and Vaudeville acts, a parade, a horse show, horseshoe-throwing contests, a Texas Christian University Band concert, and judging of homemade items and livestock. The fair program is still in good shape 75 years later.

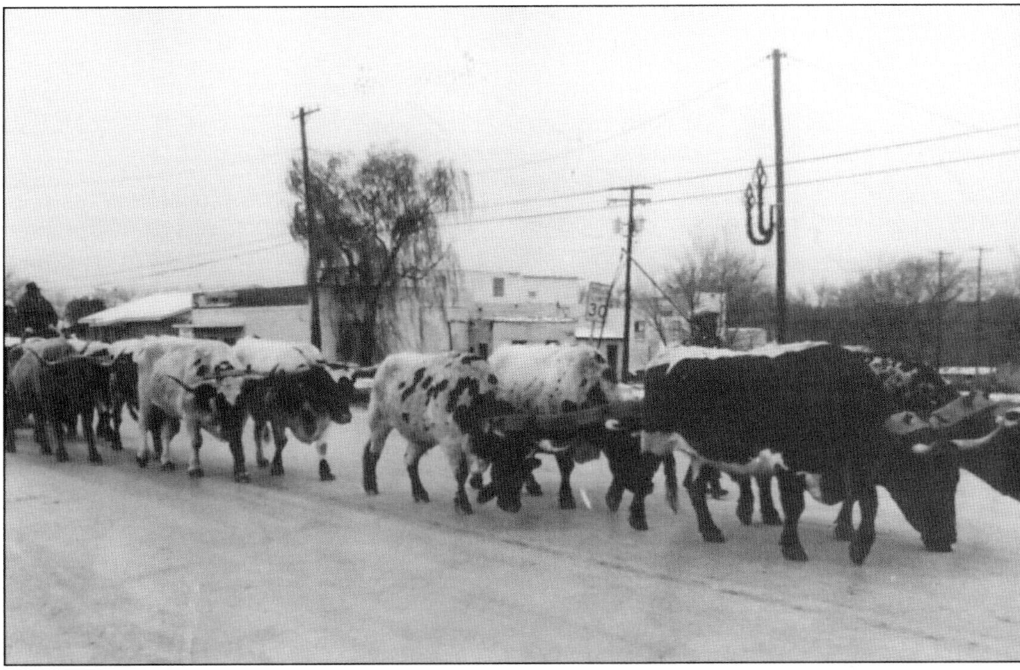

Typically Texan, these yoked longhorn steers were the highlight of Azle's annual Christmas parade in the 1980s. To the left in the photograph are two Azle buildings, the Masonic Lodge and the former Azle Food Locker on Main Street.

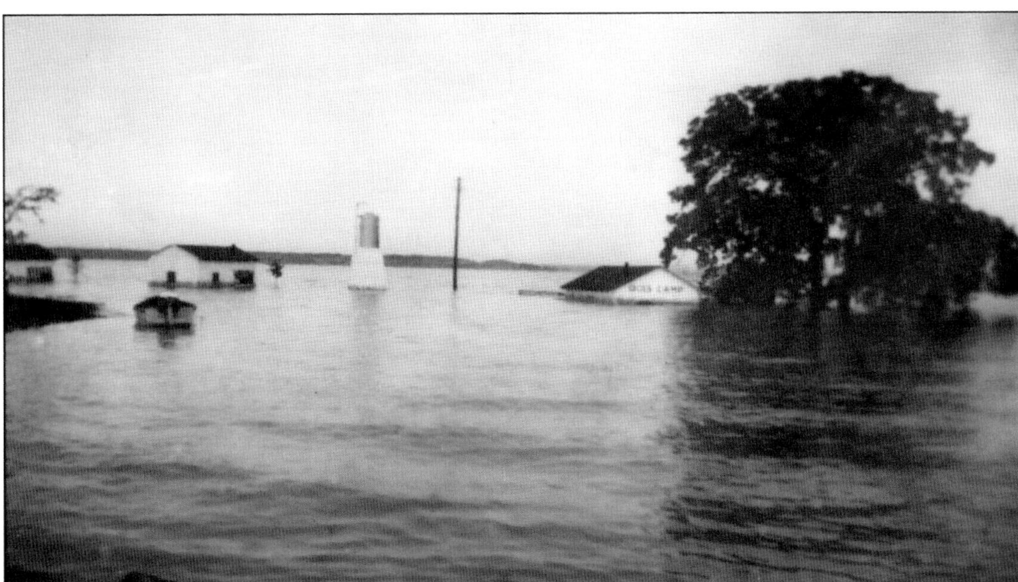

The year 1949 is remembered by old-timers as the year that Eagle Mountain Lake flooded. Torrential rains raised the level of the lake over the tops of houses. The flood is considered to be the worst in Parker and Tarrant County history. After heavy rain fell, levees broke upstream at the clear fork and west fork of the Trinity River in Fort Worth.

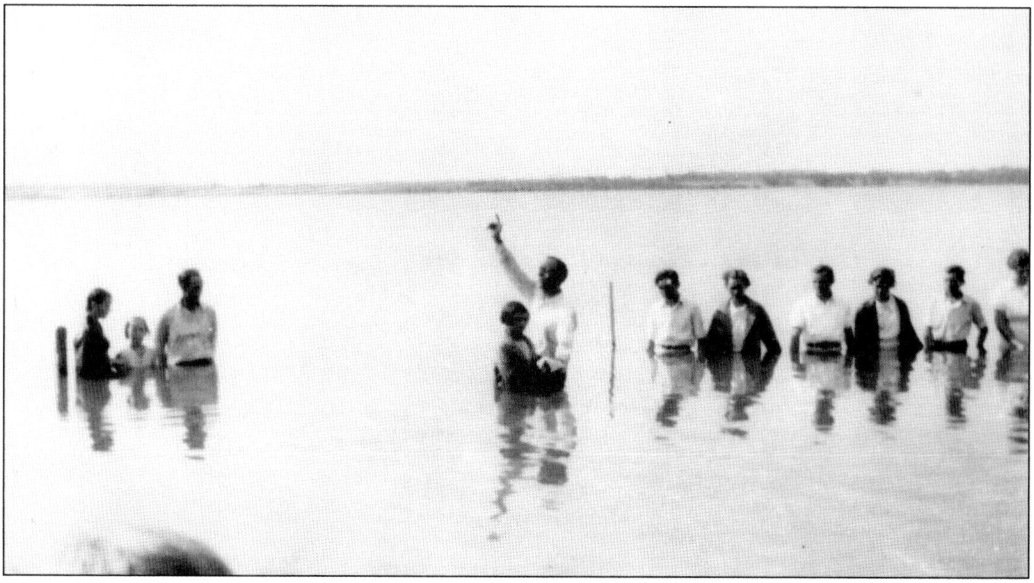

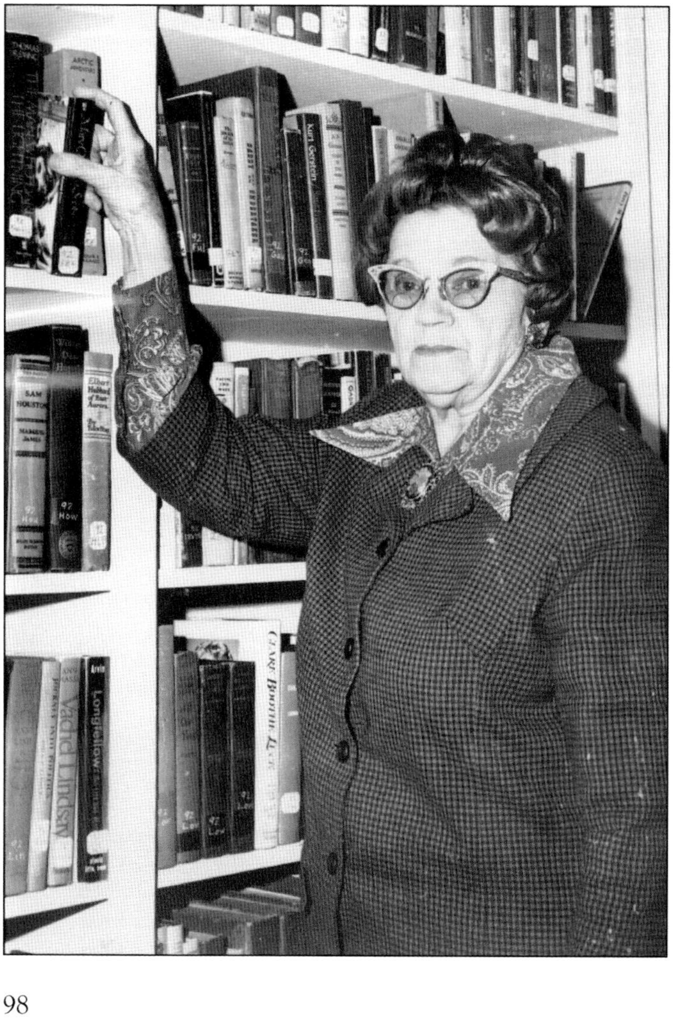

Baptismal ceremonies were a common scene on area creeks and lakes in the early 1900s. This photograph shows Laura Ledbetter Williams Aday being baptized on August 30, 1936, in Walnut Creek near the old Walnut Creek Bridge. Rev. Floyd Chaffin, the pastor at Ash Creek Baptist Church, is officiating. (Courtesy of Risa Williams Ellison, Lisa Williams, and Allan Williams.)

Eula Culberhouse Nation retired from her teaching career in Azle in 1962 to become Azle's first librarian. At the time, the only library service in Azle was a bookmobile from Fort Worth. Nation invited friends to a meeting to discuss the possibility of a public library, which was opened in April 1964 in a small rented room on Main Street and later moved to 124 West Main Street, the present location of the Azle Historical Museum.

Longtime Azle resident and Azle Historical Museum board member Marie Ethridge Welch was the first female street patrol officer in Tarrant and Parker County. She started in law enforcement in 1969 as a clerk in the Azle Police Department. She was assigned to the street in the early 1970s. Welch passed away on July 9, 2010, but left her imprint on the museum and its members.

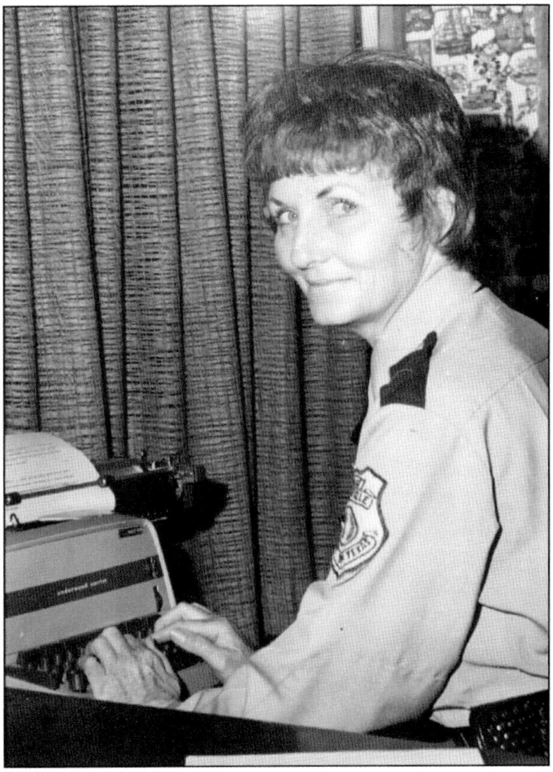

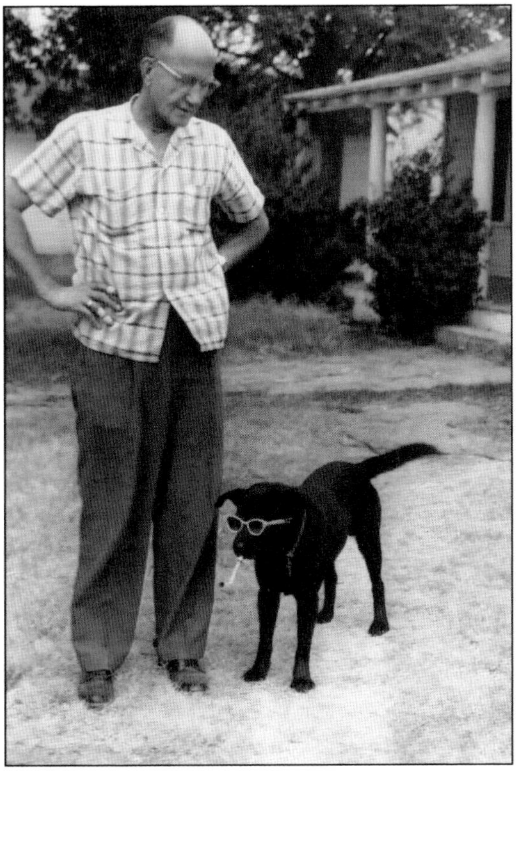

Eral Yates and his dog, Blackie, were always seen together around Azle and were captured in this 1960 photograph. When the sun was bright, Blackie preferred to go about town with his sunglasses on. He also enjoyed his corncob pipe and often wore a sign publicizing an upcoming event. Yates's father, J.N. ("Tompy") Yates, was born in Reno, Texas, in 1866, and the family has lived in the area ever since.

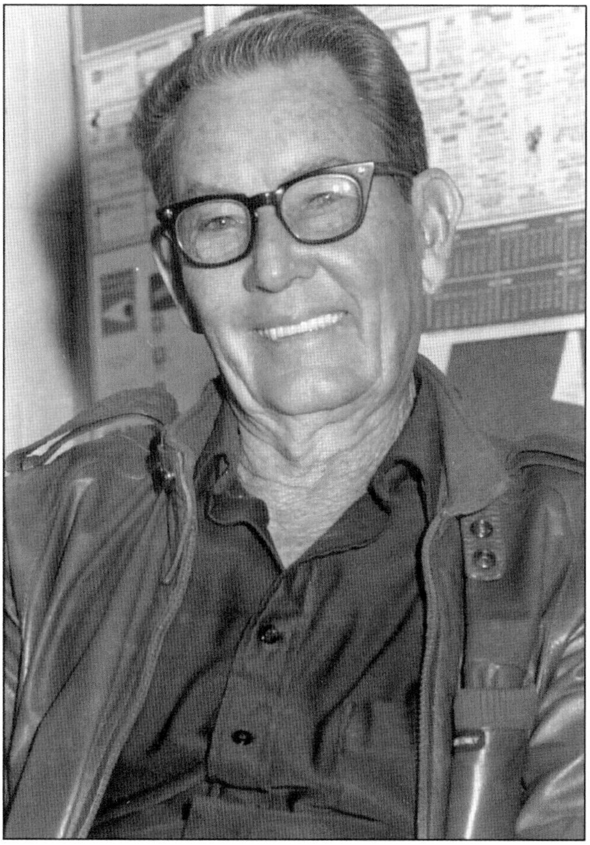

One of Azle's most beloved citizens was Jim Bob Nation. He will always be remembered as a driving force in molding young men's lives. Nation was a charter member of the volunteer fire department, the Azle Lions Club, and the Azle Chamber of Commerce. He worked with the Boy Scouts and peewee football and was a founder of Azle Little League baseball. He also announced the junior and high school football games for more than 40 years.

The Azle Lions Club held annual "Donkey Basketball" games for many years in the 1950s in the old wooden gymnasium at Azle Elementary School, better known as the Rock School. Here, Frank Lineham tries to guide his donkey to the basket. The audience had as much fun as the participants and certainly more fun than the donkeys.

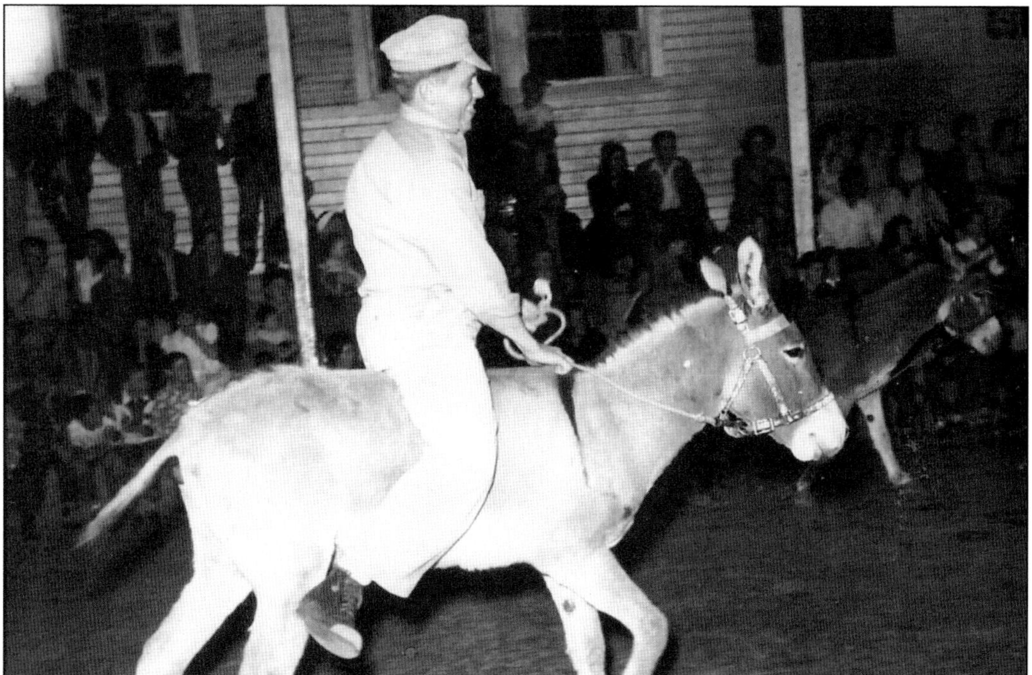

Paul Worthen, seen here in 1969, opened C and W Electronics with Frank Couch at 117 West Main Street in 1963. Paul bought out his partner in 1967. Kathryn Worthen ran the business while her husband served as city manager from 1979 to 1982. Paul was also on the city council for eight years. The Worthens were in business until Paul's death in 2008.

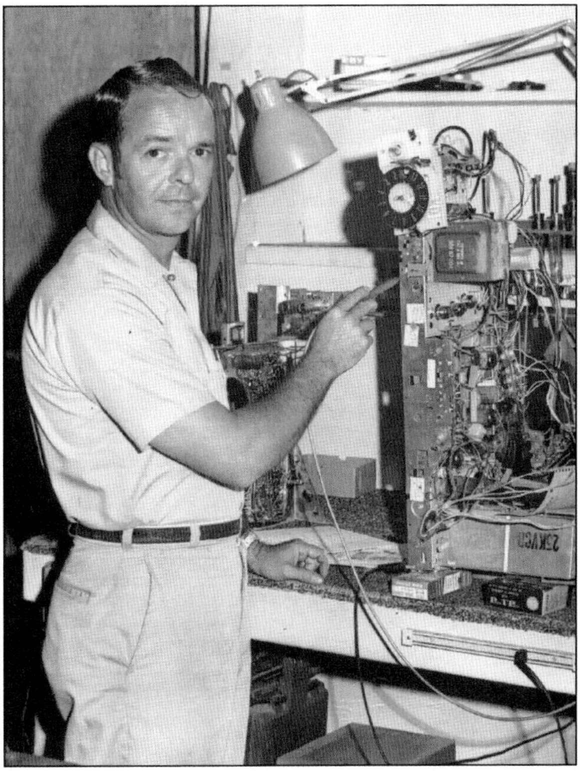

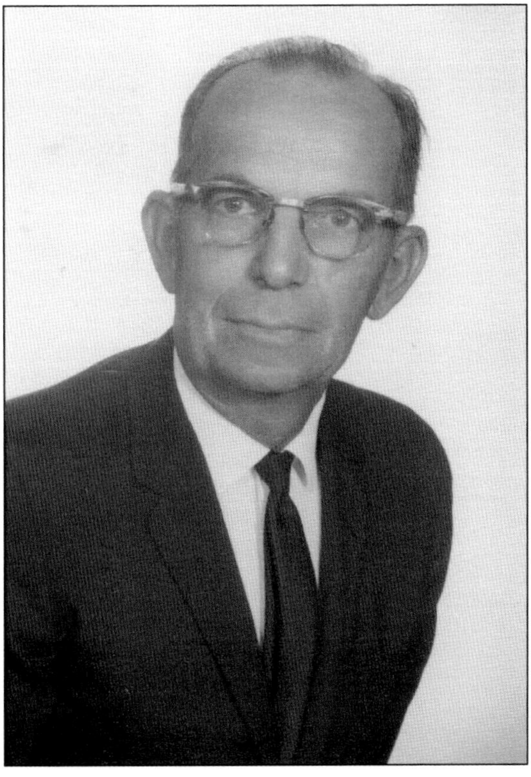

Jim Dalton, the founder of Rural Gas Supply, was one of the charter directors of the Azle State Bank, working very effectively in its organization in 1960. He was an Azle school board member for 15 years and was chosen as "Man of the Year" in 1967 by the Azle Chamber of Commerce. He was a member of Azle Masonic Lodge 601 and passed away in 1988.

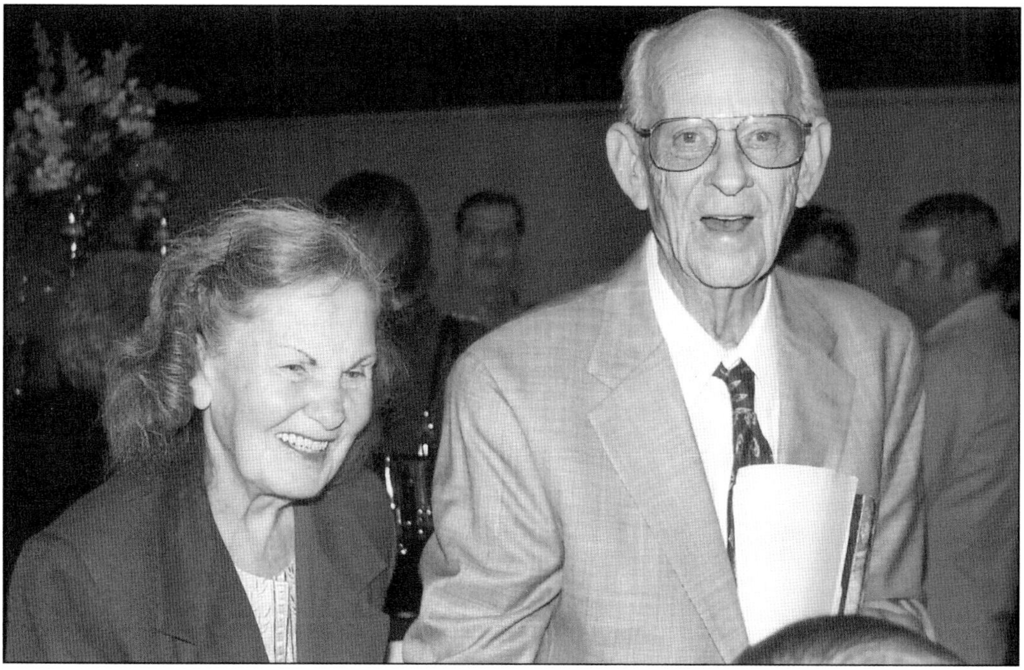

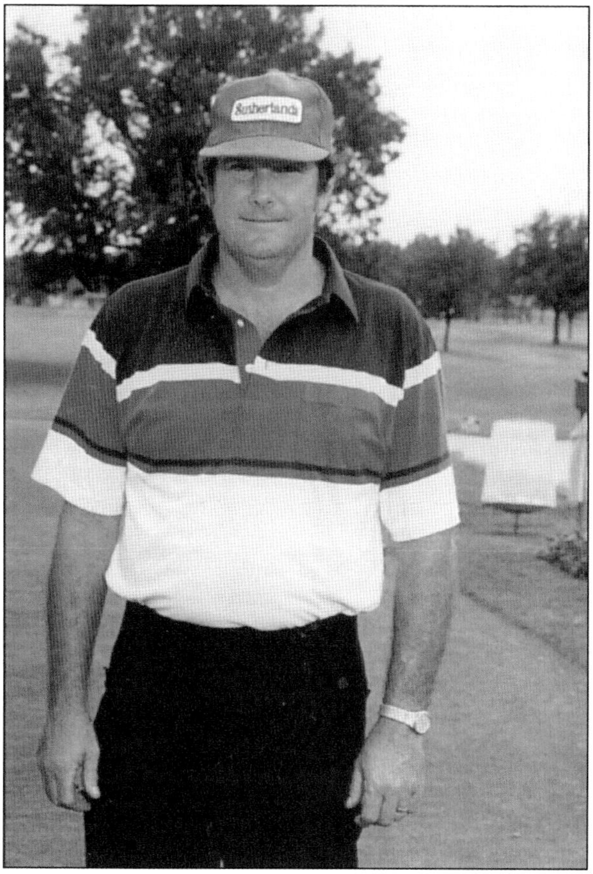

B.J. and Betty Clark came to Azle in 1952. They are the owners of Clark's Precision Machine and Tool and B.J. was on the city council for four years. The B.J. Clark Community Center was named for him in recognition of his efforts in raising money to build it. Clark was the first president of the Azle Historical Museum, serving 16 years. (Courtesy of the *Azle News*.)

Robert Landers is an Azle cattle farmer and golfer who gained fame by playing on the Senior PGA Tour. Landers took up golf at age 22 when his uncle Foster Stevens taught him the basics. He preferred playing in sneakers and using the golf clubs he assembled himself. He played on the PGA Tour in 1995 and 1996. Today, Landers still raises cattle on his farm in Azle.

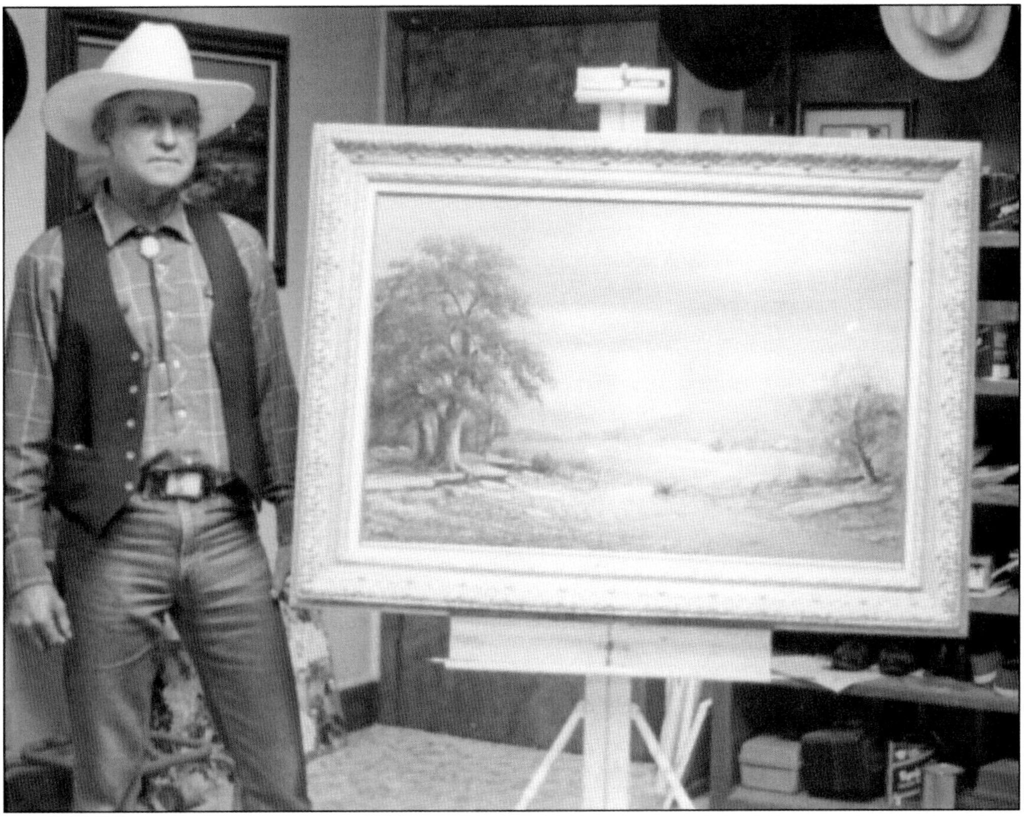

Local and nationally known artist Jack Bryant is known for his Western oil paintings and bronze sculptures. A life-size bronze of his famous bucking horse, Midnight, stands in front of the Amon G. Carter Jr. Exhibit Building in Fort Worth. Bryant's work was featured at Trammell's Flying T Gallery in Azle.

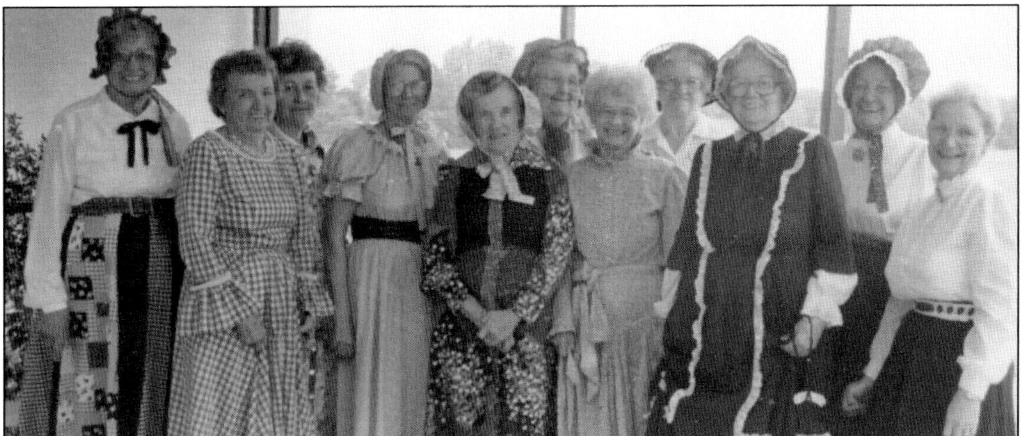

Members of the Azle Senior Citizen Center celebrated the 1890s by dressing in costume in 1990. Seen here are, from left to right, Della Rogers, Ruth Martin, Nita Miller, Pansy Lavender, Madge Sapp, Polly Moore, Pauline Cowan, Emagene Cooper, Maudie Womack, Binnie Williams, and Darlene Jones. The seniors have been meeting at the B.J. Clark Community Center since 1985.

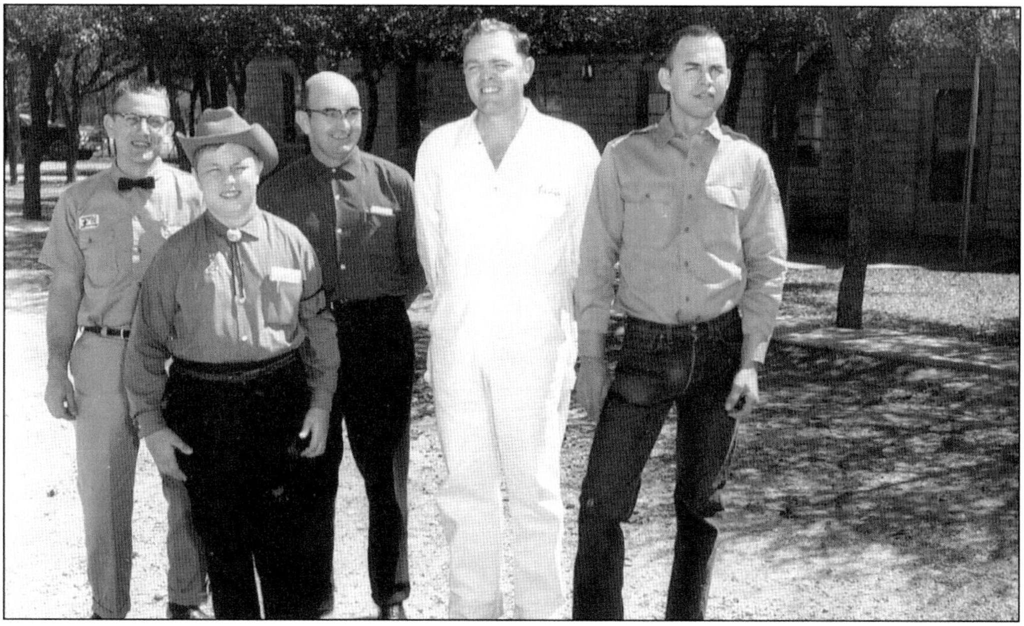

Sunday, March 15, 1968, was the day the first polio injections were given at the Medical and Surgical Clinic in Azle. Because a large crowd waited in long lines, the volunteer fire department worked traffic control. Seen here are, from left to right, Charles Covington, Jimmy Rhodes, Byrne C. Moody, Eddie Morrow, and Don Eastwood.

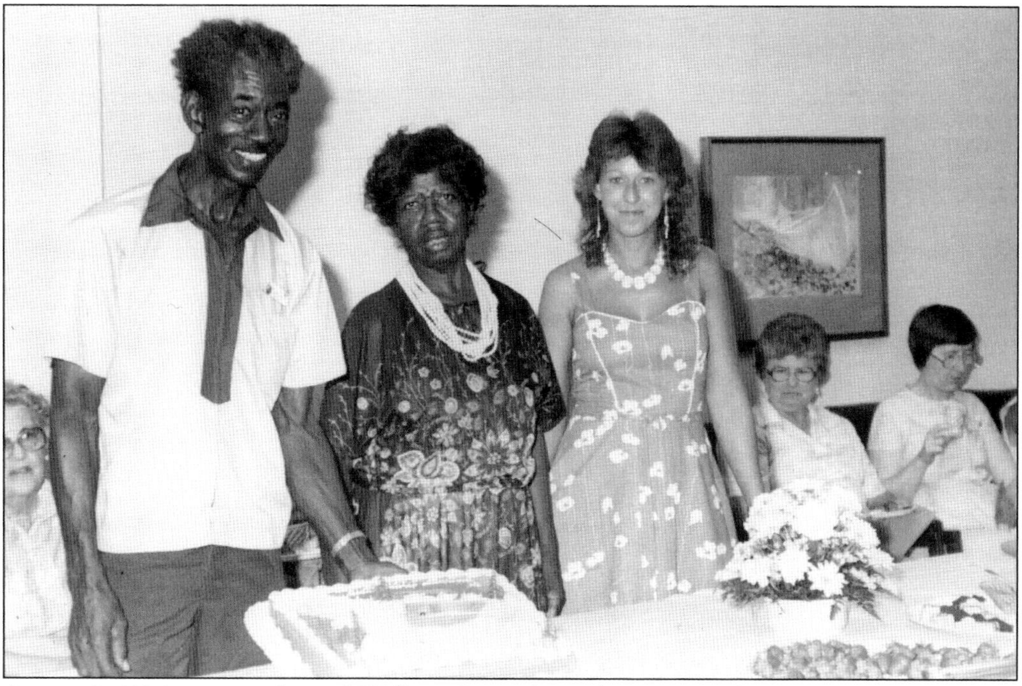

August 1, 1986, was proclaimed William Samuel Smith Day in Azle to remember him as an integral part of the growth of Harris Hospital. Smith retired from the hospital after 30 years of service and is seen with his wife, Eunice (center), and his supervisor, Robin Warrick. Smith's father, Henry Smith Sr., came to Azle with the first settlers in the 1860s.

Jim Dalton, a homebuilder in Azle in the 1950s and the owner of Rural Gas Supply, shows a piece of the landing gear of an airplane that fell through his roof in 1954. The piece was from a B-36 that was manufactured at Convair (now Lockheed Martin) and flown by an Air Force pilot stationed at Carswell. Dalton's wife, Maurine, thought the world was coming to an end when it hit the roof.

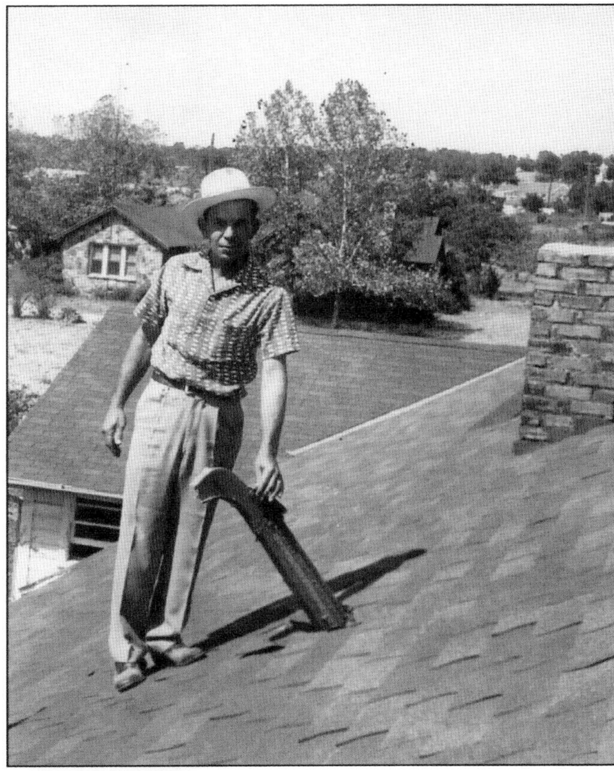

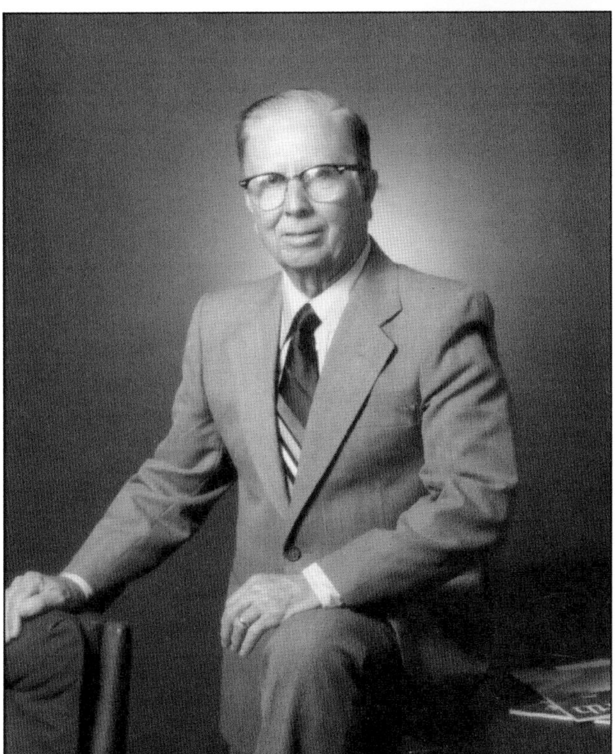

Azle's first dentist was Dr. R.A. Ivie. His first office was in the back of the Azle Funeral Home. He later built a dental office on Highway 199 by Lester's Pharmacy. Dr. Ivie practiced in Mineral Wells for 16 years before moving to Azle in 1956 with his wife, Irene, and their children, Yvonne and Lonnie.

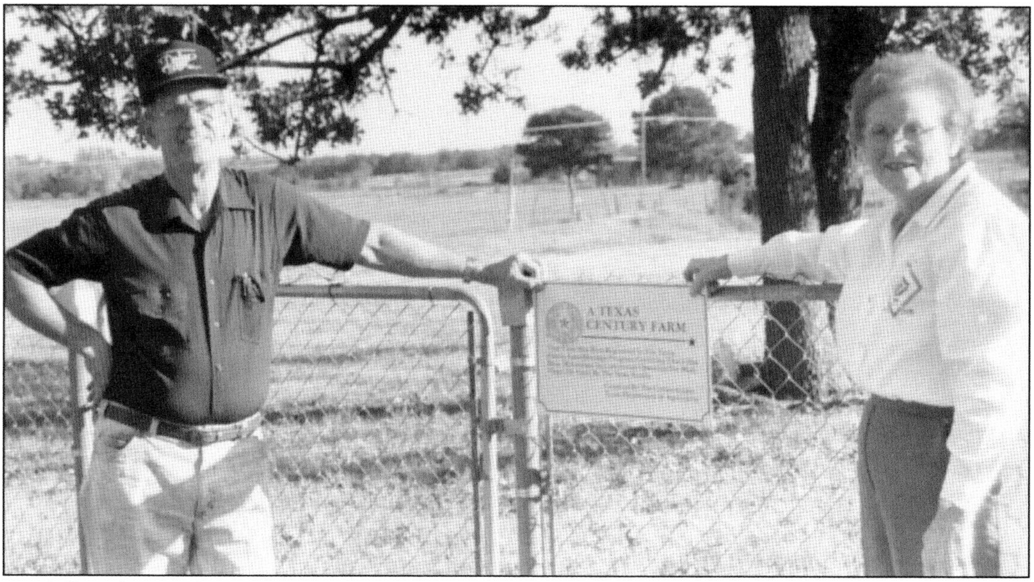


Lindell and Dorothy Harris pose beside the gate marker in 1990 that commemorates their farm as part of the Texas Department of Agriculture's Family Land Heritage. It was designated a Texas Century Farm. The 48-acre farm in Reno was founded in 1889 by Harris's grandmother Margaret Copeland Harris after the death of her husband, Buck. Harris lived on the farm from 1934 until his death in 2008.

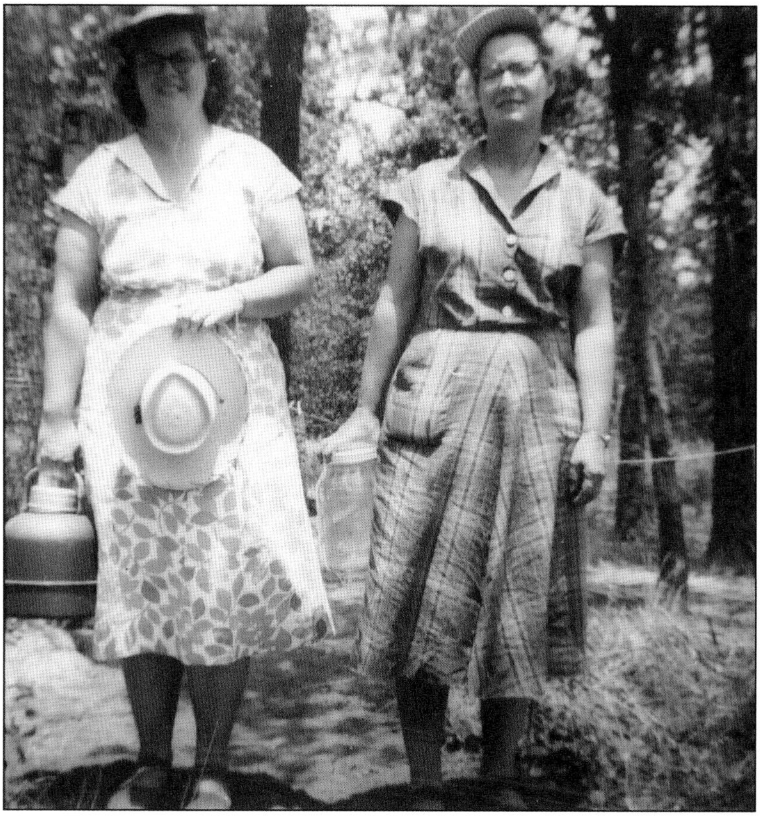

The Girl Scouts held their summer day camp on land owned by Gertie Ansley, one of the first leaders in 1953. The Scouts called it Ansley Farm, and it was located on FM 730 South. The scouts held camp there from 1954, before the highway was built, until mid-1960. Seen here in 1954 are two of the leaders, Geraldine Lane (left) and Mamie Beaver. (Courtesy of Rex Ansley Ballauer.)

James R. and Odessa Long Emanuel settled in Azle in 1949 and founded Emanuel Lumber Company. In 1970, they branched out into apartment construction and added Azleland Perpetual Care Cemetery. The Emanuels were involved in community activities, jointly holding membership in 13 clubs, lodges, and church groups. In semi-retirement, they turned the business over to their daughters and traveled extensively. (Courtesy of Betty Emanuel Haas.)

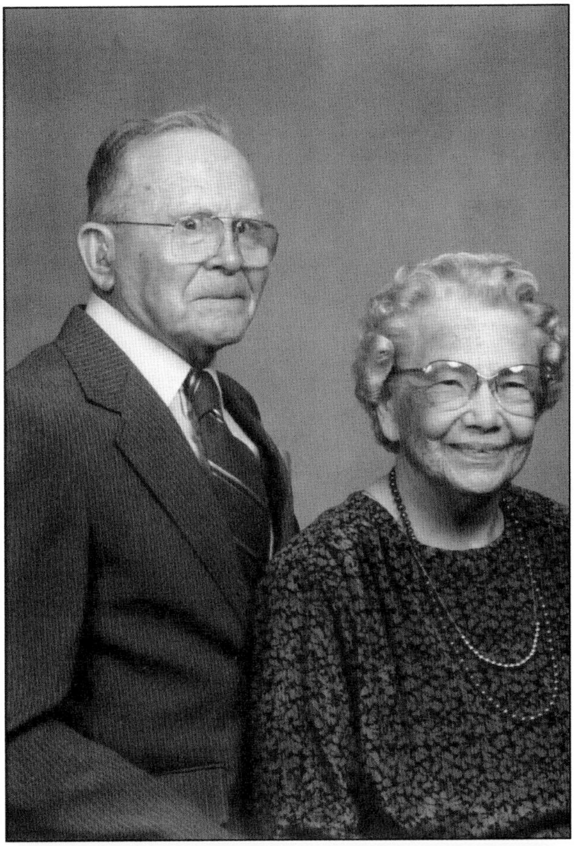

Dr. James Savage began his practice in 1955 after he and his wife, Mary Hames Savage, moved to Azle. He bought the Azle Clinic and Hospital around 1961. Dr. Savage was president of the Azle ISD board of trustees for 14 of the 15 years that he served. Mary worked diligently for the Hospital Ladies Auxiliary. (Courtesy of Brian Savage.)

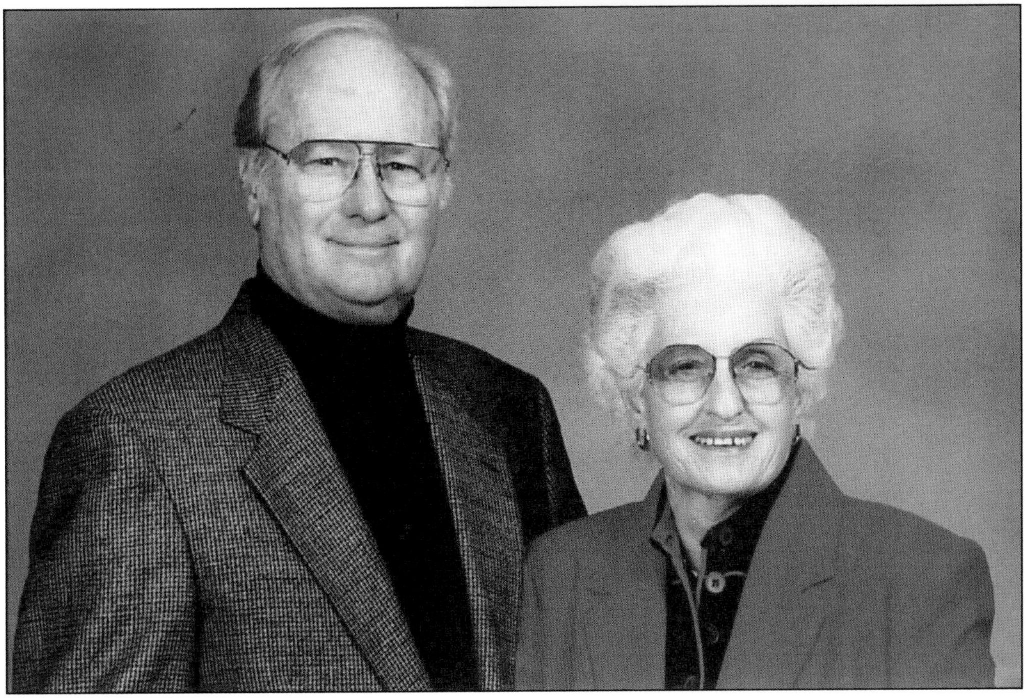

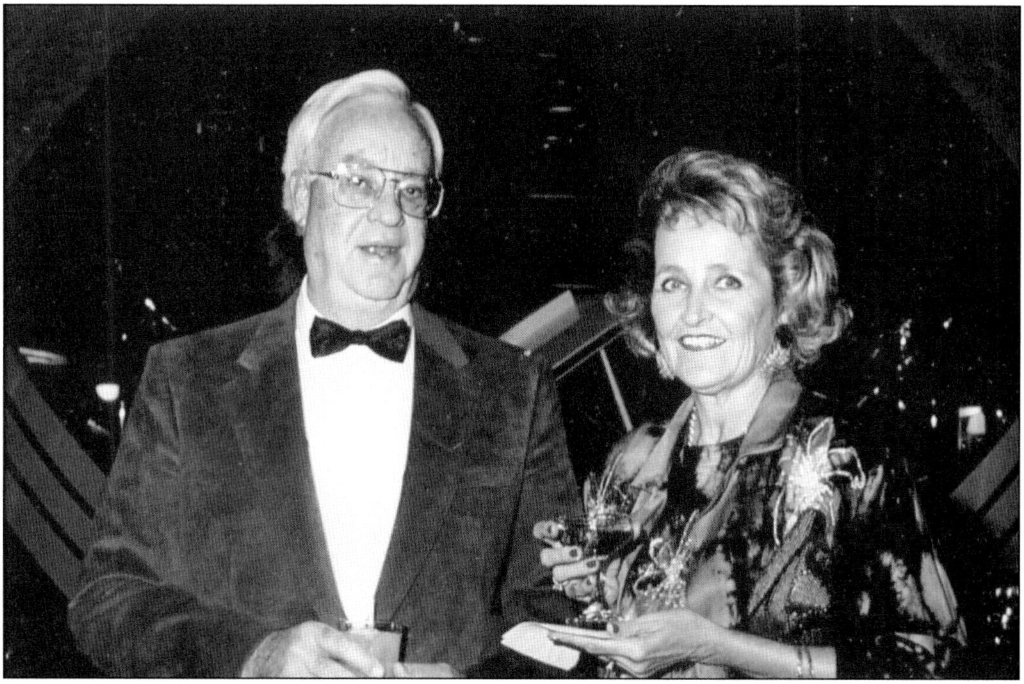

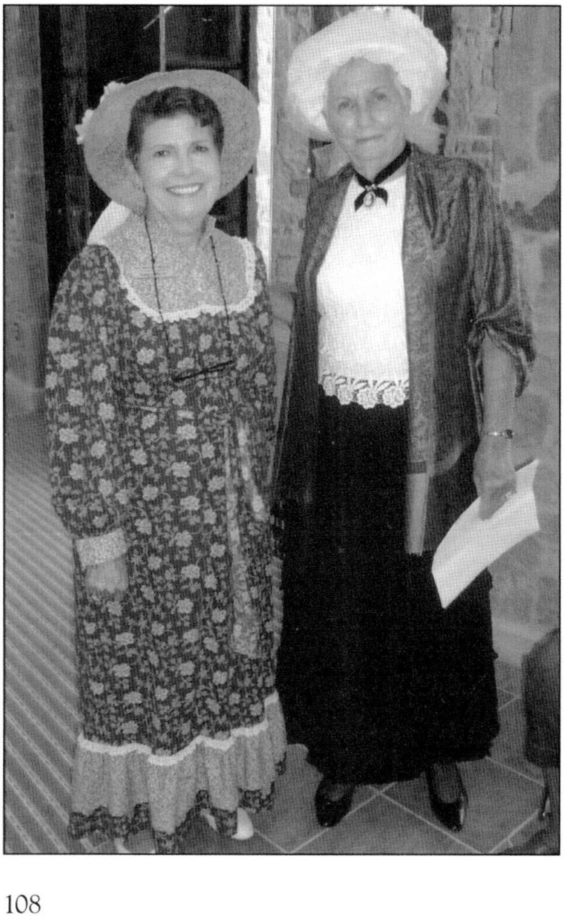

Dr. Jack Mobley and his wife, Carolyn, moved to Azle in 1960. He went into partnership with Dr. James Savage, first at 169 West Main Street and later at 108 Denver Trail. Dr. Mobley served on the Azle City Council for two years. Carolyn gave her time to special projects and organizations aimed at raising funds for Harris Methodist Hospital of Azle. (Courtesy of Jack Mobley.)

The Azle Historical Museum board members presented the history of Azle at the Grand Opening of the Azle Memorial Library on June 26, 27, and 28, 2009. The nine members dressed in costume for the three-day event. Nancy Reynolds Davis (left) and Marie Welch take a break between performances.

# *Seven*

# Government Services

One of the earliest government services in the Azle area was the post office. It originated as just a window in a general store. A postman delivered the mail in rural areas even while city dwellers still picked up mail at one place in town.

City government, with its mayors and city council members, provided numerous local services, as it still does today. An Azle Civic League unofficially began a volunteer fire department to protect citizens before city government could hire full-time firemen to do so. It was chartered officially on June 28, 1951. Even today, a few volunteers work alongside the full-time firemen as they do their work. Police, garbage collection, and other services were added as the city began to grow.

The present Azle Historical Museum building served as Azle's library until 1976, when the library moved to a white stucco building on Southeast Parkway, where it stayed for more than three decades. The new Azle Memorial Library opened in 2009 at 333 West Main Street, with the Central Park walking trail immediately south of it. Assistance to people in need in the city is provided by the Community Caring Center, at 317 Commerce Avenue, although it is partially privately funded.

Parks in Azle provide open air, free picnic tables, swimming, jogging, and other entertainment facilities. Shady Grove Park provides access to the north shore of Eagle Mountain Lake for picnicking and swimming, and it has a pavilion for family get-togethers. The 28-acre Central Park, at 263 West Main Street, is Azle's newest park, holding its grand opening on July 14, 2008. Along the banks of Ash Creek, it provides a walking path for exercise as well as an open-air amphitheater for music, a gazebo, and play areas for children.

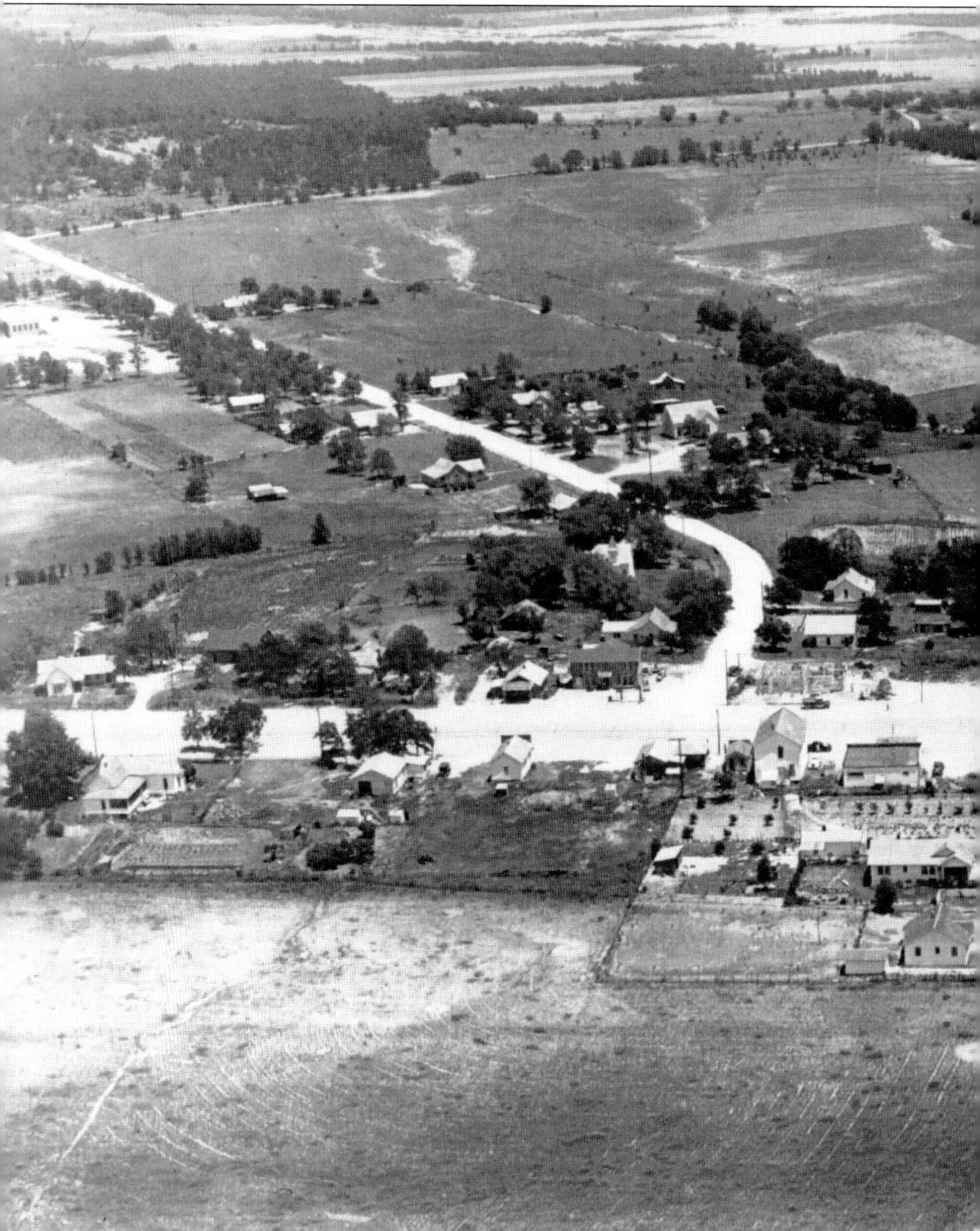

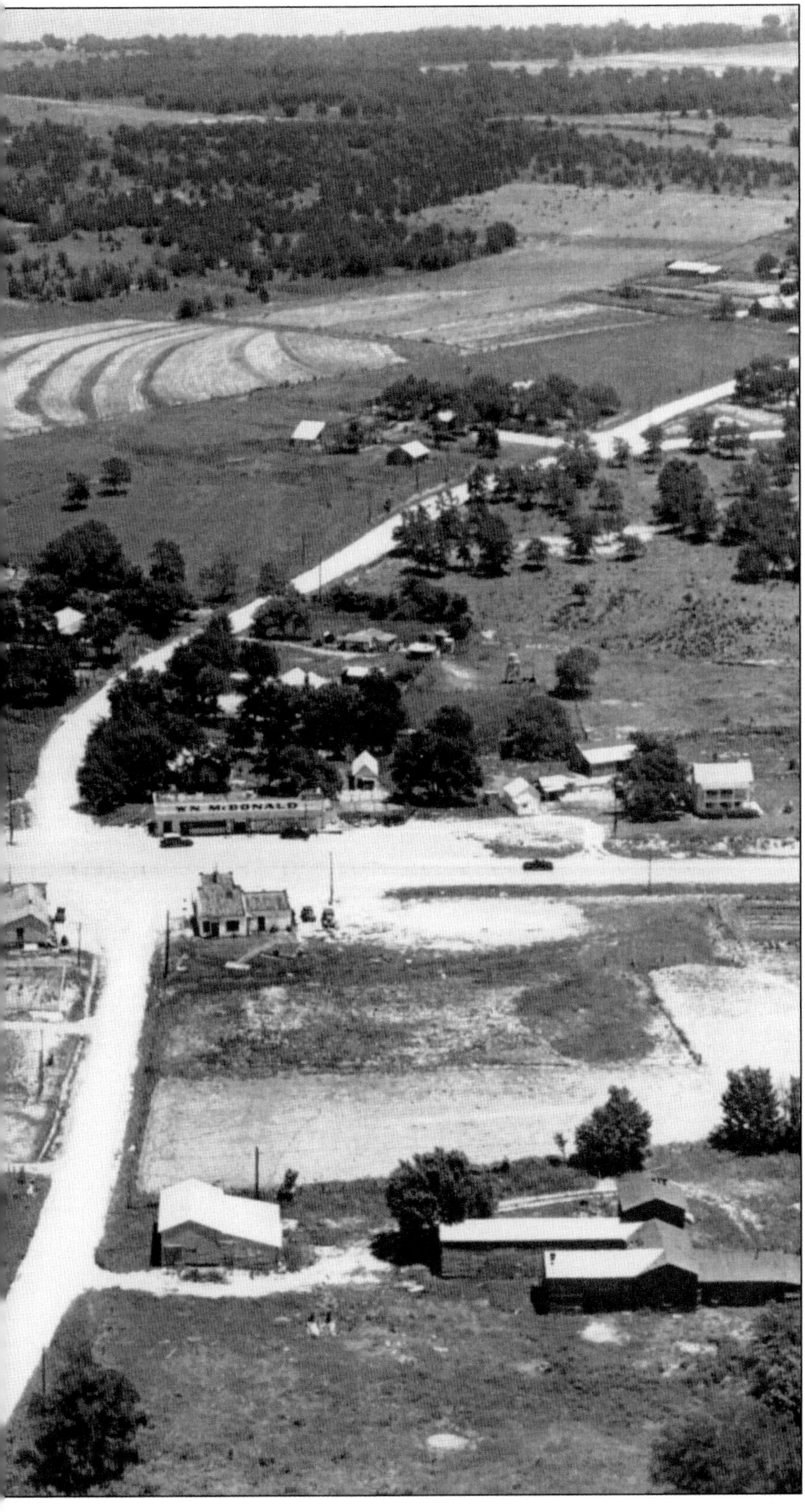


This aerial view of Azle was taken by a *Fort Worth Star-Telegram* staff photographer from a Ritchey Flying Service airplane on May 28, 1938. The street bisecting the photograph from left to right is Main Street. Crossing Main on the right and curving quickly to the right is Stewart Street. Leaving Main and curving left is the old Boyd Highway. Today, the section of it connecting to Main is Church Street, and the Azle Historical Museum stands at the northwest corner of Main and Church Streets. (Courtesy Special Collections Division of the University of Texas at Arlington Libraries.)

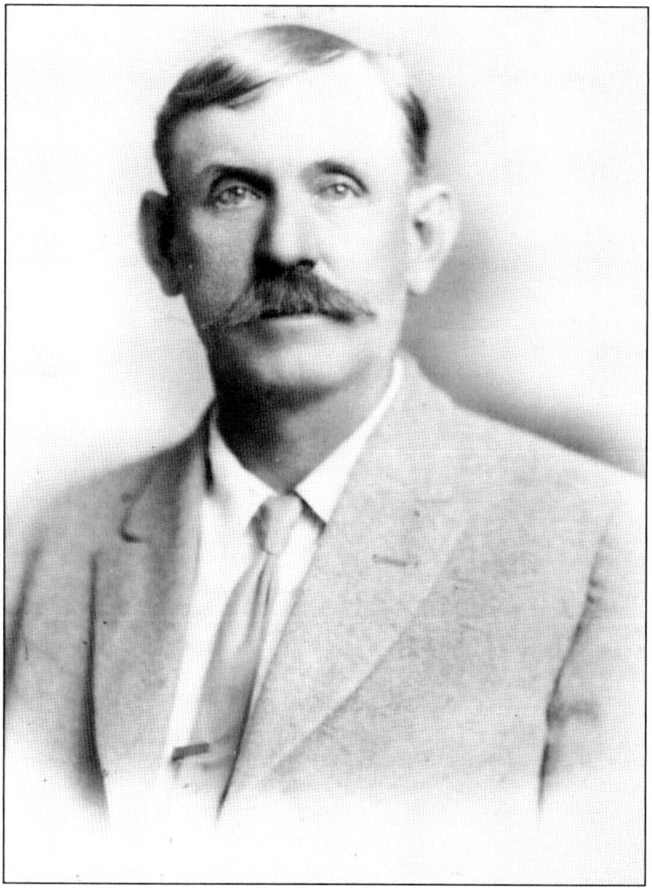

Azle's first rural mail carrier was J.R. Ross, seen here in 1904. He served for 28 years, delivering the mail even before automobiles. No mail deliveries took place in the town of Azle, as residents picked it up themselves at the postal window in the general store or drugstore in the early days.

This white frame building on West Main Street served as Azle's first actual post office. Before that, a postal window sat in part of the drugstore. This post office served Azle from 1914 to 1953. This white building became the Sweet Shop in the mid-1950s, owned by Irene and Hubert Page.

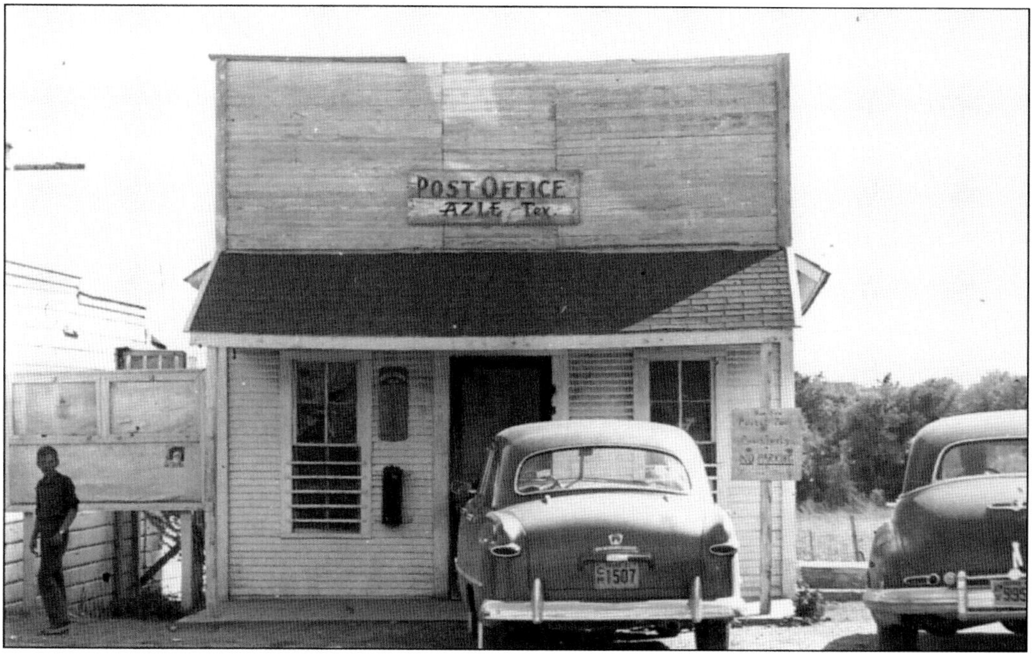

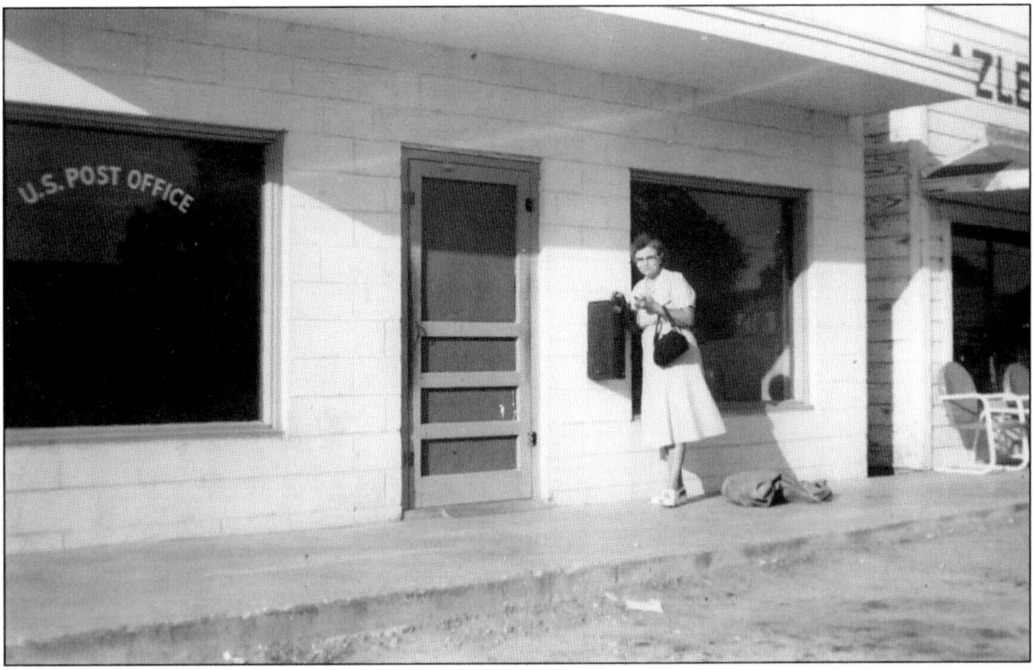


Postmaster Elsie Gipson Parker, who served from 1920 to 1958, was called "postmaster" even though she was female. Here, she heads to work at Azle's second actual post office building at 141 West Main Street. Dunn and Elam Real Estate now occupies the building.

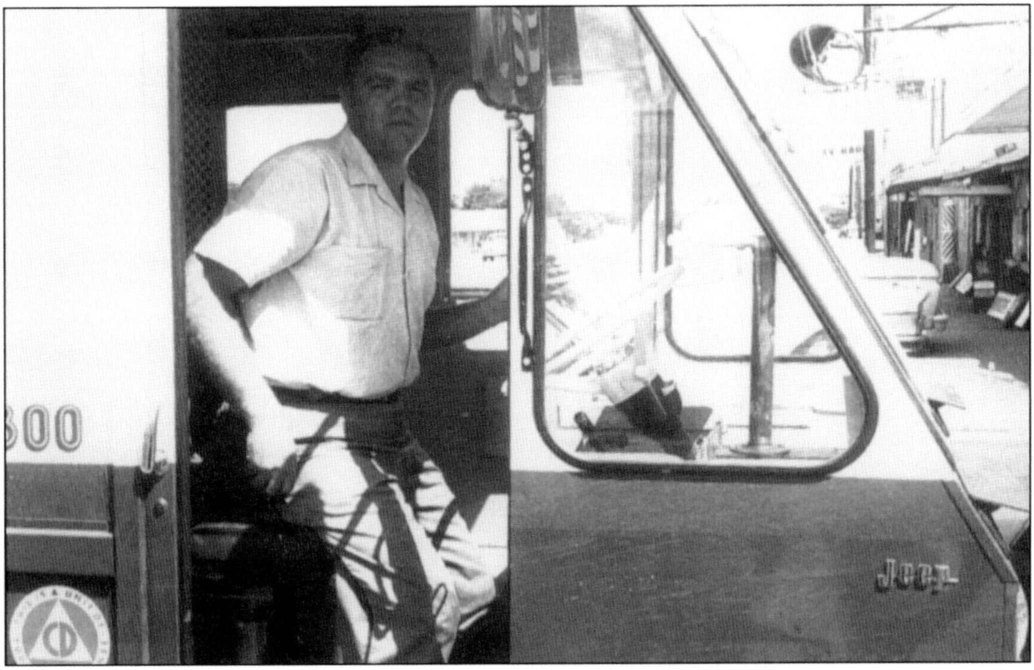

Eddie Morrow became Azle's first city mail carrier and is shown here in 1958 on the city's first postal vehicle. To facilitate the beginning of the route, he bought house numbers and put them up on all the houses, which had to be done before the US postal service would let him deliver the mail. Morrow retired from the post office in 1998 after 40 years of service.

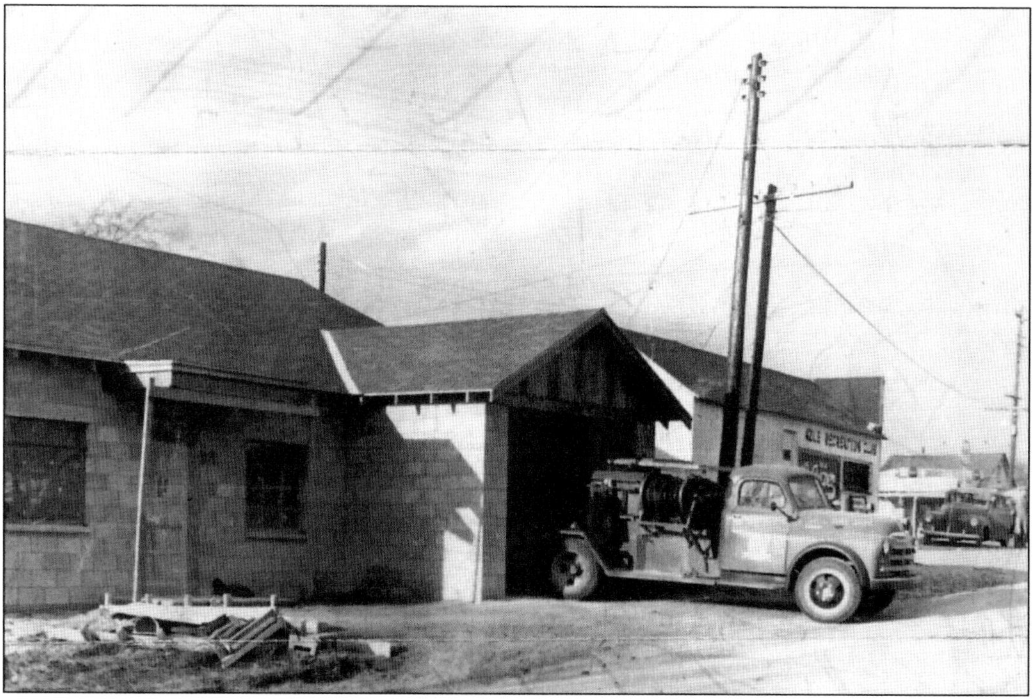

Azle's new town hall was completed in 1951 on South Stewart Street. Azle's first fire truck stands in the garage. After city government offices moved to a new location on Southeast Parkway, the town hall remained a voting site for Azle residents until the early 1970s.

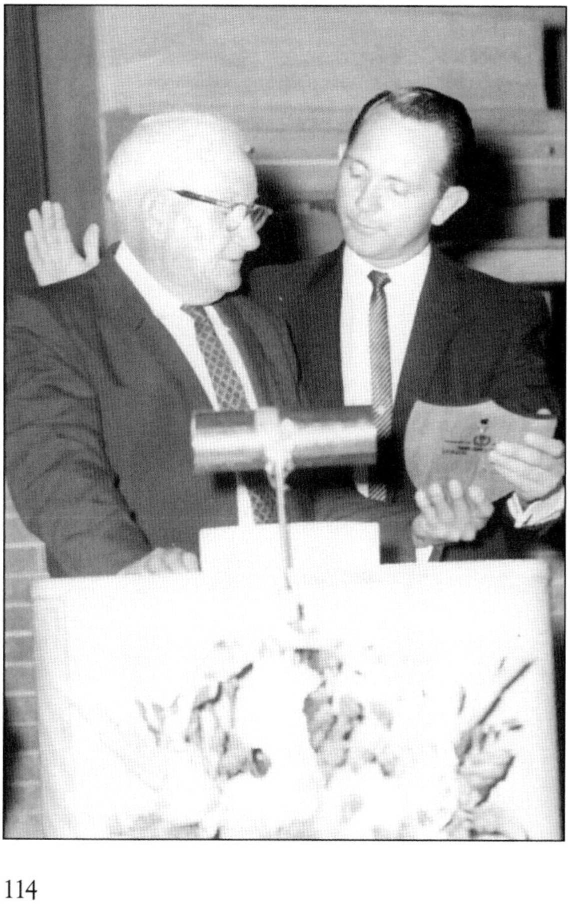

Dan Jarvis (left) served as Azle's first mayor once the city incorporated in 1957. He served one full term and 1.5 years of a second term, which he won in a write-in vote. Jarvis was the son of one of the early settlers of Fort Worth, J.J. Jarvis, who owned land in Azle. Here, Harry Heflin presents Jarvis with a plaque naming him "Citizen of the Year." He died on November 8, 1976, at the age of 91.

Jay Woody Stribling served as Azle's mayor from 1960 to June 1962. He resigned in 1962 without finishing his term. His parents, James and Byra Stribling, operated a drugstore in Azle in the 1940s and 1950s. Byra was the first telephone operator for the town. Stribling Drive in Azle bears the name of this early family.

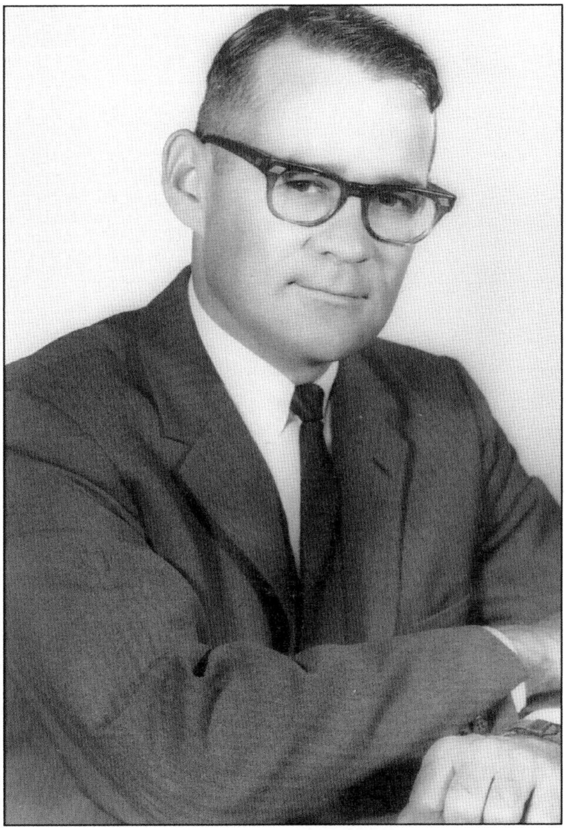

In approximately 1975, Mayor Cy Rone donated his Mercury emergency ambulance to the City of Azle, which he had been operating because his Azle Funeral Home owned it. He explained that this took him out of the ambulance business and put the City of Azle into it. Standing from left to right in front of the ambulance are B.J. Clark, Bill Pugh, Mayor Rone, city manager Cecil Forrester, and Dick Pitney.

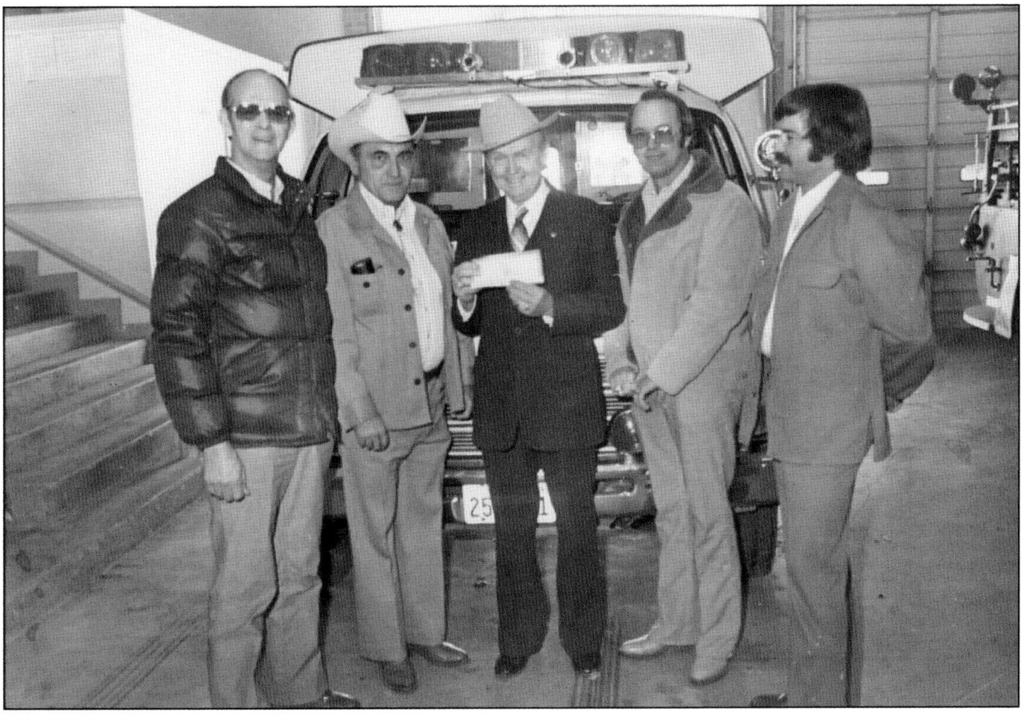

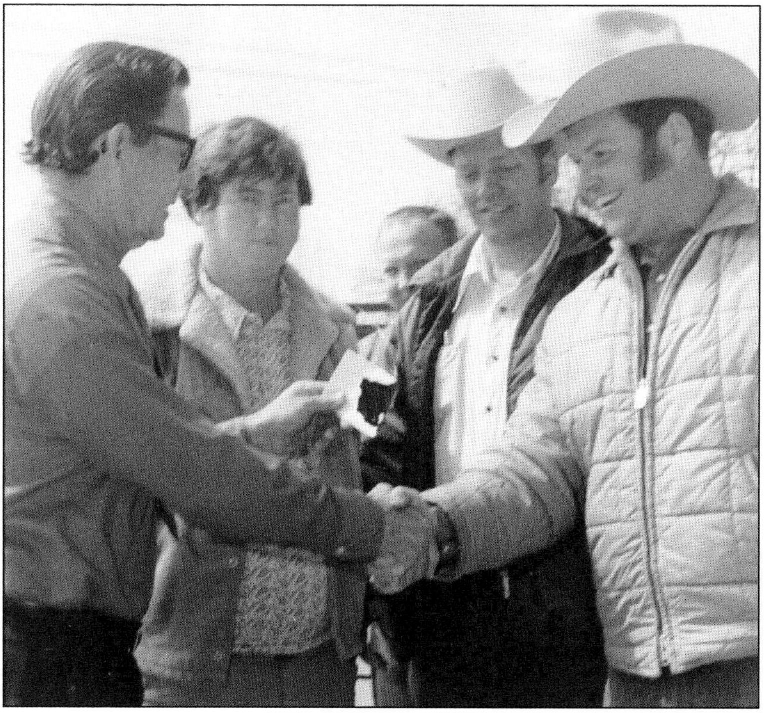

Azle borrowed money to buy a brand new fire truck and eventually celebrated by burning the paid-off note in the 1970s. From left to right, these Azleites are Jim Bob Nation, Corky Miller, Nelson Shepherd, Walter Detricks, and Tommy Bell (in back).

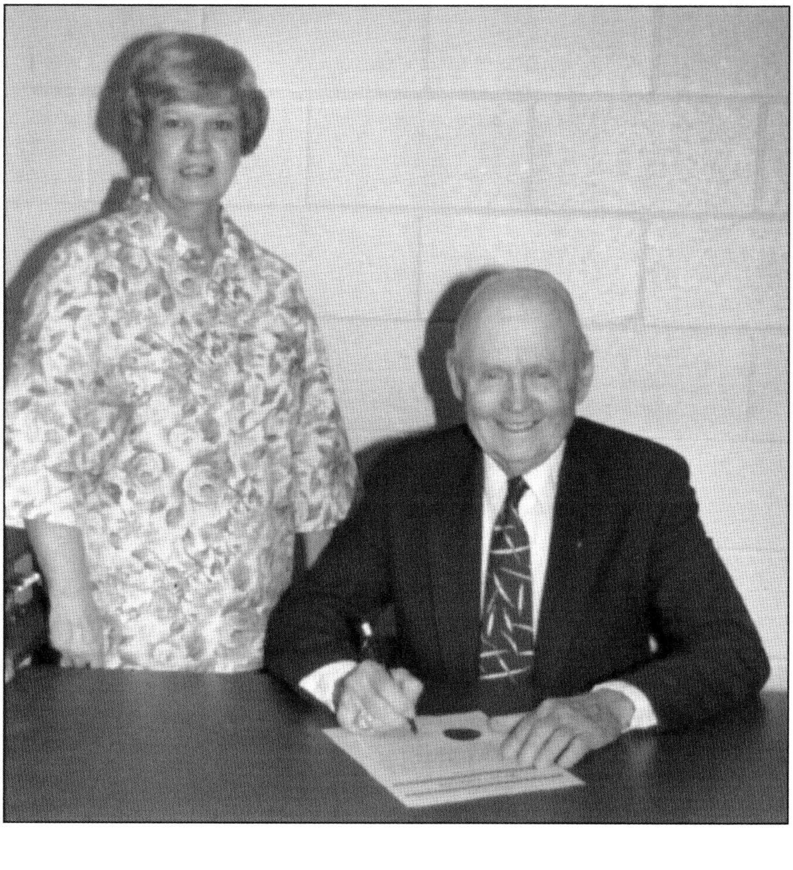

In April 1992, Mayor Cy Rone proclaimed April "Don't Mess With Azle Month." Rone and his family moved to Azle in 1960 to operate Azle Funeral Home. He was elected mayor in 1961 and served 15 terms, nine of which were consecutive, making him Azle's longest-serving mayor. Shirley Bradley (left) later served as Azle's first female mayor, from 1995 to 1999.

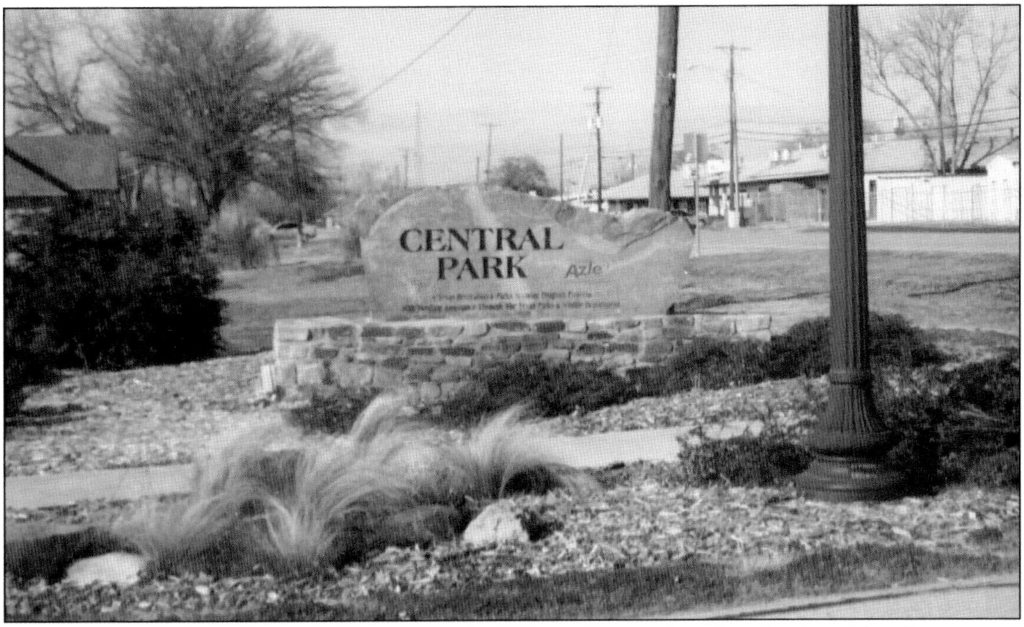


After a contest among citizens to name Azle's newest city park, officials chose the designation Central Park for the site, at 263 West Main Street. The park includes a covered picnic site, a white gazebo, climbing slides and swings for the children, a walking path, and an amphitheater. The city-owned park covers 28 acres. The three other city parks are Ash Creek, Shady Grove, and Melanie, totaling 86 acres overall.

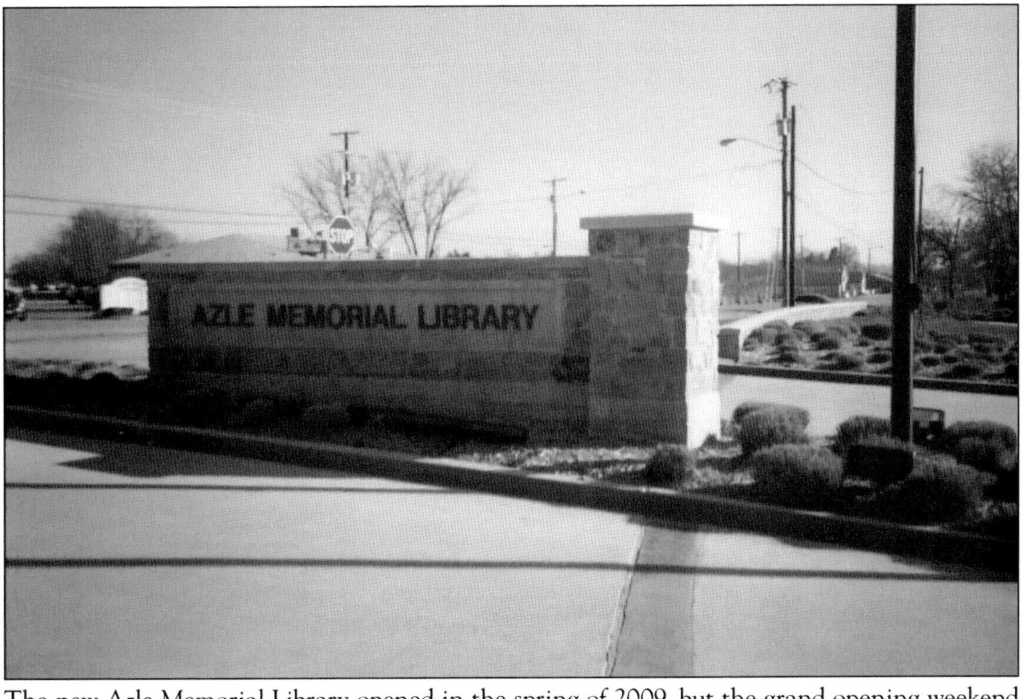


The new Azle Memorial Library opened in the spring of 2009, but the grand opening weekend was held June 26–28. It was celebrated with many activities to introduce citizens to their new facility. Janie Rector was the donor for the library, honoring her late husband, Bill Rector.

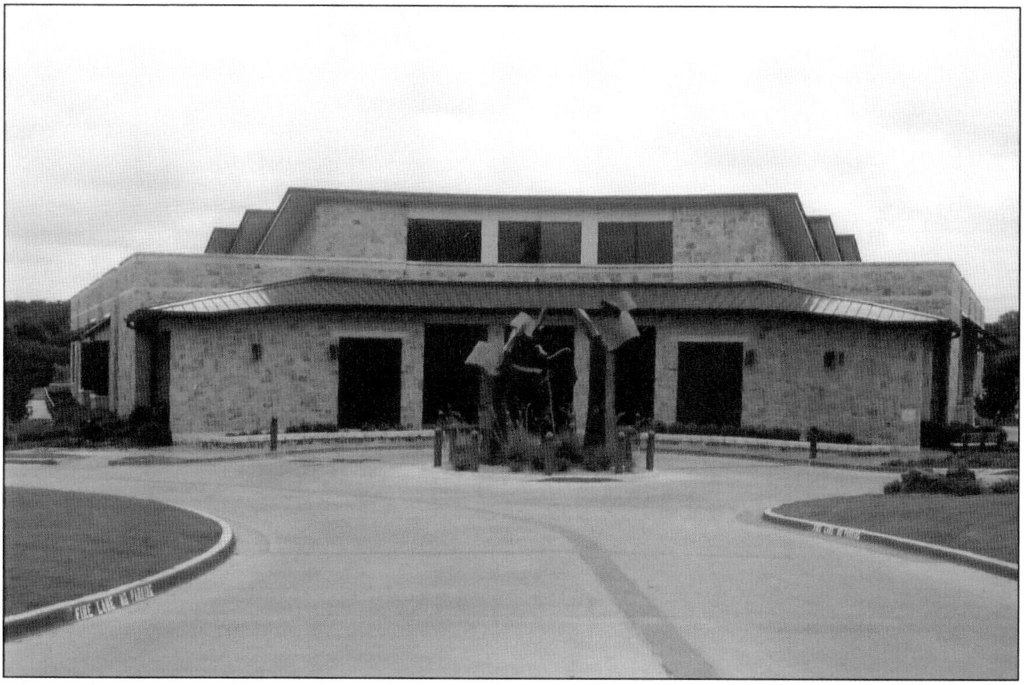

The Azle Memorial Library, at 333 West Main Street, is Azle's third library building. A white stucco building on Southeast Parkway adjacent to city hall served Azle from 1976 to 2009. Prior to that, the Rock Building at 124 West Main, which is now the Azle Historical Museum, was Azle's library. Before the library, a few shelves in a drugstore provided books for citizens to check out.

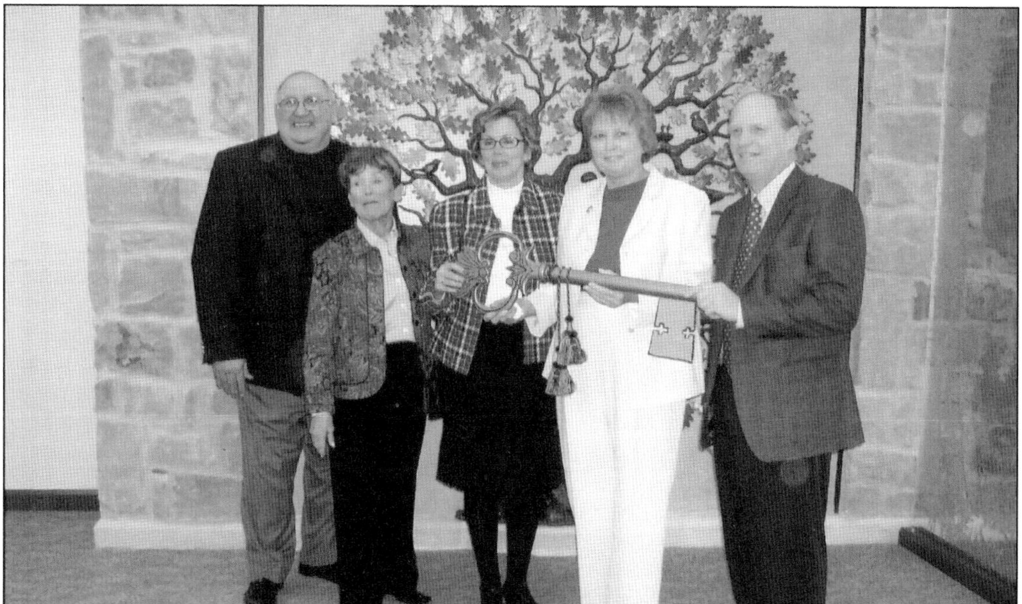

The soft opening of the new Azle Memorial Library was held on January 11, 2009. Presenting the "key" are, from left to right, Santo Forte, library board chairman; Janie Rector, library benefactor; Madeline Skinner, president of Friends of the Library; Judy Whitt, head librarian; and Steve Parker, chairman of the Library Trust.

Former mayor Russ Braudis wears a lei around his neck at Azle's first Volunteer Fair on June 7, 2008, which Braudis organized. During his two terms as mayor from May 2007 to May 2011, he presided over the opening of Azle Central Park, the Azle Memorial Library, and the Sid Dechert Bridge on Denver Trail. His administration also approved the new fire hall and the animal shelter. Having gas wells on city property made being mayor easy, Braudis affirmed.

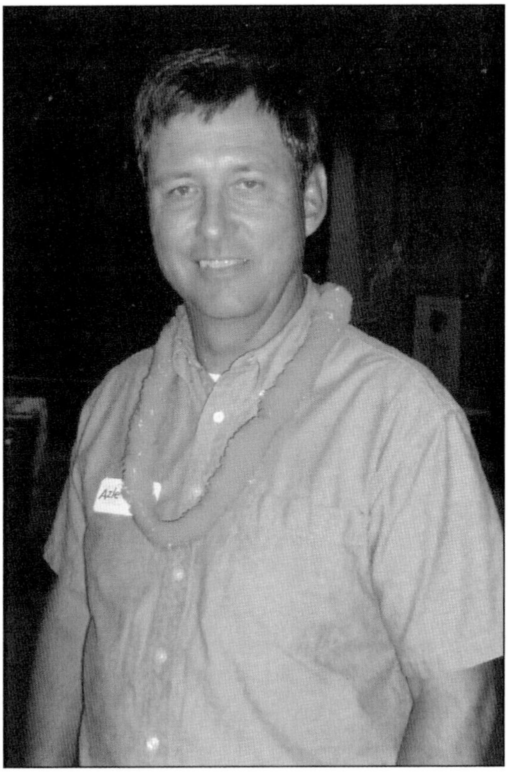

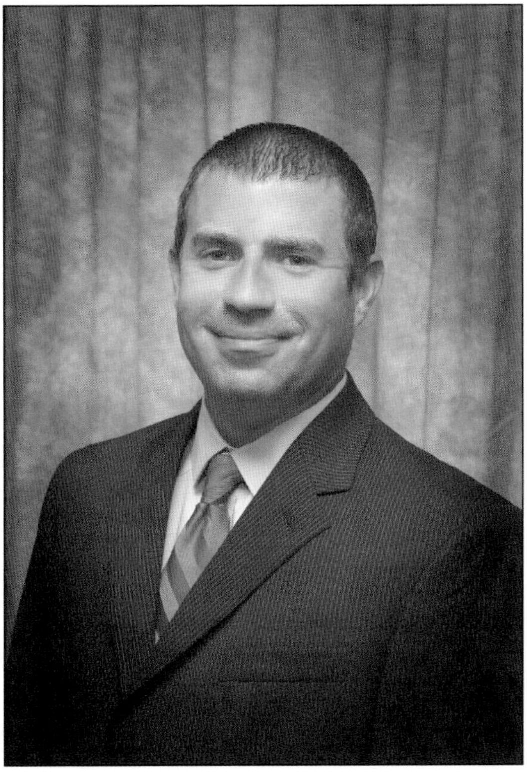

Mayor Alan Brundrett was elected to a two-year term in May 2011 after having served on the city council since filling a vacant seat in 2003. He and his family moved to Azle in 2000 from North Richland Hills. He operates the Farmers Insurance Agency in Lake Worth.

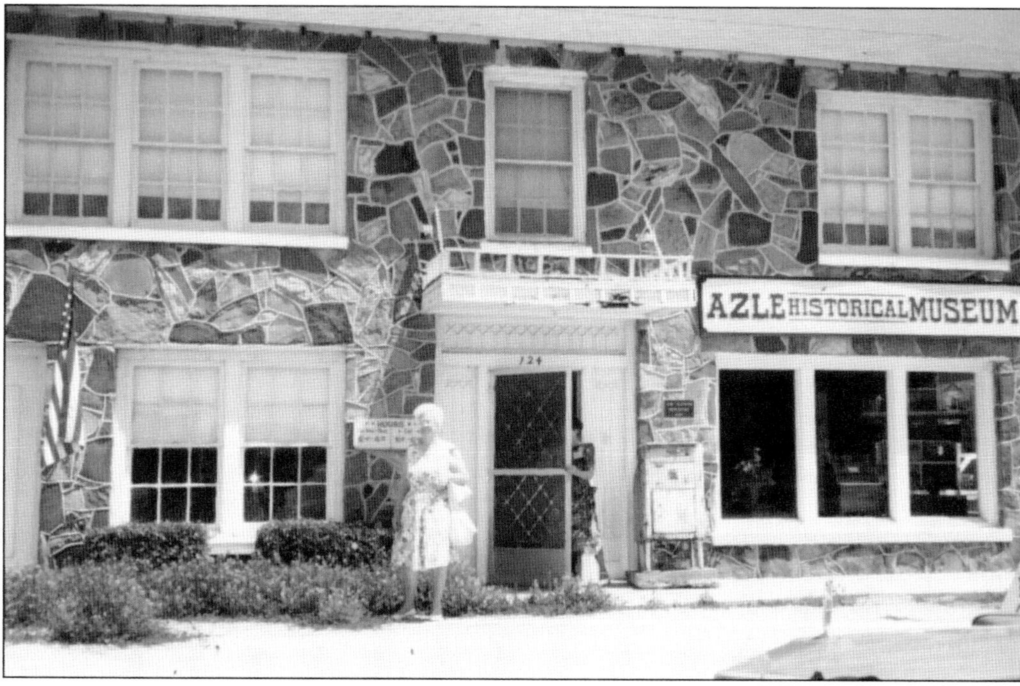


Changes came to the Azle Historical Museum in the early 1990s. Above, a large sign proclaiming "Azle Historical Museum" is posted above three front windows and small porch-like latticework is above the front door. In the 1995 photograph below, the porch has been removed and a maroon awning was installed to keep sunlight from the windows and to protect them from rain. Wind and weather later necessitated a new awning, which is now green, representing one of Azle's school colors.

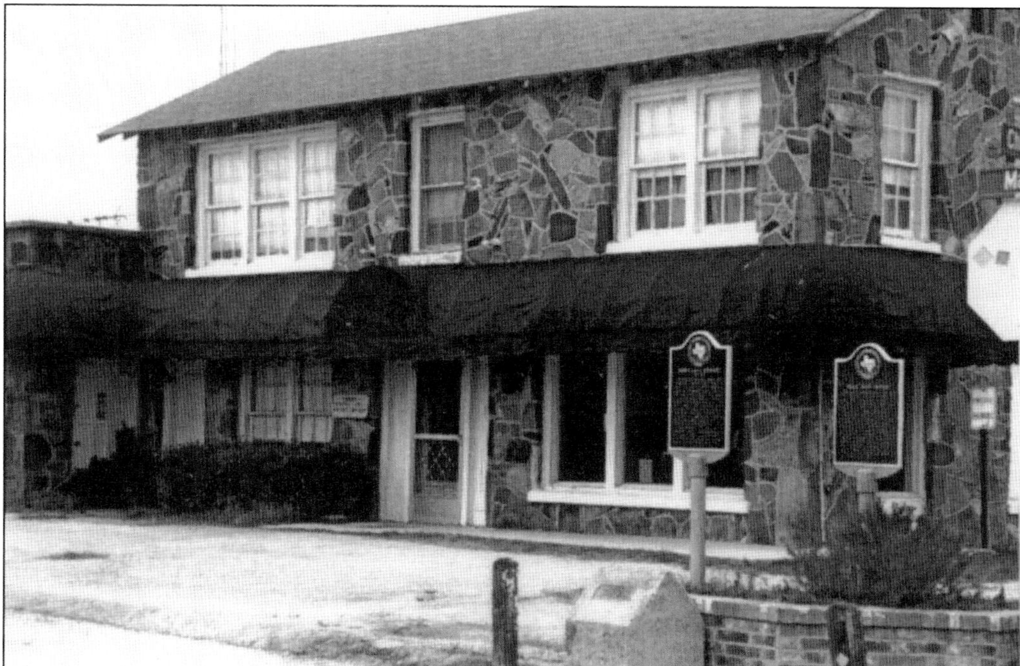

# *Eight*

# Azle Historical Museum

The bicentennial year of 1976 inspired many communities to create organizations to preserve their history. In July 1976, four locals met in the home of Byra Stribling to discuss the organization of a museum for Azle. Meeting with her were B.J. Clark, Paul Worthen, and Beatrice Carter.

They sent out letters in the coming weeks to people whom they thought might be interested, and then 10 people met in the two-story frame building at 117 West Main Street that was once Stribling Drug Store. Constructed in 1900 as Walker Drug Store, the building is the oldest structure on Main Street.

Officers elected at that meeting were B.J. Clark, president; Paul Worthen, vice president; and Bill Stribling, secretary-treasurer. The building was in use as C and W Electronics, owned by Worthen, at the time.

Once word spread about the museum, citizens began donating items to display in it. Kathryn Worthen, Paul's wife, agreed to catalogue all the donations. They were housed upstairs in the electronics building until a proper home for the museum could be found. The museum officers and volunteers entered the Fourth of July Jamboree parade in 1977 to call attention to their efforts.

In their parade entry, Herman Younger drove his "surrey with the fringe on top" and Blanche Scrimshire and Beatrice Carter rode with him while dressed in costumes from long ago. They won a second-place prize in the parade in their category.

In 1978, the city gave the members of the museum board use of the building at 124 West Main Street. The building had been Azle's library, but it recently moved to a new location on Southeast Parkway. Prior to the library occupying the building, it had served many uses.

The board members of the museum have acted as caretakers of the museum and also as a historical society. In the following years, at least 15 historical markers were researched locally and approved by the state for display at Azle sites.

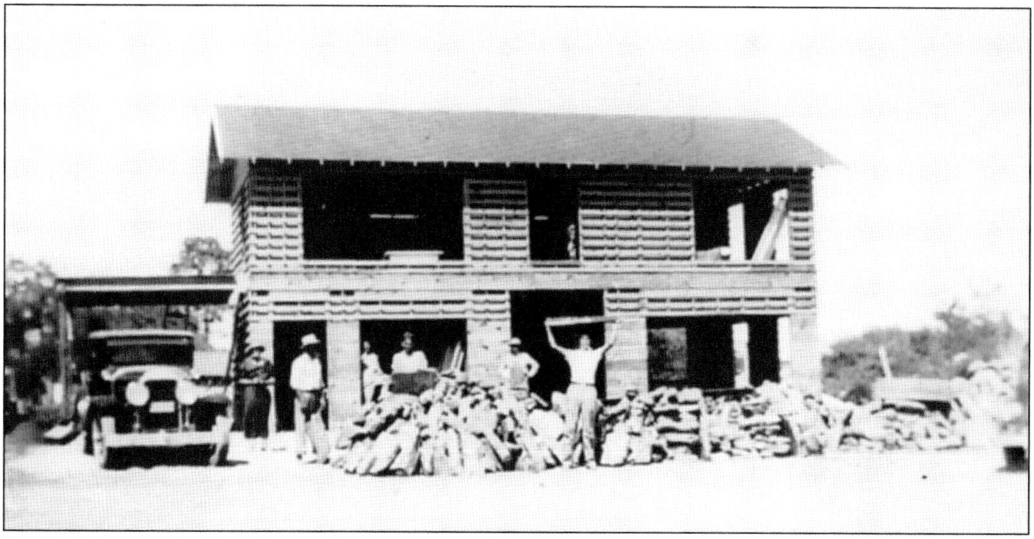

Jim Bob Nation holds a large, flat rock above his head in the center of this photograph. Others are unidentified. Nation's aunt Eula and uncle Jim Nation, constructed the building at 124 West Main Street in 1936. After serving many other uses, it is now the home of the Azle Historical Museum. Owned by the city, it bears a plaque reading, "Jim Nation Building 1936."

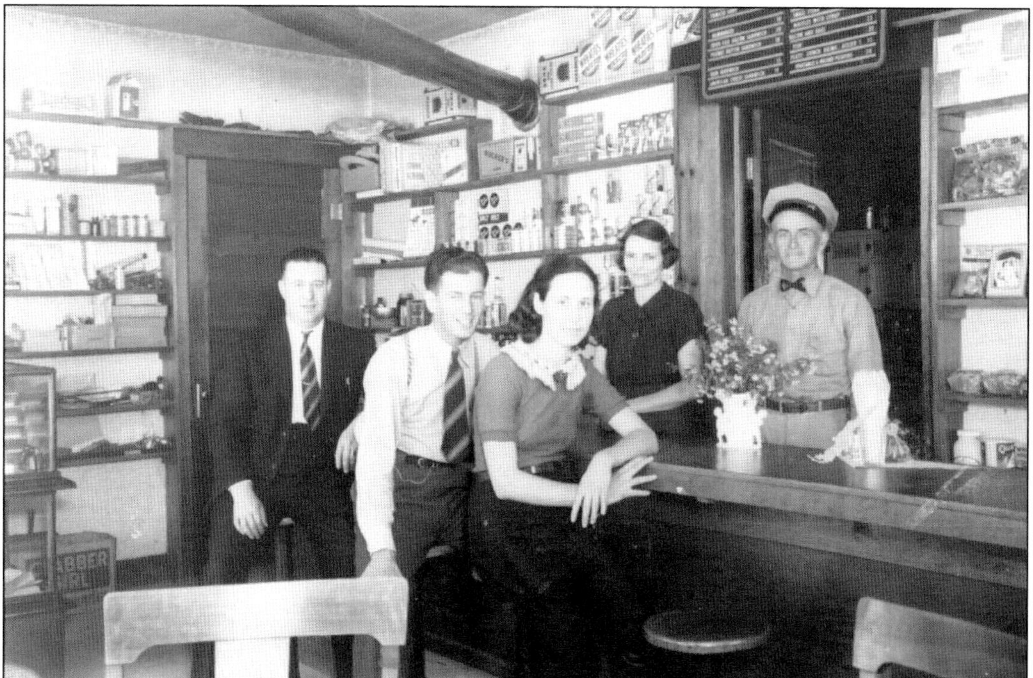

This photograph was taken inside the present Azle Historical Museum building when it was first constructed as a combination filling station and café, called Aunt Ida's Café. Through the next two decades, the building became the home for the Rural Electric Association, was made into two apartments in World War II, and then was a beauty shop and a barbershop before it became the library.

This metal post office window with 44 individual post office boxes originally sat in the very first post office in Azle in 1914. Citizens in the town of Azle picked up their mail each day after the postmaster distributed it in their boxes. Rural residents had the mail delivered to their homes. Currently, the old-time post office window is located inside the Azle Historical Museum, donated by Beatrice Carter.

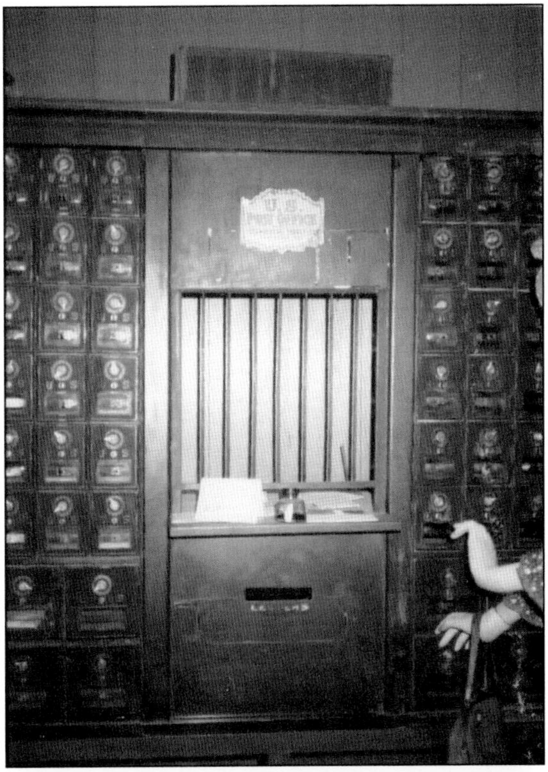

Byrne C. Moody (right) presents a waterproof leather mailbag to B.J. Clark (center), who was president of the Azle Historical Museum at the time. The mailbag was carried by Azle's first mail carriers, James Ross and Roger Hiett. Standing to the left is Fred Weaver, Ross's grandson. Moody delivered all of Azle's rural mail for many years.

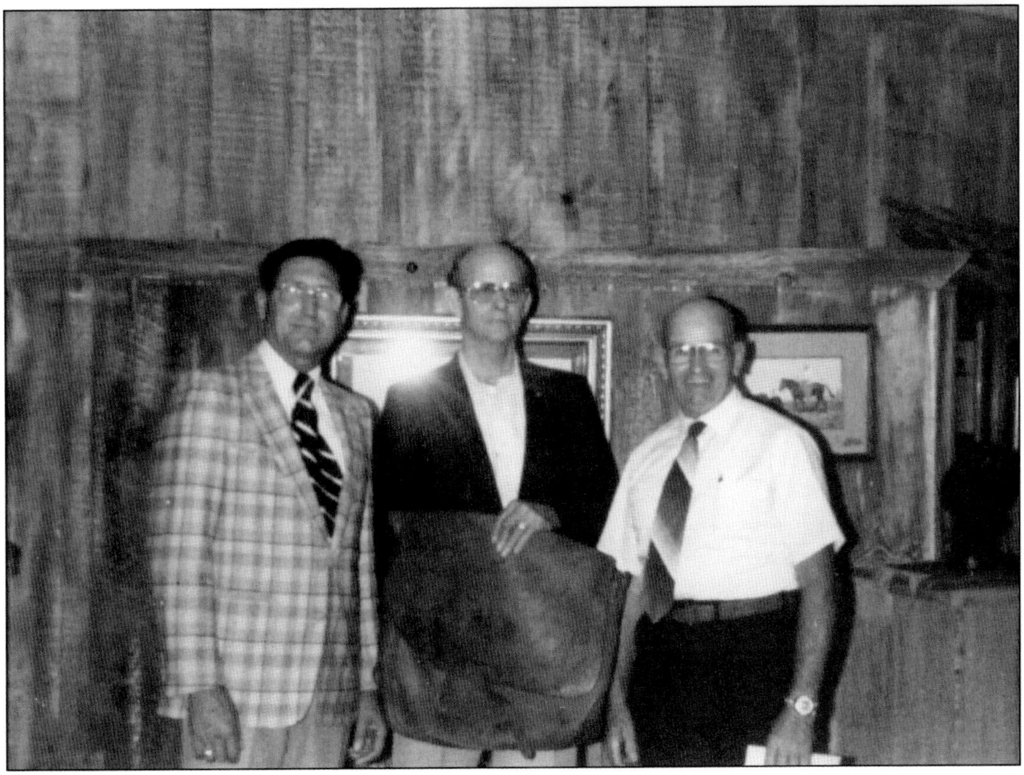

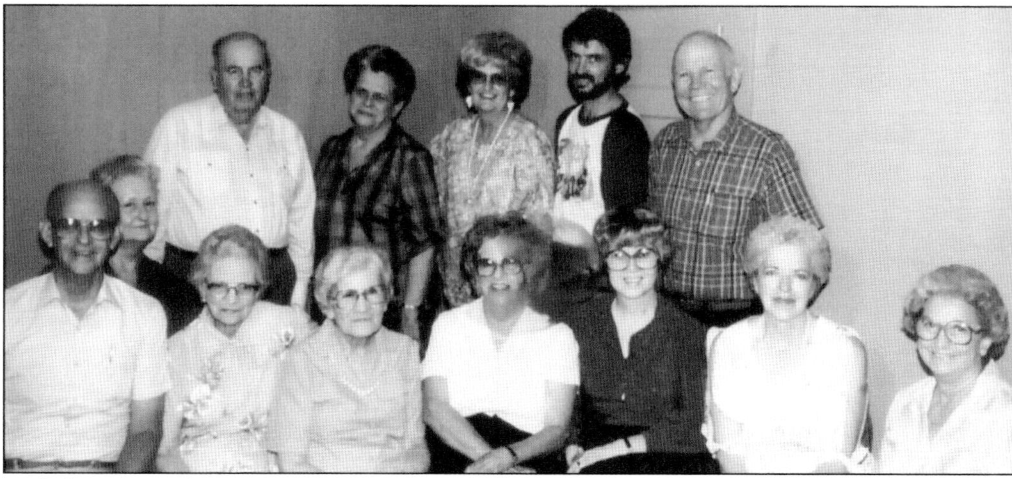

Early board members of the Azle Historical Museum in the 1980s included, from left to right, (seated) B.J. Clark, Beth Skinner, Beatrice Carter, Gertie Ansley, Lucille Young, J'Nell Pate, Naomi Hearell, and Pansy Lavender; (standing) Ford Hearell, Leska Wright, Betty Baughman, Gary Logan, and Bill Womack.

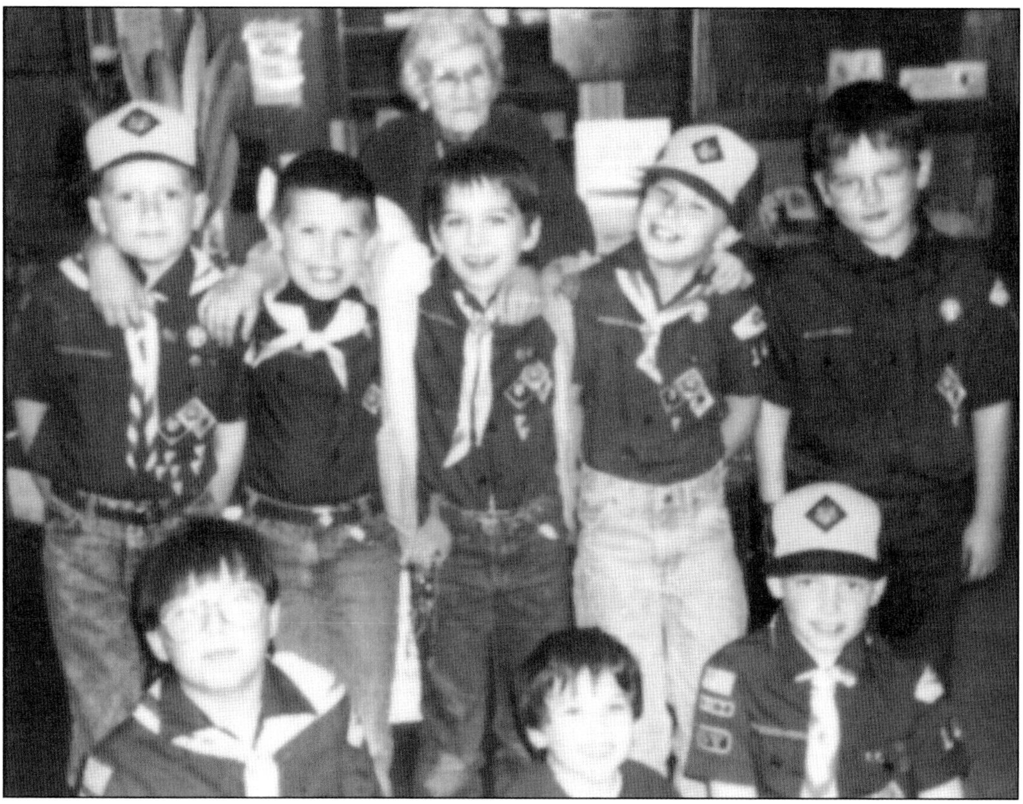

Bear Scouts from Den 7, Pack 147 visited the Azle Historical Museum in April 1993 as one of their activities. Gertie Ansley (back center), along with Johnnie Wright (not pictured), led the Scouts on a tour of the museum and related the history of Azle to the group. Ansley served as secretary-treasurer for many years for the museum. Wright was the president of the organization when the Scouts visited.

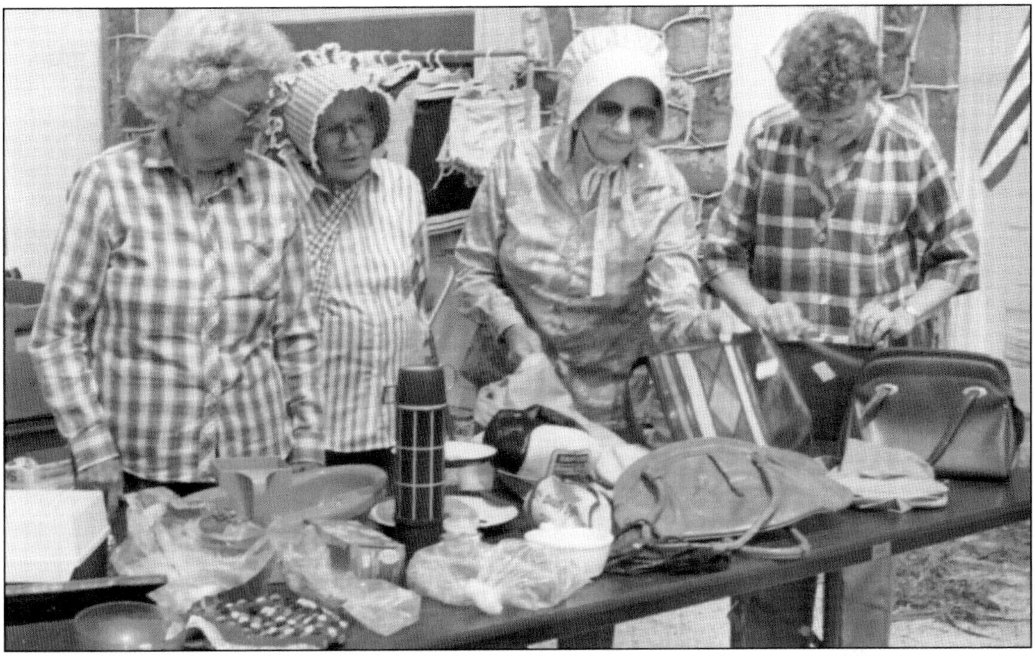

Rummaging through the items at an Azle Historical Museum yard sale in March 1988 are, from left to right, board members Lucille Young, Gertie Ansley, Pansy Lavender, and Louise Gassaway. The occasional yard sale to raise money for museum expenses turned into an annual event by 2000.

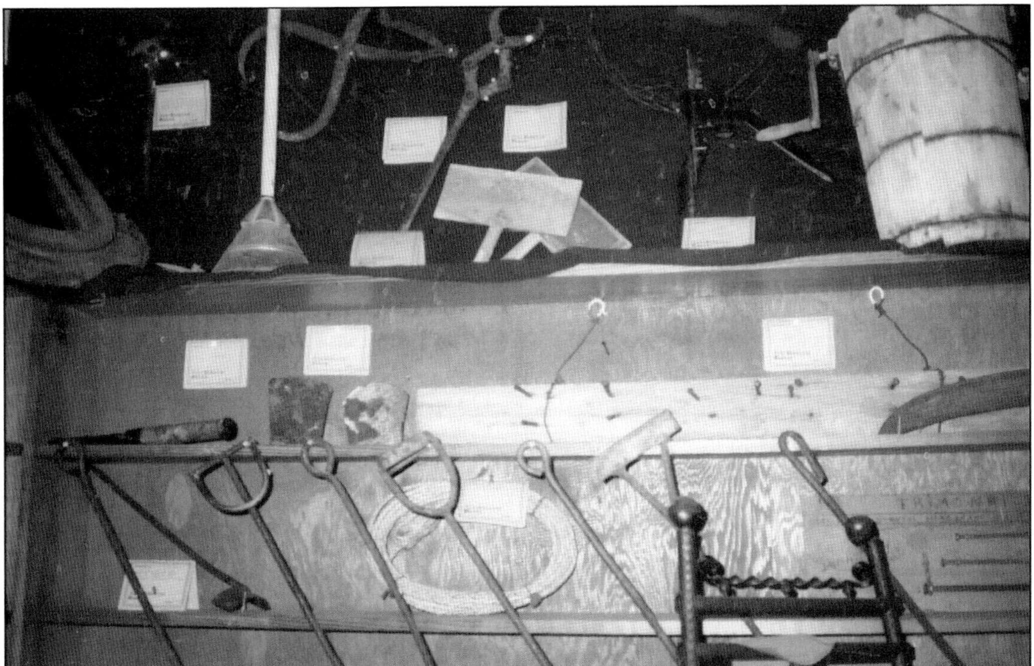

One of the downstairs rooms of the Azle Historical Museum features items from the pioneer days of Azle and its surrounding areas that working men of those days would have used. Items include branding irons, barbed wire, old guns, a primitive rope-making kit, and other items. On the top shelf is a hand-cranking ice cream freezer.

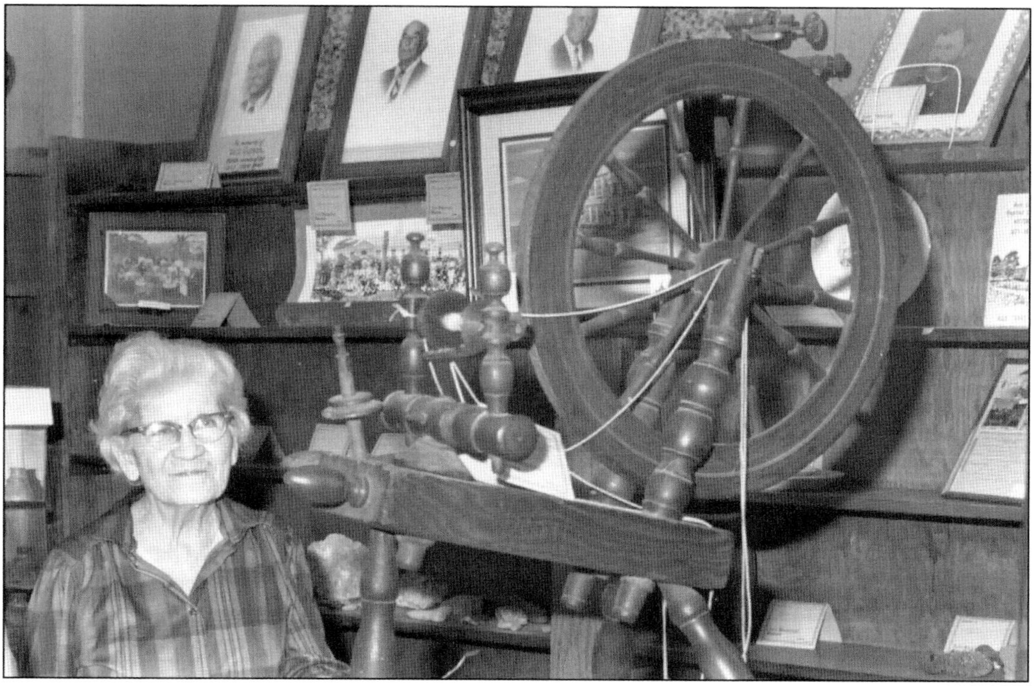

Gertie Ansley, the longtime secretary-treasurer of the Azle Historical Museum, sits by the 150-year-old spinning wheel that was later moved upstairs to complete the setting of an early-day bedroom. The photograph was taken in 1985, when Ansley was prominently involved in working on the *Azle Community History* book that came out the following year.

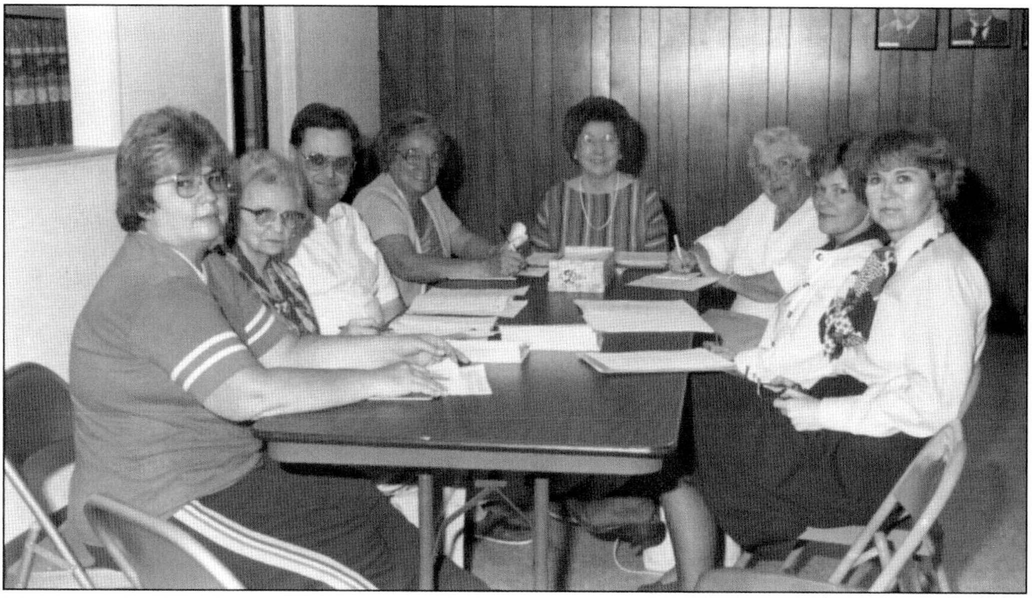

Members of Azle's Texas Sesquicentennial Committee met in 1985 to determine events in Azle to commemorate the historic event the following year. They operated as an adjunct to the Azle Historical Museum, which serves as Azle's historical society as well. Seated from left to right are Lynda Scott, Beatrice Carter, Thomas Hicks, Audrey Trammell, committee chair Laura Jane Jordan, Ada Mae Horton, Betty Haas, and J'Nell Pate.

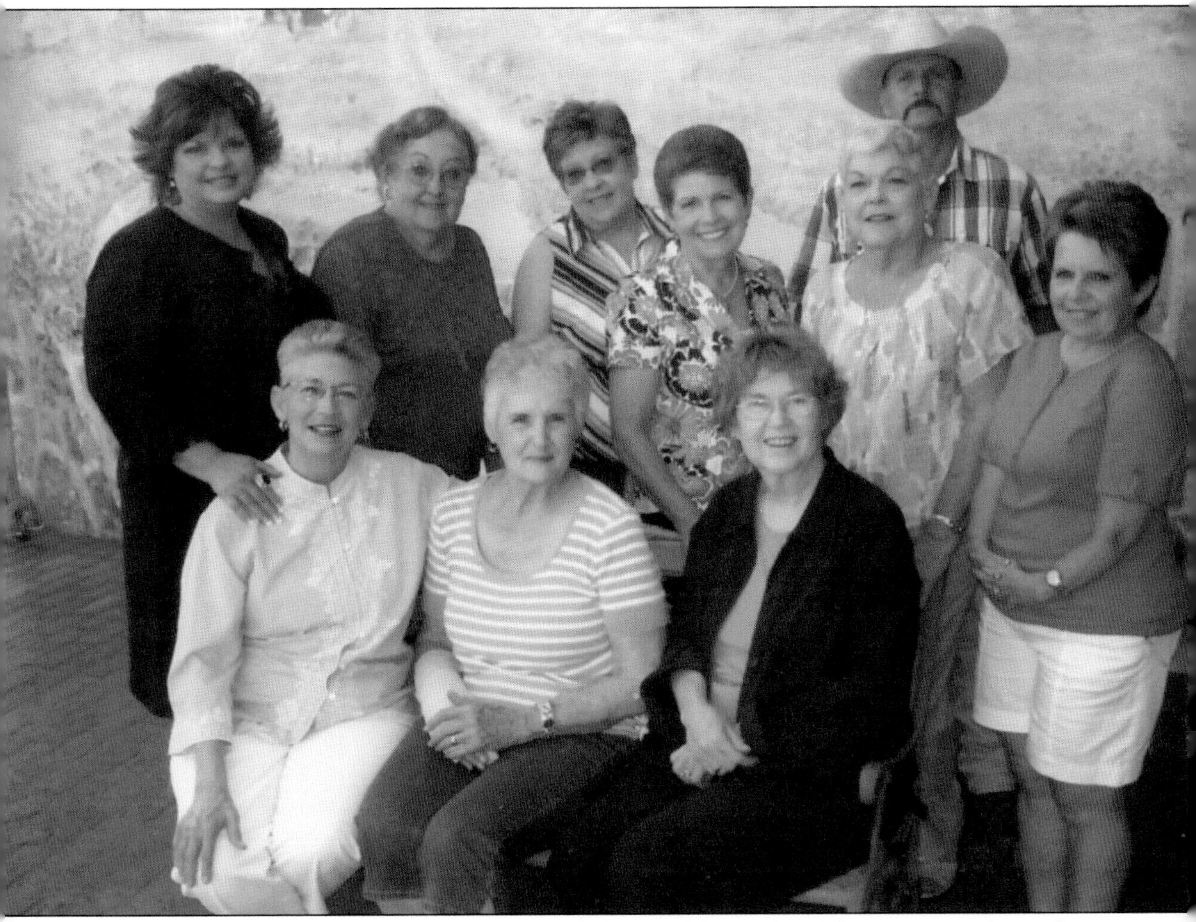

The Azle Historical Museum's board members and officers posed for this photograph on the brick plaza in front of the museum. The mural behind them was painted by Christy Carpenter Norris with the assistance of her mother, Peggy Carpenter, on the wall of Rural Gas Supply, next door to the museum. The plaza is made from engraved bricks that are available for purchase by anyone interested in leaving a permanent reminder of their family, friends, and organization, or as a memorial to loved ones. The proceeds from the bricks benefit the museum. The nine board members are elected in staggered elections every two years by the museum members at their annual meeting in August. The officers are elected from the board by the board members. From left to right are (first row) Rex Ballauer, president; Patsy Glover, treasurer; and J'Nell Pate, secretary; (second row) Debbie Hall, vice president; Dicey Rowden; Christine Sellers; Nancy Davis; Hurene Morrow; and Kim Dunaway; (third row) Britt Eason, the museum's newest member.

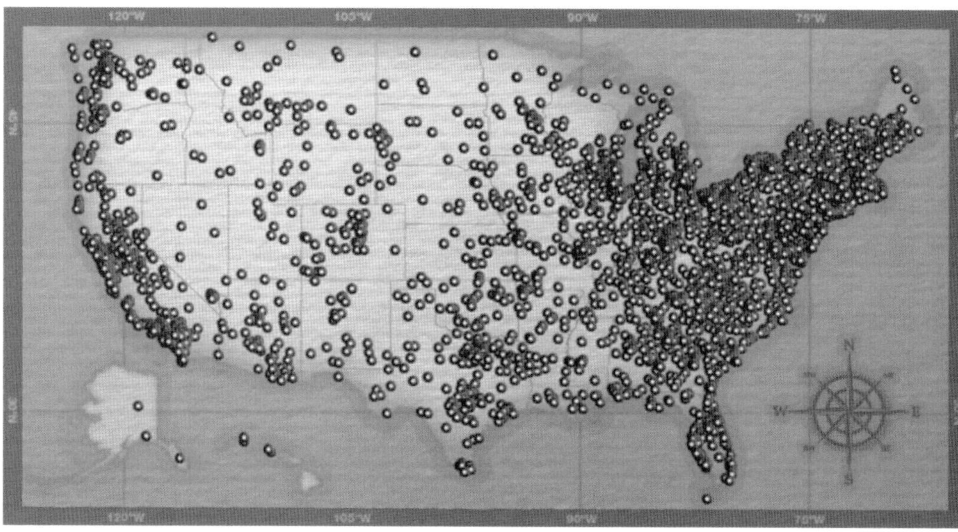